CONTENTS

Part 3: Practical: Divine Righteousness Producing Practical Righteousness in the Believer (Romans 12–16)

LECTURES ON THE EPISTLE TO THE GALATIANS

Part 1: Personal (Galatians 1–2)

Part 2: Doctrinal (Galatians 3–4)

Part 3: Practical (Galatians 5–6)

LECTURES ON THE EPISTLE TO THE
ROMANS

PREFACE

The present volume consists of notes of lectures on the Roman Letter, substantially as given to the students of the Moody Bible Institute of Chicago, Illinois; the Evangelical Theological College of Dallas, Texas; and at various Bible conferences throughout the United States and Canada in recent years.

They are sent forth in printed form in response to the earnest solicitation of many who heard them, and in the hope that they will be used of God to the blessing of numbers who cannot be reached by the spoken word.

The author is indebted far more than he realizes to writers and speakers who have gone over the same ground before him. No claim is made for originality. It is God's truth—not that of any teacher—and as such it is committed to His care for His glory.

H. A. IRONSIDE

PART 1

DOCTRINAL

The Righteousness of God Revealed in the Gospel

Romans 1–8

THE THEME AND ANALYSIS

The epistle to the Romans is undoubtedly the most scientific statement of the divine plan for the redemption of mankind that God has been pleased to give us. Apart altogether from the question of inspiration, we may think of it as a treatise of transcendent, intellectual power, putting to shame the most brilliant philosophies ever conceived by the minds of men.

It is noteworthy that the Holy Spirit did not take up an unlettered fisherman or provincial Galilean to unfold His redemption plan in all its majesty and grandeur. He selected a man of international outlook: a Roman citizen, yet a Hebrew of the Hebrews. A man whose education combined familiarity with Greek and Roman lore, including history, religion, philosophy, poetry, science and music, together with closest acquaintance with Judaism both as a divine revelation and as a body of rabbinical traditions and additions to the sacred deposit of the Law, the Prophets, and the Psalms. This man, born in the proud educational center, Tarsus of Cilicia, and brought up at the feet of Gamaliel in Jerusalem, was the chosen vessel to make known to all nations for the obedience of faith the gospel of the glory of the blessed God, as so marvelously set forth in this immortal letter.

It was evidently written somewhere along the journey from Macedonia to Jerusalem, and very likely, as tradition asserts, at Corinth.

About to leave Europe for Palestine to carry to the Jewish Christians, his brethren after the flesh and in the Lord, the bounty provided by the Gentile assemblies, his heart turns longingly to Rome, the "eternal city," the mistress of the ancient world, where already apart from direct apostolic ministry a Christian church had been formed. To a number of its members he was already known, to others he was a stranger, but he yearned over them all as a true father in Christ and earnestly desired to share with them the precious treasure committed to him. The Spirit had already indicated that a visit to Rome was in the will of God for him, but the time and circumstances were hidden from him. So he wrote this exposition of the divine plan and sent it on by a godly woman, Phebe, a deaconess of the assembly at Cenchrea, who had been called to Rome on business. The letter served the double purpose of introducing her to the Christians there and ministering to them the marvelous unfolding of the righteousness of God revealed in the gospel in accordance with the testimony committed to Paul. Think of the grace that entrusted this matchless epistle to the feeble hand of a woman in times such as those! The whole church of God throughout the centuries owes to Phebe a debt of gratitude and to the God who watched over her unending praise, for the preservation of the valuable manuscript that she delivered safely into the hands of the elders at Rome and through them to us.

The theme of the epistle is the righteousness of God. It forms one of an inspired trio of expositions that together give us an amazingly rich exegesis of a very brief Old Testament text. The text is found in Habakkuk 2:4: "The just shall live by his faith." As quoted three times in the New Testament, there are just six words. The pronoun *his* being omitted. The three letters referred to are Romans, Galatians, and Hebrews, each of which is based upon this text.

Romans has to do particularly with the first two words. Its message is, *"The just* shall live by faith" (1:17), answering the question that is raised in the book of Job, "How [shall] man be just with God?" (9:2).

Galatians expounds the two central words, "The just *shall live* by faith" (3:11). The Galatian error was in supposing that while we begin in faith, we are perfected by works. But the apostle shows that we live by that same faith through which we were justified. "Having begun in the Spirit, are ye now made perfect by the flesh?" (v. 3).

Hebrews takes up the last two words, "The just shall live *by faith"* (10:38). It emphasizes the nature and power of faith itself, by which alone the justified believer walks. Incidentally, this is one reason why, after having carefully examined many arguments against the Pauline authorship of Hebrews, I have not the slightest doubt that it is correctly attributed to the same one who wrote Romans and Galatians. This is confirmed by the testimony of the apostle Peter in his second epistle, 2 Peter 3:15–16, for it was to converted Hebrews Peter was addressing himself and to them Paul had also written.

The epistles to the Romans may be readily divided into three great divisions:

1. Chapters 1–8 are *doctrinal* and give us the righteousness of God revealed in the gospel.
2. Chapters 9–11 are *dispensational* and give us the righteousness of God harmonized with His dispensational ways.
3. Chapters 12–16 are *practical* and set forth the righteousness of God producing practical righteousness in the believer.

Each of these divisions will be found to break naturally into smaller subdivisions, and these into sections and subsections.

In submitting the following outline, I do so only suggestively. The careful student may think of more apt designations for each particular part and may possibly find it simpler to separate the different paragraphs according to some other arrangement. But I suggest the following analysis as one that seems to me to be simple and illuminating.

PART 1: DOCTRINAL: THE RIGHTEOUSNESS OF GOD REVEALED IN THE GOSPEL (ROM. 1–8)
   A. The need of the gospel (1:1–3:20)
      1. Salutation (1:1–7)
      2. Introduction (1:8–17)
         a. The apostle's stewardship (1:8–15)
         b. The theme stated (1:16–17)
      3. The ungodliness and unrighteousness of the entire human family demonstrated; or, the need of the gospel (1:18–3:20)
         a. The state of the degraded heathen: The barbarian world. (1:18–32)
         b. The state of the cultured Gentiles: The moralists (2:1–16)
         c. The state of the religious Jews (2:17–29)
         d. The complete indictment of the entire world (3:1–20)
   B. The gospel in relation to the question of our sins (3:21–5:11)
      1. Justification by grace through faith on the ground of accomplished redemption (3:21–31)
      2. The witness of the Law and the Prophets (4:1–25)
         a. Abraham's justification (4:1–6)

b. David's testimony (4:7–8)
c. For all mankind on the same principle (4:9–25)
3. Peace with God: Its basis and results (5:1–5)
4. The summing "up" (5:6–11)
C. The gospel in relation to indwelling sin (5:12–8:39)
1. The two races and two heads (5:12–21)
2. The two masters: Sin and righteousness (6:1–23)
3. The two husbands, two natures, and two laws (7:1–25)
4. The triumph of grace (8:1–39)
a. No condemnation in Christ (8:1–4)
b. The Spirit of Christ in the believer (8:5–27)
c. God for us (8:28–34)
d. No separation (8:35–39)

PART 2: DISPENSATIONAL: THE RIGHTEOUSNESS OF GOD HARMONIZED WITH HIS DISPENSATIONAL WAYS (ROM. 9–11)
A. God's past dealings with Israel in electing grace (9:1–33)
B. God's present dealings with Israel in governmental discipline (10:1–21)
C. God's future dealings with Israel in fulfillment of the prophetic Scriptures (11:1–36)

PART 3: PRACTICAL: DIVINE RIGHTEOUSNESS PRODUCING PRACTICAL RIGHTEOUSNESS IN THE BELIEVER (ROM. 12–16)
A. God's good, acceptable, and perfect will revealed (12:1–15:7)
1. The walk of the Christian in relation to his fellow believers and to men of the world (12:1–21)
2. The Christian's relation to worldly governments (13:1–14)
3. Christian liberty and consideration for others (14:1–23)
4. Christ: The believer's pattern (15:1–7)
B. Conclusion (15:8–33)
C. Salutations (16:1–24)

EPILOGUE: THE MYSTERY REVEALED (ROM. 16:25–27)

I would earnestly press upon the student the importance of committing to memory, if possible, this outline or some similar analysis of the epistle, before attempting the study of the letter itself. Failure to get the great divisions and subdivisions firmly fixed in the mind leaves the door open for false interpretations and confused views later on. Many, for instance, through not observing that the question of justification is settled in chapters 3–5, are greatly perplexed when they come to chapter 7. But if the teaching of the first chapters referred to be clearly understood, then it will be seen that the man in chapter 7 is not raising again the question of a sinner's acceptance with God, but is concerned about a saint's walk in holiness. Then again, how many a soul has become almost distracted by reading eternal issues into chapter 9, altogether beyond what the apostle intended, and endeavoring to bring heaven and hell into it as though these were here the chief questions at issue, whereas God is dealing with the great dispensational question of His sovereign electing grace toward Israel, and His temporary repudiation of them nationally, while in a special way His grace goes out to the Gentiles. I only mention these instances at this time in order to impress upon each student the importance of having an "[outline] of sound words" (2 Tim. 1:13) in studying this or any other book of the Bible.

I add an additional suggestion or two. It is good to have "catchwords" sometimes to fix things in the mind. Someone has aptly designated Romans as "The Epistle of the *Forum.*" This, I think, is most helpful. In this letter the sinner is brought into the courtroom, the forum, the place of judgment, and shown to be utterly guilty and undone. But through the work of Christ a righteous basis has been laid upon which he can be justified from every charge. Nor does God stop here, but He openly acknowledges the believing sinner as His own son, making him a citizen of a favored race and owning him as His heir. Thus the challenge can be hurled at all objectors, "What shall we then say to these things? If God be for us, who can be against us?" Every voice is silenced, for "it is God that justifieth" (Rom. 8:33), and this not at the expense of righteousness but in full accord therewith. This view readily accounts for the use of legal and judicial terms so frequently found in the argument.

A dying sinner was once asked if he would not like to be saved. "I certainly would," he replied. "But," he added earnestly, "I don't want God to do anything wrong in saving me." It was through the letter to the Romans he learned how "[God can] be just, and the justifier of him which believeth in Jesus" (Rom. 3:26). You will remember how Socrates expressed himself five hundred years before Christ. "It may be," he said, addressing himself to Plato, "that the Deity can forgive sins, but I do not see how." It is this that the Holy Spirit takes up so fully in this epistle. He shows us that God does not save sinners at the expense of His righteousness. In other words, if saved at all, it will not be because righteousness has been set aside in order that mercy might triumph, but mercy has found a way whereby divine righteousness can be fully satisfied and, yet, guilty sinners justified before the throne of high heaven.

The apostle John suggests the same wondrous truth when in his first epistle, he says, "If we confess our sins, he is faithful and just to forgive us our sins, and to cleanse us from all unrighteousness" (1 John 1:9). How much more natural the sense would seem to our poor minds before being divinely instructed, if it read, "He is merciful and gracious to forgive." Although the gospel is in the most marvelous way the unfolding of the mercy of God and exalts His grace as nothing else can, yet it is because it rests on a firm foundation of righteousness that it gives such settled peace to the soul who believes it. Since Christ has died, God could not be faithful to Him nor just to the believing sinner if He still condemned the one who trusts in Him who bore "our sins in his own body on the tree" (1 Peter 2:24).

It is, therefore, the righteousness of God that is magnified in this epistle to the Romans, even as David of old cried, "[Save (or deliver)] me in thy righteousness" (Pss. 31:1; 71:2). It was as Luther was meditating on this verse that light began to dawn upon his darkened soul. He could understand how God could damn him in His righteousness, but it was when he saw that God can save in righteousness that his soul entered into peace. And untold myriads have found the same deliverance from perplexity when through this glorious unfolding of the righteousness of God as revealed in the gospel, they saw how "God can save, yet righteous be." If we fail to see this as we study the epistle, we have missed the great purpose for which it was given of God.

I would add one other thought, which I believe is of moment, particularly for those who seek to present the gospel to others. It is this: in Romans, we have the gospel taught to saints rather than the gospel preached to unsaved sinners. I believe it is very important to see this. In order to be saved it is only necessary to trust in Christ. But in order to understand our salvation and, thus, to get out of it the joy and blessing God intends to be our portion, we need to have the work of Christ unfolded to us. This is what the Holy Spirit has done in this precious epistle. It is written to people who are already saved to show them the secure foundation upon which their salvation rests: namely, the righteousness of God. When faith apprehends this, doubts and fears are gone and the soul enters into settled peace.

SALUTATION AND INTRODUCTION

Romans 1:1–17

As we come to a verse-by-verse examination of this epistle, we may well remind ourselves once more of the precious truth that "all scripture is God-breathed and profitable" (2 Tim. 3:16). God has spoken through His Word, and this letter contains some of the most important messages He has ever given to mankind. It will be well for us, therefore, to approach the study of it in a prayerful and self-judged spirit, putting all our own preconceived ideas to one side and letting God through the inspired Word correct our thoughts, or, better still, supplant them with His own.

The first seven verses, as we have already noticed, form the salutation and demand a careful examination. Some most precious truths are here communicated in what might seem a most casual manner. The writer, Paul, designates himself a servant—literally, bondman—of Jesus Christ. He does not mean, however, that his was a service of bondage, but rather the wholehearted obedience of one who realized that he had been "bought with a price" (1 Cor. 6:20; 7:23), even the precious blood of Christ.

There is a story told of an African slave whose master was about to slay him with a spear when a chivalrous British traveler thrust out his arm to ward off the blow, and it was pierced by the cruel weapon. As the blood spurted out, he demanded the person of the slave, saying he had bought him by his suffering. To this the former master ruefully agreed. As the latter walked away, the slave threw himself at the feet of his deliverer, exclaiming, "The blood-bought is now the slave of the son of pity. He will serve him faithfully." And he insisted on accompanying his generous deliverer and took delight in waiting upon him in every possible way.

Thus had Paul, thus has each redeemed one, become the bondman of Jesus Christ. We have been set free to serve and may well exclaim with the psalmist, "O LORD, truly I am thy servant; I am thy servant and the son of thine handmaid: thou hast loosed my bonds" (Ps. 116:16).

Not only was Paul in the general sense a servant, but he was a servant of peculiar and exalted character. He was a called apostle, not as in the Authorized Version, "called *to be* an apostle" (Rom. 1:1). The words "to be" are in italics and are not required to complete the sense. It may seem a small thing to which to call attention, but the same interpolation occurs in verse 7, where it is altogether misleading as we shall see when we come to consider it.

We need not think of Paul as one of the Twelve. Some question the regularity of the appointment of Matthias, but it seems to me we may well consider his selection by casting lots as the last official act of the old economy. It was necessary that one who had kept company with the Lord and His disciples from the baptism of John should fill the place that Judas had forfeited. Thus the number of the twelve apostles of the Lamb who are (in the glorious days of earth's regeneration that we generally call the Millennium) to sit upon twelve thrones judging the twelve tribes of Israel, would be completed. Paul's ministry is of a different character. He was preeminently the apostle to the Gentiles and to him was committed the special "dispensation of the mystery." This puts his apostleship on an altogether different plane from that of the Twelve. They knew Christ on earth, and their ministry in a very definite way was linked with the kingdom and the family of God. Paul knew him first as the glorified Lord Jesus, and his was distinctively the gospel of the glory.

He was "separated unto the gospel of God" (v. 1). We may rightfully think of this separation from several different viewpoints. He had been set apart for his special ministry before his birth. As in the instances of Moses, Jeremiah, and John the Baptist, he was separated from his mother's womb (Gal. 1:15). But he must first learn the weakness and unprofitableness of the flesh. Then God had mercy on him, and he was separated from the Christless mass and called by divine grace. But there was more than this. He was in a peculiar sense delivered from both the people of Israel and the Gentile nations to be a minister and witness of the things he had seen and heard. And lastly, he was separated with

Barnabas for the specific work of carrying the gospel to the Gentiles, when at Antioch in Pisidia, the brethren, in accordance with the divine command, laid their hands upon them and sent them away to carry the gospel to the regions beyond. This gospel is here called "the gospel of God." In verse 9 it is called "the gospel of his Son," and in verse 16, "the gospel of Christ," although there is a possibility that the words "of Christ" should be dropped, as they do not appear in some of the best manuscripts.

Verse 2 is parenthetical and identifies the gospel with the glad tidings promised in Old Testament times and predicted by the prophets in the Holy Scripture. "To him give all the prophets witness, that through his name whosoever believeth in him shall receive remission of sins" (Acts 10:43). Timothy had been taught from childhood the Holy Scriptures, and the apostle says that these "are able to make thee wise unto salvation through faith which is in Christ Jesus" (2 Tim. 3:15).

This gospel is not a new law. It is not a code of morals or ethics. It is not a creed to be accepted. It is not a system of religion to be adhered to. It is not good advice to be followed. It is a divinely given message concerning a divine Person, the Son of God, Jesus Christ our Lord. This glorious Being is true Man, yet very God. He is the Branch that grew out of the root of David, therefore true Man. But He is also the Son of God, the virgin-born, who had no human father, and this His works of power demonstrate. To this blessed fact the Spirit of Holiness bare witness when He raised dead persons to life. The expression, "by the resurrection from the dead," is literally, "by resurrection of dead persons" (Rom. 1:4). It includes His own resurrection, of course; but it also takes in the resurrection of the daughter of Jairus, of the widow's son, and of Lazarus. He who could thus rob death of its prey was God and man in one blessed, adorable Person, worthy of all worship and praise, now and forevermore.

From Him, the risen One, Paul had received grace (not only unmerited favor, but favor against merit, for he had deserved the very opposite) and apostleship by divine call that he might make known the gospel unto all nations to the obedience of faith for Christ's name's sake.

His apostleship, therefore, extended to those who were in Rome. Hitherto, he had not been able to visit them personally, but his heart went out to them as the called of Jesus Christ, and so he writes "to all that be in Rome, . . . called . . . saints" (v. 7). Observe that they were saints in the same way that he was an apostle, namely, by divine call. We do not become saints by acting in a saintly way, but because we are constituted saints we should manifest saintliness.

As is customary in his letters, he wishes them grace and peace from God our Father and the Lord Jesus Christ. Saved by grace in the first place, we need grace for seasonable help all along the way. Having peace with God through the blood of His cross, we need the peace of God to keep our hearts at rest as we journey on toward the eternal Sabbath-keeping that remains for the people of God.

Verses 8–17 are the introduction, which make clear his reasons for writing.

It is evident that a work of God had begun in Rome a number of years before the writing of this letter, for already the faith of the Christian assembly there was spoken of throughout the whole world, that is, throughout the Roman Empire. There is no evidence whatever that this work was in any sense linked with apostolic ministry. Both Scripture and history are silent as to who founded the church in Rome. Certainly Peter did not. There is not the remotest reason for connecting his name with it. The boast of the Roman Catholic Church that it is founded on Peter as the rock and that the Roman Bishop is the successor of St. Peter is all the merest twaddle. We have no means of knowing whether any apostle visited Rome until Paul himself was taken there in chains.

There seems to have been a providential reason why he was hindered from going there earlier. He calls God to witness (that God whom he served not merely outwardly but in his spirit, the inward man, in the gospel of His Son) that he had never ceased to pray for those Roman believers since he first heard of them. Coupled with his petitions for them was his earnest request that if it was the will of God he might have the opportunity to visit them and "have a prosperous journey" (v. 10). How differently that prayer was answered from what he might have expected, we well know. It gives us a little idea of the overruling wisdom of God in answering all our prayers. No man is competent to say what is prosperous and what is not. God's ways are not ours.

Paul longed to see them, hoping that he might be used of God to impart unto them some spiritual gift which would be for their establishment in the truth. Nor did he think only of being a blessing to them, but he fully expected that they would be a blessing to him. Both would be comforted together.

Many times during the past years he had prepared to go to Rome, but his plans had miscarried. He longed to have some fruit there as in other Gentile cities, for he felt himself to be a debtor to all mankind. The treasure committed to him was not for his own enjoyment but that he might make it known to others, whether Greeks or barbarians, cultured or ignorant. And realizing this he was ready to preach the gospel in Rome as elsewhere.

When in verse 16 he says, "I am not ashamed of the gospel of Christ," I understand that he means far more than people generally attach to these words. It was not merely that he did not blush to be called a Christian or that he was always ready boldly to declare his faith in Christ, but the gospel was to him a wonderful, because inspired, scheme for the redemption of mankind, a divinely revealed system of truth transcending all the philosophies of earth, which he was ready to defend on every occasion. It was not, as some might have supposed, that he had refrained from visiting Rome because he did not feel competent to present the claims of Christ in the metropolis of the world in such a manner that they could not be answered and logically repudiated by the cultured philosophers who thronged the great city. He had no fear that they would be able to overthrow by their subtle reasonings that which he knew to be the only authoritative plan of salvation. It is beyond human reason, but it is not illogical or unreasonable. It is perfect because of God.

This gospel had been demonstratively proven to be the divine dynamic bringing deliverance to all who put faith in it, whether the religious Jew or the cultured Greek. It was the power of God and the wisdom of God unto salvation. It met every need of the mind, the conscience, and the heart of man, for in it the righteousness of God was revealed faith-wise. This I take to be the real meaning of the somewhat difficult expression translated "from faith to faith" (v. 17). It is really "out of faith unto faith." That is, on the principle of faith to those who have faith. In other words, it is not a doctrine of salvation by works, but a proclamation of salvation entirely on the faith principle. This had been declared to Habakkuk long centuries before when God said to the troubled prophet, "The just shall live by faith."

This is the text of the entire epistle, as we have already seen, and of Galatians and Hebrews likewise.

It gives us the quintessence of the divine plan. It has been the rest of millions throughout the centuries. It was the foundation of what has been designated the Augustinian Theology. It was the key that opened the door of liberty to Martin Luther. It became the battle cry of the Reformation. And it is the touchstone of every system since that professes to be of God. If wrong here, they are bound to be wrong throughout. It is impossible to understand the gospel if the basic principle be misunderstood or denied. Justification by faith alone is the test of orthodoxy. But no mind untaught by the Holy Spirit will ever receive it, for it sets the first man aside altogether as in the flesh and unprofitable in order that the Second Man, the Man of God's counsels, the Lord Jesus Christ, may alone be exalted. Faith gives all honor to Him as the One who has finished the work that saves and in whom alone God has been fully glorified, His holiness maintained, and His righteousness vindicated, and that not in the death of the sinner but in the salvation of all who believe. It is a gospel worthy of God, and it has demonstrated its power by what it has accomplished in those who have received it in faith.

THE NEED OF THE GOSPEL

Romans 1:18–3:20

We have seen that the gospel reveals the righteousness of God. The apostle now proceeds to show the need of such a revelation and piles proof upon proof, evidence upon evidence, and Scripture upon Scripture to demonstrate the solemn fact that man has no righteousness of his own, but is both by nature and practice utterly unsuited to a God of infinite holiness whose throne is established on righteousness. This he does in the next section of the epistle, Romans 1:18–3:20. In a masterly way he brings the whole world into court and shows that condemnation rests upon all because all have sinned. Man is guilty, hopelessly so, and can do nothing to retrieve his condition. If God has not a righteousness for him his case is ended.

In verses 18–32 of the first chapter the case of the barbarian is considered. "The wrath of God is revealed from heaven against all ungodliness and unrighteousness of men, who hold the truth in unrighteousness" (v. 18). The first class is the pagan world. The second, those to whom a divine revelation had come. The barbarians and heathen generally are ungodly. They know not the true God and so are "without God in the world" (Eph. 2:12). Therefore, their behavior is described as ungodliness.

On the other hand, to the Jew had been committed the knowledge of God

22

and a divine code of righteousness. He gloried in this while walking in unrighteousness. He held the truth (as something on which he had a "corner") in unrighteousness. Against both classes the wrath of God is revealed.

The heathen are without excuse. Paganism and idolatry are not steps in human evolution as man advances from slime to divinity. Heathenism is a declension not an upward reach. The great pagan nations once knew more than they do now. The knowledge of God brought through the flood was disseminated throughout the ancient world. Back of all the great idolatrous systems is pure monotheism. But men could not stand this intimate knowledge of God, for it made them uncomfortable in their sins. So a host of lesser deities and divinities were invented as go-betweens and, eventually, the knowledge of the true God was entirely lost. But even today creation is His constant witness: "That which may be known of God is manifest [to] them; for God hath shown it unto them" (Rom. 1:19). This orderly universe with its succession of the seasons and the mathematical accuracy of the movements of the heavenly bodies bears testimony to the Divine Mind. The stars in their courses proclaim the great Creator's power:

> Forever singing as they shine,
> The Hand that made us is divine.

So, "the invisible things of him from the creation of the world are clearly seen, being understood by the things that are made, even his eternal power and Godhead" (v. 20). One word in the original is rendered by four words in English: "Things-that-are-made" is *Poima,* and from this we get our word *poem.* Creation is God's great epic poem, every part fitted together like the lines and verses of a majestic hymn. In Ephesians 2:10 we find the same word again. "We are his *workmanship* [His poem] created in Christ Jesus unto good works which God hath before ordained that we should walk in them." This is God's greatest poem: the epic of redemption.

> 'Twas great to call a world from naught;
> 'Twas greater to redeem.

These two wondrous poems are celebrated in Revelation 4–5. In chapter 4 the enthroned and crowned saints worship Christ as Creator. In chapter 5 they adore Him as Redeemer.

Pursuing Paul's argument we note in verses 21–23 that the barbarous nations are without excuse for their present ignorance and bestial condition,

Because that, when they knew God, they glorified him not as God, neither were thankful; but became vain in their imaginations, and their foolish heart was darkened. Professing themselves to be wise they became fools, and changed the glory of the incorruptible God into an image made like to corruptible man, and to birds, and fourfooted beasts and creeping things.

Observe the downward steps on the toboggan-slide of idolatry—God first thought of as an idealized man, then likened to the birds that soar into the heavens, next to the beasts that prowl over the earth, and finally to serpents and other detestable creeping things, whether reptilian or insectivorous. Even the Egyptian worshiped the serpent and the scarabaeus, and yet back of all Egyptian mythology is hidden the original revelation of one true and living God! What degradation does this imply on the part of one of the most enlightened nations of antiquity! And others bear similar marks of declension and deterioration.

Because men gave God up, He gave them up. Twice in the verses that follow we read, "God gave them up," first to uncleanness and then to vile affections. Once we are told, "God gave them over to a reprobate mind" (v. 28). The vile immoralities depicted here are the natural result of turning from the Holy One. The picture of heathenism in its unspeakable obscenities is not overdrawn, as any one acquainted with the lives of idolatrous people will testify. The awful thing is that all this vileness and filthiness is being reproduced in modern high society where men and women repudiate God. If people change the truth of God into a lie and worship and serve the creature rather than the Creator, the whole order of nature is violated. For apart from the fear of God there is no power known that will hold the evil desires of the natural heart in check. It is part of the very nature of things that flesh will be manifested in its worst aspects when God gives men up to follow the bent of their unholy lusts.

What a picture of mankind away from Him do we get in the closing verses. Sin and corruption are everywhere triumphant. Righteousness is not to be found when the back is turned on God. Nor are men sensitive about their sins or ashamed of their evil ways, but "knowing the judgment of God, that they which commit such things are worthy of death, not only do the same, but have pleasure in them that do them."

That the apostle's picture of heathenism is still true, the following clipping bears witness: "A Chinese teacher once told a missionary that the Bible could not be so ancient a book after all, because the first chapter of Romans gave an account of Chinese conduct, such as the missionary could only have written after full acquaintance with the people. The mistake was not an unnatural one, but it is a heathen's testimony to the truth of the Bible."

In the first sixteen verses of the next chapter another class is brought into view: it is the world of culture and refinement. Surely among the educated, the followers of the various philosophic systems, will be found men who lead such righteous lives that they can come into the presence of God claiming His blessing on the ground of their own goodness! Certainly there were those who professed to look with disgust and abhorrence upon the vile lewdness of the ignorant rabble, but were their private lives any holier or any cleaner than those whom they so loudly condemned?

It is now their turn to be summoned into court, so to speak, where the apostle fearlessly arraigns them before the august tribunal of "the righteous LORD [who] loveth righteousness" (Ps. 11:7). "Therefore thou art inexcusable, O man, whosoever thou art that judgest; for wherein thou judgest another thou condemnest thyself; for thou that judgest doest the same things" (Rom. 2:1). Philosophy does not preserve its devotee from the indulgence of the flesh. A recognition of the evil is not necessarily power to overcome the evil. Culture does not cleanse the heart nor education alter the nature. It is against the doer of evil that the judgment of God according to truth will be rendered. To praise virtue while practicing vice may enable one to get by with his fellows, but it will not deceive Him who is of purer eyes than to behold iniquity.

Sternly he asks, "Thinkest thou this, O man, that judgest them which do such things and doest the same, that thou shalt escape the judgment of God? Or despisest thou the riches of His goodness and forbearance and longsuffering; not knowing that the goodness of God leadeth thee to repentance?" (vv. 2–3). Men are inclined to consider that God is condoning their ways, if "sentence against an evil work is not executed speedily" (Eccl. 8:11), whereas He waits in longsuffering mercy that men may have opportunity to face their sins and own their guilt, thus finding mercy. Instead of doing this, after the hardness and impenitence of their hearts, men untouched by divine grace "treasurest up unto themselves wrath against the day of wrath and revelation of the righteous judgment of God; who will render to every man according to his deeds" (Rom. 2:5–6).

What a solemn expression is this—"treasurest up [or storing up] . . . wrath against the day of wrath!" How apt was the answer of the poor old colored woman who when taunted with the folly of believing in a "lake of fire and brimstone" (Rev. 20:10) because "no such an amount of brimstone could be found in one place," exclaimed solemnly, "Ebryone takes his own brimstone wif' him!" Ah, that is it! Each rebel against God, each sinner against light, each violator of his own conscience carries his own brimstone with him! He is making his own destiny.

Properly, I believe, we should consider verses 7–15 as parenthetical, not merely 13–15, as indicated in the Authorized Version. In these verses great principles of judgment are laid down that should forever silence the caviler who would charge God with unrighteousness because some have light and privileges that others do not enjoy.

Judgment will be "according to truth" (Rom. 2:2) and "according to . . . deeds" (v. 6). Men will be judged by the light they have had, not by the light they never knew. Eternal life is offered to all who "by patient continuance in well doing seek for glory and honour and [incorruptibility]" (v. 7). (Observe it is not immortality, but incorruptibility. The distinction is of great importance, though the two terms are often confounded in the Authorized Version.) If any were so characterized, it would prove that there was a divine work in the soul. But where is the natural man who so lives? Well then, "unto them that are contentious and do not obey the truth, but obey unrighteousness," there can but be meted out in the day of judgment "indignation and wrath, tribulation and anguish, upon every soul of man that doeth evil," whether privileged Jew or ignorant Gentile (vv. 8–9).

It is not that God will deal in indiscriminate judgment with all men, therefore, but light given will be the standard by which they are judged. None can complain, for if one but "follow the gleam" he will find light enough to guide his steps and ensure his salvation. If, by the light of nature, men realize their responsibility to their Creator, He will make Himself responsible to give them further light unto the salvation of their souls.

With Him there is no respect of persons. The greater the privileges, the greater the responsibility. But where privileges are comparatively few, He regards ignorant men with no less interest and tender compassion than He does those whose outward circumstances are seemingly better.

"As many as have sinned without law shall also perish without law: and as many as have sinned in the law shall be judged by the law" (v. 12). No principle could be sounder. Men are held responsible for what they know, or might know if they would. They are not condemned for ignorance unless that ignorance be the result of the willful rejection of light. "Men [love] darkness rather than light, because their deeds [are] evil" (John 3:19).

The parenthetical verses 13–15 of Romans 2 emphasize the plain principle already laid down so forcibly. Judgment is according to deeds. To know the law and fail to obey it only increases the condemnation. Doers of the law will be justified, if such there are. But elsewhere we learn that from this standpoint all would be lost, for "by the deeds of the law there shall no flesh be justified in his sight" (3:20). The Jew prided himself upon being in possession of the divine oracles and thought this made him superior to the Gentile nations round about. But God has not left Himself without wit ness. To these nations He has given both the light of conscience and the light of nature. They "show the work of the law written in their hearts" (2:15).

Observe, it is not that the law is written in their hearts. That is new birth and is the distinctive blessing of the new covenant. If the law were written there, they would fulfill its righteousness. But the *work* of the law is quite another thing. "The law worketh wrath" (4:15). It is a "[ministry] of condemnation" (2 Cor. 3:9). And Gentile sinners who never heard of the Sinaitic code have a sense of condemnation resting upon them when they live in violation of the dictates of their divinely-implanted conscience which testifies either for or against them— "accusing or else excusing one another" (Rom. 2:15). This is experimental proof that they are on the ground of responsibility and that God will be righteous in judging them in that solemn day when the Man Christ Jesus will sit upon the august tribunal of the ages and manifest the secret motives and springs of conduct. This, Paul says is "according to my gospel" (v. 16). He declares that the Crucified will sit upon the throne at the last great assize. "[God] hath appointed a day, in which he will judge the world in righteousness by that man whom he hath ordained; whereof he hath given assurance unto all men, in that he hath raised him from the dead" (Acts 17:31).

With all that the apostle had written concerning the sinfulness and degeneracy of the Gentiles, whether barbarian or highly civilized, the Jew would be in fullest agreement. They were "dogs," outside of the Abrahamic covenant, "aliens [to] the commonwealth of Israel" (Eph. 2:12). Their judgment was just, for they were the enemies of God and His chosen people. But it was otherwise with the Hebrews. They were the elect of Jehovah, the chosen race to whom God had given His holy law and favored with abundant tokens of His special regard. So they reasoned, forgetting that holding correct doctrine does not avail if practical righteousness be overlooked or disregarded.

The apostle suddenly summons the proud worldly Sadducee and the complacent Pharisee into court, and proceeds to arraign them along with the despised Gentiles. Verses 17–29 give us the examination of the chosen people.

> Behold, [he exclaims,] thou art called a Jew, and restest in the law, and makest thy boast of God, and knowest his will, and approvest the things

that are more excellent [or, triest things that differ; see margin], being instructed out of the law; and art confident that thou thyself art a guide of the blind, a light of them which are in darkness, an instructor of the foolish, a teacher of babes, which hast the form of knowledge and of the truth in the law. (vv. 17–20)

In these masterly clauses he sums up all their pretensions. And when I say pretensions, I do not mean pretenses. These were the things in which they gloried and they were largely true. God had revealed Himself to this people as to no other, but they were wrong in supposing that this exempted them from judgment if they failed to keep His covenant. He had said long before, "You only have I known of all the families of the earth: therefore I will punish you for all your iniquities" (Amos 3:2).

Privilege increases responsibility. It does not, as they seemed to think, set it aside. The knowledge of the divine oracles gave to the Jew a standard of judgment that no others had. Therefore, how much holier should be his life! Were the Israelites then a more righteous people than the nations about them? On the contrary, they failed more miserably than those of less light and fewer privileges.

Incisively the Spirit of God drives home the truth as to their actual state in four questions calculated to expose the inmost secrets of their hearts and to lay bare the hidden sins of their lives. "Thou therefore which teachest another, teachest thou not thyself?" (Rom. 2:21). You are so confident that you are fitted to instruct the ignorant, have you heeded the instruction given in the law? No answer!

"Thou that preachest a man should not steal, dost thou steal?" (v. 21). Throughout the ancient world the Jew was looked upon as the arch-thief, using every cunning device known to the money lender and usurer to part his clients from their wealth. True, driven by desperation, the Gentile voluntarily put himself into the hand of the Jewish pawnbroker, but he knew as he did so that he was dealing with one who had no niceties of pity or compassion for an indigent debtor when the debtor was a hated Gentile dog. The Jew is again speechless.

"Thou that sayest a man should not commit adultery, dost thou commit adultery?" (v. 22). Lechery of the gravest kind was not an uncommon offense in Israel, as the divine records prove and as history bears witness. The evil is in the very nature of man. Out of the heart proceed fornication, lasciviousness, and every unclean thing. In this respect the Jew is as guilty as his Gentile neighbor. He has no reply.

Perhaps the keenest thrust is in the last question of all. "Thou that abhorrest idols, dost thou commit sacrilege?" (v. 22). The word translated "commit sacrilege" really means "to traffic in idols." This was an offense of which the Jew was peculiarly guilty. Abhorring images, he nevertheless was often known to act as a go-between in disposing of idols stolen from the temples of a conquered people and those ready to purchase them in other districts. He was even charged with systematically robbing temples and then selling the images. The town clerk of Ephesus had this in mind when he said, "Ye have brought hither these men, which are neither robbers of [temples, not churches], nor yet blasphemers of your goddess" (Acts 19:37). So this was indeed a home thrust, exposing at once the hypocritical character of the man who professed detestation of idolatry and all its works, and yet was not above profiting financially at the expense of idolaters in a manner so thoroughly dishonest.

So the apostle drives home the tremendous indictment! "For the name of God is blasphemed among the Gentiles through you, as it is written" (Rom. 2:24). This their own prophets had declared, and he but insists upon what Scripture and their consciences confirmed.

To trust in circumcision, the sign of the Abrahamic covenant, while walking in so carnal a manner was but deceiving themselves. Ordinances do not profit if that of which the ordinance speaks is neglected. The uncircumcised Gentile, if he walk before God in righteousness, will be accounted as circumcised, whereas the covenant mark on the flesh of a Jew will only add to his condemnation if he lives in opposition to the law.

It is reality that counts with God. The true Jew (and "Jew" is a contraction of "Judah," meaning, "Praise") is not one who is such by natural birth alone or by outward conformity to ritual, but one who is circumcised in heart, who has judged his sinfulness in the sight of the Lord, and who now seeks to walk in accordance with the revealed will of God (see vv. 26–29). "Whose *praise* [note the play on the word Jew] is not of men, but of God" (v. 29).

In Romans 3:1–20 we have the great indictment, the summing up of all that has gone before. There is no moral distinction between Jew and Gentile. All are bereft of righteousness. All are shut up to judgment, unless God has a righteousness of His own providing for them.

That the Jew has certain advantages over the Gentile is acknowledged as self-evident, and of these the chief is the possession of the Holy Scripture, the oracles of God. But these very Scripture passages only made his guilt the more evident. Even if they did not really have faith in these sacred writings yet their unfaith cannot make void the faithfulness of God. He will fulfill His Word even if it be in the setting aside of the people He chose for Himself. He must be true though all others prove untrue. In judgment He will maintain His righteousness, as David confesses in Psalm 51:1–4.

Does man's unrighteousness then but prepare the way for God to display His righteousness, and is it a necessity of the case? If so, sin is a part of the divine plan and man cannot be held accountable. But this the apostle indignantly refutes. God is just. He will judge men for their sins in righteousness. And this could not be if sin were foreordained and predetermined. If the latter were true, man might have just cause to complain: "If the truth of God hath more abounded through my lie unto his glory; why yet am I also judged as a sinner?" (Rom. 3:7). And in that case what was being slanderously reported by some as the teaching of Paul, "Let us do evil that good may come" (v. 8), would be correct. But all who so plead show themselves deficient in moral principle. Their judgment is just.

Then in verses 9–20 we have the divine verdict on the entire human race. The Jew is no better than the Gentile. All alike are under—that is, slaves to—sin. And this the Old Testament confirms. Like a masterly lawyer he cites authority after authority to prove his case. The quotations are largely from the Psalms, and one from the prophet Isaiah (see Pss. 5:9; 10:7; 14:1–3; 36:1; 53:1–3; 140:3; Isa. 59:7–8). These are testimonies the Jew could not attempt to refute, coming as they do from his own acknowledged Scripture. There are fourteen distinct counts in this indictment or summary of evidence.

1. "There is none righteous, no, not one" (v. 10). All have failed in something.
2. "There is none that understandeth" (v. 11a). All have become willfully ignorant.
3. "There is none that seeketh after God" (v. 11b). All seek their own.
4. "They are all gone out of the way" (v. 12a). They have deliberately turned their backs on the truth.
5. "They are together become unprofitable" (v. 12b). They have dishonored God instead of glorifying Him.
6. "There is none that doeth good, no, not one" (v. 12c). Their practices are evil. They do not follow after that which is good.
7. "Their throat is an open sepulchre" (v. 13a). because of the corruption within.
8. "With their tongues they have used deceit" (v. 13b). Lying and deception are characteristic.
9. "The poison of asps is under their lips" (v. 13c). It is the poison inserted

into the very nature of man by "that old serpent, . . . the Devil, and Satan" (Rev. 12:9; 20:2) at the very beginning.

10. "Whose mouth is full of cursing and bitterness" (v. 14) for "out of the abundance of the heart the mouth speaketh" (Matt. 12:34).

11. "Their feet are swift to shed blood" (v. 15). Hatred produces murder and, alas, in how many ways it is manifested!

12. "Destruction and misery are in their ways" (v. 16), because they have forgotten God the source of life and blessing.

13. "The way of peace have they not known" (v. 17), for they have deliberately chosen the ways of death.

14. "There is no fear of God before their eyes" (v. 18). Hence there is no wisdom in them.

Can any plead "Not guilty" to all of these charges? If so, let him speak. But none can honestly do so. And so he concludes, "We know that what things soever the law saith, it saith to them who are under the law: that every mouth may be stopped, and all the world become guilty before God. Therefore by the deeds of the law there shall no flesh be justified in his sight, for by the law is the knowledge of sin" (vv. 19–20).

It is God saying again, as in the days of Noah, "The end of all flesh is come before me" (Gen. 6:13). "They that are in the flesh cannot please God" (Rom. 8:8). "The flesh profiteth nothing" (John 6:63). How slow we are to learn this! How hard it is for the natural man to give up all pretension to righteousness and to fall down in the dust of self-judgment and repentance before God, only to find he is then in the very place where grace can meet him!

The law was given to a special people as we have seen. They alone were "under the law." That Gentiles were not, we have already been told in Romans 2:12–14. How, then, does the failure of those under the law bring in all the world as guilty before God? An illustration may help. A man has a desert ranch of large extent. He is told it is worthless as pasturage or farming land. He fences off twelve acres; breaks it, harrows it, fertilizes it, sows it, cultivates it, and reaps only sagebrush and cactus! It is no use trying out the rest, for all is of the same character. He says it is all good-for-nothing, so far as agriculture is concerned. Israel was God's twelve acres. He gave them His law, instructed them, disciplined them, warned them, restrained them, protected them, and sent His Son to them. It was Him they rejected and crucified. In this act the Gentiles joined. All are under judgment to God. There is no use of further test. There is nothing in the flesh for God. Man is hopelessly corrupt. He is not only guilty but is utterly unable to retrieve his condition. The law but accentuates his guilt. It cannot justify. It can only condemn.

How hopeless is the picture! But it is the dark background on which God will display the riches of His grace in Christ Jesus!

THE GOSPEL IN RELATION TO OUR SINS

Romans 3:21–5:11

It is with a sense of the greatest relief that we turn from the sad story of man's sin and shame to contemplate the wondrous grace of God as told out in the gospel, the divine remedy for the ruin that came in by the fall. And this presentation of the Good News is in two parts: it presents the gospel first as having to do with the question of our sins and, then when that is settled, as having to do with our sin—the sin-principle, sin in the flesh, the carnal mind which dominates the unsaved, unregenerated man. The first theme is fully taken up in Romans 3:21–5:11, and this we will now consider.

"But now," exclaims the apostle. It marks a decided change of subject. *Now* that man has been fully shown up, God will be revealed. Now upon the proven unrighteousness of all mankind "the righteousness of God . . . is manifested" (3:21). Of old He had declared, "I [will] bring near my righteousness" (Isa. 46:13). This is in no sense a wrought-out, legal righteousness, such as man was unable to produce for God. It is a righteousness "without the law," that is, altogether apart from any principle of human obedience to a divinely-ordained code of morals. It is a righteousness of God for unrighteous men and is in no wise dependent upon human merit or attainment.

The righteousness of God is a term of wide import. Here it means a righteousness of God's providing—a perfect standing for guilty men for which God makes Himself responsible. If men are saved at all, it must be in righteousness. But of this, man is utterly bereft. Therefore, God must find a way whereby every claim of His righteous throne shall be met, and yet guilty sinners be justified from all things. His very nature demands that this must not be at the expense of righteousness but in full accord with it.

And this has been in His mind from the beginning. It is "witnessed," or borne testimony to, "by the law and the prophets" (v. 21). Moses depicts it in many types of remarkable beauty. The coats of skin wherein our first parents were clothed, the sacrificial victims accepted in behalf of the offerers, the wonderful symbolism of the tabernacle all tell out the story of a righteousness provided by God for the unrighteous sinner who turns to Him in faith. The prophets, too, take up the same story. They predict the coming of the Just One who was to die to bring unjust men nigh to God. "Deliver me in thy righteousness," cries David (Ps. 31:1). "Purge me with hyssop and I shall be clean: wash me, and I shall be whiter than snow," he prays (51:7). "He hath clothed [us in] the garments of salvation, . . . in the robe of righteousness" (Isa. 61:10), says Isaiah, for "the chastisement of our peace was upon him" who was "bruised for our iniquities" (53:5). "This is his name," exclaims Jeremiah, "whereby he shall be called, the Lord our Righteousness" (Jer. 23:6). "I will save you from all your uncleannesses," is the promise through Ezekiel (36:29). To Daniel the angel Gabriel foretells the making of "reconciliation for iniquity" and the bringing in of "everlasting righteousness" (Dan. 9:24). The so-called Minor Prophets take up the same strain, and all point forward to the Coming One through whom salvation will be secured for all who repent—Jehovah's Fellow, who will become the smitten Shepherd for man's redemption. "To him give all the prophets witness, that through his name whosoever believeth in him shall receive remission of sins" (Acts 10:43).

The righteousness of God is a "by faith" righteousness. It is not "by works." Faith is taking God at His word. So He has sent a message to man to be believed. It is the offer of an unimpeachable righteousness to all, but is only upon all them who believe. There is a question as to the reading here. Some editors reject "and upon all" (Rom. 3:22). But there can be no question of the underlying truth. God freely offers a righteousness to all. It is the covering of all those who believe and of them only. All need it alike, for all have sinned. There is no difference as to this. No man has come up to the standard. All have come short of the glory of God. But He is not looking for merit in man. He offers His righteousness as a free gift. So we read, "Being justified freely by his grace through the redemption that is in Christ Jesus" (v. 24).

To be justified is to be declared righteous. It is the sentence of the judge in favor of the prisoner. It is not a state or condition of soul. We are not justified because we have become righteous in heart and life. God justifies first, then He enables the justified one to walk in practical righteousness. We are justified *freely.* The word means "without price!" It is the same as in John 15:25, "They hated me without a cause." There was nothing evil in the ways or life of Jesus, for which men should hate Him. They hated Him *freely.* So there is no good in man for which God should justify him. He is justified freely, *without a cause,* when he believes in Jesus.

This is "by grace." Grace is not only unmerited favor. Grace is favor against merit. It is the goodness of God, not alone to men who have done and can do nothing to deserve it, but it is favor shown to men who have deserved the very opposite. "Where sin abounded, grace did much more abound" (Rom. 5:20).

> Sovereign grace, o'er sin abounding;
> Ransomed souls the tidings swell,
> 'Tis a deep that knows no sounding;
> Who its length and breadth can tell?
> On its glories
> Let my soul forever dwell.

In order thus to show grace in righteousness to admittedly guilty sinners, God must have a just and satisfactory basis. Sin cannot be overlooked. It must be atoned for. This has been effectuated "through the redemption that is in Christ Jesus" (3:24). Redemption is a buying back. Man's life is forfeited because of his iniquitous ways. He is sold under judgment. Christ the Holy One—God and Man in one glorious Person upon whom the violated law had no claim—took the guilty rebel's place, paid the utmost penalty, thus redeeming the believing sinner from the wrath and curse to which he had sold himself.

> He bore on the tree, the sentence for me,
> And now both the Surety and sinner are free.

And He who died lives again and is Himself the abiding propitiation—literally, the mercy seat, the place where God can meet with man through Christ's atoning blood—available to faith. The apostle clearly alludes to the blood-sprinkled mercy seat on the ark of the covenant of old. Within the ark were the tables of the law. Above were the cherubim, "justice and judgment" the habitation of God's throne. They are ready, as it were, to leap from that throne to execute God's righteous wrath against the violators of His law. But sprinkled upon the mercy seat is the blood that typifies the sacrifice of the cross. Justice and judgment ask no more. "Mercy rejoiceth against judgment" (James 2:13), for God Himself has found a ransom.

Until the Lord Jesus suffered for sins, the Just for the unjust to bring us to God, the sin question was not really settled. "It [was] not possible that the blood of bulls and of goats should take away sins" (Heb. 10:4). Old Testament saints therefore were all saved "on credit," as we say. Now that Christ has died the account is closed, and God declares His righteousness in pretermitting sins down through the past ages when men turned to Him in faith. It is not *our* past sins He refers to in verse 25. It is the sins of believers in the ages before the cross. And now God declares *at this time*—since the work is done—His righteousness, for He has shown how He can be just and yet justify ungodly sinners who believe in Jesus. This leaves no room for boasting on man's part, rather for shame and contrition in view of what our sins cost the Savior, and of joyful praise as we contemplate the grace that wrought so wondrously on our behalf. Human merit is barred out in the very nature of the case. Salvation is through grace by faith. "Therefore we conclude that a man is justified by faith apart from the deeds of the law" (Rom. 3:28). This then embraces lawless Gentiles as well as law-breaking Jews. The same evangel is for all. He who is the Creator of all has passed none by. He will justify the circumcised not by ritual but by faith, and the uncircumcised Gentile through faith likewise.

Does this invalidate or ignore the law? Not at all. The law condemned the breaker of it and demanded vengeance. This Christ has borne, so the majesty of the law is upheld, yet sinners are saved.

> On Christ Almighty vengeance fell
> That would have sunk a world to hell;
> He bore it for a chosen race,
> And thus became a Hiding-place.

In chapter 4 the apostle proceeds to show, by means of Abraham and David, how all this is witnessed by the law and the prophets. Abraham is taken from the Pentateuch, the books of the law; David from the Psalms, which are linked with the Prophets.

What then do we see in Abraham? Was he justified before God by his works? If so, he had this to boast in, that he had righteously deserved the divine approval. But what does the Scripture say? In Genesis 15:6 we are told that "[Abraham] believed in the LORD; and he counted it to him for righteousness." Romans 4:3 reads, "Abraham believed God, and it was counted unto him for righteousness." This is the very principle the apostle has been pressing and explaining so clearly.

To earn salvation by works would be to put God in man's debt. He would owe it to the successful worker to save him. This is the very opposite of grace, which is mercy shown "to him that worketh not, but believeth on him that justifieth the ungodly" (Rom. 4:5). It is his faith that is counted for righteousness. To this then Abraham bears testimony. And David too is heard singing the blessedness of the man to whom God imputes righteousness without works, when he cries in Psalm 32:1–2: "Blessed is he whose transgression is forgiven, whose sin is covered. Blessed is the man unto whom the LORD imputeth not iniquity." Romans 4:7–8 reads, "Blessed are they whose iniquities are forgiven, and whose sins are covered. Blessed is the man to whom the Lord will not impute sin." In the psalm the Hebrew word for "covered" means "atoned for." This is the gospel. Atonement has been made. Therefore, God does not impute sin to the believer in His Son but imputes righteousness instead.

Luther called the Thirty-second Psalm "a Pauline Psalm." It teaches in no uncertain way the same glorious doctrine of justification apart from human merit. The non-imputation of sin is equivalent to the imputation of righteousness. Augustine of Hippo had these words painted on a placard and placed at the foot of his bed where his dying eyes could rest upon them. To myriads more they have brought peace and gladness in the knowledge of transgression forgiven and sin atoned for, as the Hebrew word in the Old Testament translated "covered" really means.

This blessedness was not—is not—for a chosen few only, but is freely offered to all. Faith was reckoned to Abraham for righteousness when he was on Gentile ground before the covenant sign of circumcision was placed upon his flesh. It was really a seal of what was already true, as in the case of Christian baptism. Because he was justified he was commanded to be circumcised. In the centuries since the Jews had come to regard the sign as of more importance than the faith. People ever exalt the visible at the expense of the invisible.

Abraham is called "the father of circumcision" (Rom. 4:12), for through him the ordinance began. But he is father not only to them who are of the circumcision literally, but to all who have no confidence in the flesh, who have judged it as weak and unprofitable, and who, like him, trust in the living God.

The promise that he should be heir of the world was not given to him "through the law" (v. 13), that is, it was not a reward of merit, something he had earned by obedience. It was on the ground of sovereign grace. Hence his righteousness, like ours if we believe, was a "by faith righteousness." The heirs of the promise are those who accept it in the same faith, otherwise it would be utterly invalidated. It was an unconditional promise.

The law promised blessing upon obedience and denounced judgment on disobedience. None have kept it. Therefore, "the law worketh wrath" (v. 15). It cursed. It could not bless. It intensified sin by giving it the specific character of transgression, making it the willful violation of known law. It could not be the means of earning what was freely given.

The promise of blessing through the Seed—which is Christ—is of faith that it might be by grace. And so it is "sure" to all the seed, that is, to all who have faith. All such are "of the faith of Abraham" (v. 16). He is thus the father of us all who believe in Jesus. And so the word is fulfilled that said, "I have made thee a father of many nations" (v. 17). This comes in parenthetically. The words, "Before Him whom he believed," properly follow the words, "the father of us all." That is to say, Abraham, though not literally our father by natural generation, is the father of all who believe in the sight of God. The same faith characterizes them all.

God is the God of resurrection. He works when nature is powerless. He so wrought in the case of Abraham and Sarah, both beyond the time when they could naturally be the parents of a child. He so wrought when He raised up Christ, the true Seed, first by bringing Him into the world contrary to nature, of a virgin mother; and second by bringing Him up from the dead. Abraham believed in the God of resurrection and staggered not at the divine promise though fulfillment seemed impossible. God delights to do impossibilities! What He promises He performs. Fully persuaded of this, Abraham believed God, and "it was imputed to him for righteousness" (v. 22). In the same way we are called upon to believe on Him who raised up Jesus our Lord from the dead—He who was, in infinite grace, delivered up to death to make atonement for our offenses, and who, upon the completion of His work to God's satisfaction, was raised again for our justification. His resurrection is the proof that God is satisfied. The divine justice has been appeased. The holiness of God has been vindicated. The law has been established. And so the believing sinner is declared justified from all things. Such is the testimony of chapter 4.

In the first eleven verses of chapter 5 we have a marvelous summing up, concluding this phase of the subject. "Therefore," that is, in view of all that has been so clearly established, "being justified by faith we have peace with God through our Lord Jesus Christ" (v. 1). Some would render it, "Let us have peace." But this is to weaken the force of the entire argument. Peace, as used here, is not a state of mind or heart. It is a prevailing condition between two who were once alienated. Sin had disturbed the relations of Creator and creature. A breach had come in which man could not mend. But peace has been made by the blood of Christ's cross. There is no longer a barrier. Peace with God is now the abiding state into which every believer enters. The sin question is settled. If two nations be at war, there is no peace. If peace is made, there is no war. "There is no peace, saith my God, to the wicked" (Isa. 57:21). "But Christ has made peace," yea, "He is our peace" (Eph. 2:14). We believe it, and we have peace with God.

We might say, "Let us enjoy peace with God." But, "Let us have peace with God," is absurd on the face of it. We have the peace. It is a settled thing. He made it, not we.

> 'Tis everlasting peace,
>   Sure as Jehovah's name;
> 'Tis stable as His steadfast throne,
>   Forevermore the same.
>
> My love is ofttimes low,
>   My joy still ebbs and flows,
> But peace with Him remains the same,
>   No change Jehovah knows.
>
> I change; He changes not,
>   My Christ can never die;
> This blood-sealed friendship changes not,
>   His truth, not mine, the tie.

"The peace of God" is another thing, as in Philippians 4:6–7. That is experimental. It is the abiding portion of all who learn to cast every care on Him who is the great Burden-bearer.

To see this distinction and to really grasp it in faith is of prime importance. Until the soul realizes that the peace made by the blood of His cross is eternal and undisturbed, even though one's experience may be very different owing to personal failure or lack of appropriating faith, there will be no certainty of one's ultimate salvation.

But knowing this peace to be based, not on my frames or feelings, but on accomplished redemption, I have conscious access by faith into this grace wherein I stand. I stand in grace, not in my own merit. I was saved by grace. I go on in grace. I shall be glorified in grace. Salvation from first to last is altogether of God, and therefore altogether of grace.

> Grace is the sweetest sound
>> That ever reached our ears:
> When conscience charged and justice frowned,
>> 'Twas grace removed our fears.

> Grace is a mine of wealth
>> Laid open to the poor,
> Grace is the sov'reign spring of health,
>> 'Tis *life for evermore.*

> Of grace then, let us sing,
>> A joyful wondrous theme;
> Who grace has brought shall *glory* bring,
>> And we shall reign with Him.

This is the golden scepter held out by the King of Glory to all who venture to approach in faith.

Note it is *access and standing* that are before us in this second verse of the fifth chapter of our epistle. Access is based on standing not on state. The terms are to be carefully distinguished. In Philippians we read much about "your state." Paul was greatly concerned about that. He never had a fear about the standing of the children of God. That is eternally settled.

Standing refers to the new place in which I am put by grace as justified before the throne of God and in Christ risen, forever beyond the reach of judgment. State is condition of soul. It is experience. Standing never varies. State is fluctuating and depends on the measure in which I walk with God. My standing is always perfect because it is measured by Christ's acceptance. I am accepted in Him. "As He is, so are we *in this world*" (1 John 4:17). But my state will be good or bad as I walk in the Spirit or walk after the flesh.

My standing gives me title to enter consciously as a purged worshiper into the Holiest and to boldly approach the throne of grace in prayer. Of old God sternly said, "Stand afar off and worship." Access was not known under the legal covenant. God was hidden; the veil was not yet rent. Now all is different, and we are urged to "draw near with a true heart in full assurance of faith, having our hearts sprinkled from an evil conscience, and our bodies washed with pure water" (Heb. 10:22).

> And now we draw near to the throne of grace.
> For His blood and the Priest are there;
> And we joyfully seek God's holy face
> With our censer of praise and prayer.
> The burning mount and the mystic veil
> With our terrors and guilt are gone;
> Our conscience has peace that can never fail,
> 'Tis the Lamb on high on the throne.

Thus we do indeed rejoice in the hope of the glory of God. It is hope—not as uncertainty—but hope that is sure and certain, because it is based on the finished work of the Christ of God and a seated Priest on the right hand of the Majesty in the heavens. The glory is assured for all who are justified by faith and so have peace with God.

But before we reach the glory we must tread the sands of the wilderness. This is the place of testing. Here we learn the infinite resources of our wonderful God. So we are enabled to glory in tribulations, contrary though these may be to all that the natural man rejoices in. Tribulation is the divinely appointed flail to separate the wheat from the chaff. In suffering and sorrow we learn our own nothingness and the greatness of the power that has undertaken to carry us through. These are lessons we could never learn in heaven.

> The touch that heals the broken heart
> Is never felt above;
> His angels know His blessedness,
> His wayworn saints His love.

Thus "tribulation worketh patience" (Rom. 5:3) if we accept it as from our loving Lord Himself, knowing it is for our blessing. Out of patient endurance springs fragrant Christian experience, as the soul learns how wonderfully Christ can sustain in every circumstance. And experience blossoms into hope, weaning the heart from the things of earth and occupying them with the heavenly scene to which we are hastening.

Thus "hope maketh not ashamed, [for] the love of God is shed abroad in our hearts by the Holy [Spirit] which is given unto us" (v. 5). This is the first mention of the Spirit's work in the epistle. We read of the Spirit of Holiness in chapter 1 in connection with Christ's work and resurrection, but not a syllable about the Spirit's work in the believer until the soul enters into peace through the apprehension of the finished work of Christ. This is all-important. I am not saved by what goes on within myself. I am saved by what the Lord Jesus did for me. But the Spirit seals me when I believe the gospel, and by His indwelling the love of God is shed abroad within my heart.

> Soon as my all I ventured
> On the atoning blood,
> The Holy Spirit entered,
> For I was born of God.

It is a great mistake to rely upon my own recognition of the Spirit's work within me as the ground of my assurance. Assurance is by the word of the truth of the gospel. But upon believing, I receive the Spirit. Of this the eighth chapter largely treats. This gives corroborative evidence. "We know that we have passed from death unto life because we love the brethren" (1 John 3:14).

Verses 6–11 constitute a separate section. In this portion we have the summing up of all that has gone before, before the apostle goes on in the next division to take up the second phase of the gospel—in relation to our *sin*.

We were helpless, without strength, when God in grace gave His Son, who died for ungodly sinners in whom no merit could be found.

This is not like man. Few indeed could be found who would voluntarily die for an upright man, a righteous man, known and acknowledged to be such— much less for a wicked man. Some indeed might be willing to die for a good man, a kindly, benevolent man who has won their hearts by his gracious demeanor. But God has "[commended] his [own] love [see Greek] toward us, in that, while we were yet sinners [neither righteous nor good], Christ died for us" (Rom. 5:8), thus becoming the Substitute for guilty rebels. If love gave Him up to the death of the cross while we were so lost and vile, we may know beyond any doubt that since we have been justified by His blood He will never allow us to come into judgment: "We shall be saved from wrath through him" (v. 9).

This has been called the chapter of "the five much mores," and of these we have the first one in verse 9. "Much more then," he exclaims, since now, cleared of every charge by the blood of the Son of God, we are forever beyond the reach of the divine vengeance against sin.

The second use of this term is in verse 10: "For if, when we were enemies, we were reconciled to God by the death of his Son, much more, being reconciled, we shall be saved by his life." How blind are they who read into this a reference to the earthly life of our blessed Lord. That life—pure and holy as it was—could never have saved one poor sinner. It was by His death He made atonement for our sins. Even the love of God told out so fully in the ways of Jesus only drew out the envenomed hate of the human heart. It is His death that destroys the enmity—when I realize He died for me I am reconciled to God. The hatred was all on my side—there was no need for God to be reconciled to me—but I needed reconciliation, and I have found it in His death. Now, since it is already an accomplished fact, I may know for a certainty I "shall be saved by his life." He says, "Because I live, ye shall live also" (John 14:19). It is, of course, His resurrection life that is in view. "Wherefore he is able . . . to save [evermore] them . . . that come unto God by him, seeing he ever liveth to make intercession for them" (Heb. 7:25, margin reading). A living Christ at God's right hand is my pledge of eternal redemption. He lives to plead our cause, to deliver through all the trials of the way, and to bring us safely home to the Father's house at last. We are bound up in the same bundle of life as Himself, though this properly is the subject of the last part of the chapter and has to do with the second phase of salvation.

Secure for time and eternity we "joy in God through our Lord Jesus Christ, by whom we have now received the [reconciliation]" (Rom. 5:11, see margin). It is not we who received the atonement, but God. We needed to make an atonement for our sins but were unable to do so. Christ has made it for us by offering up Himself without spot unto God. Thus it is God who has accepted the atonement, and we, who once were "enemies" and "alienated . . . in [our] minds by wicked works" (Col. 1:21), have received the reconciliation. The enmity is gone. We are at peace with God, and we joy in Him who has become our everlasting portion.

This is the glorious end—for the present—to which the Holy Spirit has been leading us. Our salvation is full and complete. Our sins are gone. We are justified freely by His grace. We have peace with God and look forward with joyous certainty to an eternity of bliss with Him who has redeemed us.

The other three "much mores" occur in the next section, where the question of the two Headships is thoroughly gone into. We shall notice them in order when we come to them.

THE GOSPEL IN RELATION TO INDWELLING SIN

Romans 5:12–7:25

It will be necessary to take up this third part of the great doctrinal division in two lectures because of the wide scope of Romans 5:12 to the end of chapter 8. We shall look first therefore at that portion which ends with chapter 7. In the last half of chapter 5 we have the two heads—Adam and Christ. In chapter 6 we have two masters, sin personified and God as revealed in Jesus. In chapter 7 there are two Husbands to be considered—the Law and Christ risen.

The awakened sinner is concerned about one thing: how to be delivered from the judgment his sins have righteously deserved. This aspect of salvation has all been gone into and settled in the portion we have recently gone over. It is never raised again. As we go on into this next part of the epistle, the question of guilt does not come up. The moment a sinner believes the gospel his responsibility as a child of Adam under the judgment of God is over forever. But that very moment his responsibility as a child of God begins. He has a new nature that craves what is divine. But he soon discovers that his carnal nature has not been removed nor improved by his conversion to God, and from this fact arises many trying experiences. It often comes as a great shock when he realizes that he has still a nature capable of every kind of vileness. He is rightly horrified, and may be tempted to question the reality of his regeneration and his justification before God. How can a Holy God go on with one who has such a nature as this? If he tries to fight sin in the flesh, he is probably defeated and learns by bitter experience what Philip Melanchthon, Luther's friend, put so tersely, "Old Adam is too strong for young Philip."

Happy is the young convert if at this crisis he comes under sound scriptural instruction instead of falling into the hands of spiritual charlatans who will set him to seeking the elimination of the fleshly nature and the death of the carnal mind. If he follows their advice he will be led into a quagmire of uncertainty and dazzled by the delusive will-o'-the-wisp of possible perfection in the flesh, will perhaps flounder for years in the bog of fanaticism and self-torture before reaching the rest that remains for the people of God. I have tried to tell of my own early experiences along this line in a little volume titled, *Holiness: The False and the True,* which I am thankful to know has been blessed to the deliverance of many thousands of souls. It was the truth we are now to consider that saved me at last from the wretchedness and disappointments of those early years.

In taking up these chapters, I desire to antagonize no one but, simply, to constructively open up the line of truth here set forth for the soul's blessing.

And first we have to consider the two great families and the two federal heads of Romans 5:12–21.

The moment a man is justified by faith he is also born of God. His justification is, as we have seen, his official clearance before the throne of God. His regeneration involves his introduction into a new family. He becomes a part of the new creation of which the risen Christ is the Head. Adam the first was federal head of the old race. Christ Risen, the Second Man and the Last Adam, is Head of the new race. The old creation fell in Adam, and all his descendants were involved in his ruin. The new creation stands eternally secure in Christ, and all who have received life from Him are sharers in the blessings procured by His cross and secured by His life at God's right hand.

> Joyful now the new creation
>   Rests in undisturbed repose,
> Blest in Jesus' full salvation,
>   Sorrow now nor thraldom knows.

It is the apprehension of this that settles the question of the believer's security and thus gives a scriptural basis for the doctrine of deliverance from the power of sin.

It will be observed that the subject begun in verse 12 is concluded in verses 18–21. The intervening passage (vv. 13–17) is parenthetical, or explanatory. It may be best therefore for us to examine the parenthesis first. Sin was in the world dominating man from Adam's fall even before the law was given by Moses. But sin did not as yet have the distinct character of transgression until a legal code was given to man, which he consciously violated. Therefore, apart from law, sin was not imputed. Nevertheless, that it was there and to be reckoned with is manifest, for "by sin came death" and death reigned as a despotic monarch over all men from Adam to Moses, save as God interfered in the case of Enoch who was translated that he should not see death. Even where there was no willful sin, as in the case of infants and irresponsible persons, death reigned, thus proving that they were part of a fallen race federally involved in Adam's sin and actually possessing Adam's fallen nature. He who was originally created in the image and likeness of God defaced that image by sin and lost the divine likeness. We read that "Adam . . . begat a son in his own likeness, after his image" (Gen. 5:3). This is characteristic of all the race of which he is the head. "In Adam all die" (1 Cor. 15:22).

Theologians may wrangle about the exact meaning of all this and rationalists may utterly refuse to accept it, but the fact remains, "It is appointed unto men once to die" (Heb. 9:27). Apart from divine interference each one may well say with the poet:

> I have a rendezvous with death,
> I shall not fail my rendezvous.

You have doubtless heard of the epitaph, often mentioned in this connection, that is engraven on a tombstone marking the resting place of the bodies of four young children in St. Andrew's churchyard in Scotland:

> Bold infidelity, turn pale and die.
> Beneath this stone four sleeping infants lie:
> Say, are they lost or saved?
> If death's by sin, they sinned, for they are here.
> If heaven's by works, in heaven they can't appear,
> Reason, ah, how depraved!
> Turn to the Bible's sacred page, the knot's untied:
> They died, for Adam sinned; they live, for Jesus died.

There is no other solution to the problem of childhood suffering than that of the fall of the race in Adam.

But Adam was a figure, an antitype, of Him who was to come—yea, who has come and has Himself taken the responsibility of undoing the effects of the fall for all who, trusting in Him, become recipients of His resurrection life. With this is linked a perfect righteousness that is eternal in duration and divine in origin. There is a difference as to the offense and the gift, however. Adam's one offense involved his race in the consequences of his fall. Christ, having satisfied divine justice, offers the gift of life by grace to all who will believe and so it abounds unto many. Notice that here in verse 15 we have the third "much more."

Nor is it merely that as by one that sinned so is the gift—for the one sin brought universal condemnation, putting the whole race under judgment. But the reception of the gift of life and righteousness in faith places the recipient in the position of justification from all things irrespective of the number of offenses. Death reigned because of one offense. But we are told that "much more," those who receive this abundance of grace and this free gift of righteousness now reign triumphant over death in life by Jesus Christ, the one who has overcome death and says, "Because I live, ye shall live also."

This is the substance of the parenthesis. Now let us go back—with all this in mind—to verse 12 and link it with verses 18–21. Sin entered into the world by one man and death by sin. So death passed upon all men for all have sinned, inasmuch as all were in the loins of Adam when he fell and all the race is involved in the defection of its head.

Now look at verse 18. "Therefore as by [one] offense" there came universal condemnation, even so by one accomplished act of righteousness on the cross there comes an offer to all—that of justification of life. In other words, a life is offered as a free gift to all who are involved in the consequences of Adam's sin, which is the eternal life manifested in the Son of God who once lay low in death under the sentence of condemnation but arose in triumph having abolished death. Now as Head of a new race He imparts His own resurrection life—a life with which no charge of sin can ever be linked—to all who believe in Him. They share henceforth in a life to which sin can never be in any sense attached. This is a new creation, of which Paul writes so fully in 2 Corinthians 5 and in 1 Corinthians 15: "If any man be in Christ, [it] is . . . new creation" (2 Cor. 5:17). And it is in new creation that "all is of God"; "Old things [have] passed away; [and] all things [have] become new" (v. 17). So we get the full force of the word, "As in Adam all die, . . . so in Christ shall all be made alive" (1 Cor. 15:22).

It is not universal salvation nor is it merely that He will raise all the dead, but the two races, the two creations, the two Headships, are in contrast. Christ is the beginning, the origin, the federal Head of the creation of God (Rev. 3:14). As the risen Man at God's right hand, having passed through death He now is the fountain of life—pure, holy, unpolluted life—to all who believe. So we are now before God in justification of life.

By one man's disobedience the many were constituted sinners. "Much more," by one glorious act of obedience unto death on the part of Him who is now our new Head, the many are constituted righteous.

The coming in of the law added to the gravity of the offense. It gave sin the specific character of transgression. "But where sin abounded [had reached its flood-tide, so to speak], grace did *much more abound*" (Rom. 5:20). That is, grace superabounded, so that as sin reigned like a despotic monarch throughout the long centuries before the cross, unto the death of all his subjects, now grace is on the throne and reigns through accomplished righteousness unto eternal life by Jesus Christ our Lord!

What a gospel! What a plan! It is perfect! It is divine—like God Himself! How gloriously do these five "much mores" bring out the marvels of grace!

In the light of all this, is it any wonder that the apostle, recognizing the innate tendency of the human heart to turn the grace of God into lasciviousness, puts into the mouth of the reader the question, "Shall we continue in sin, that grace may abound?" (Rom. 6:1). Chapter 6 answers this cavil (for it is really that) in a masterly way.

"Far be the thought!" he exclaims indignantly. "How shall we, [who have died] to sin, live any longer therein?" (v. 2). In what sense did we die to sin? If actually dead to it, we would not be concerned about either the question or its answer. That which perplexes us is the fact that while we hate sin we find within ourselves a tendency to yield to it. But we are said to have died to it. How and where? The next verses give the answer.

The very fact that our link with Adam as federal head was broken by our association with Christ in His death tells us that we have the right to consider ourselves as having died, in that death of His, to the authority of sin as a master. Israel was redeemed from judgment by the blood of the Lamb. This answers to the first aspect of salvation. By the passage through the Red Sea they died to Pharaoh and his taskmasters. This illustrates the aspect we are now considering. Sin is no longer to hold sway over us, we served it in the past. But death has changed all that. Our condition of servitude is over. We are now linked with Christ risen and thus have been brought to God.

Of this the initiatory ordinance of Christianity speaks. "Know ye not, that so many of us [have been] baptized into [or unto] Jesus Christ were baptized into [or unto] his death?" (v. 3). Israel was "baptized unto Moses in the cloud and in the sea" (1 Cor. 10:2). They passed through death in figure, and Moses was their new leader. Pharaoh's dominion was ended so far as they were concerned (1 Cor. 10). So we who are saved are now baptized unto, or into, the death of Christ. We have accepted His death as ours, knowing that He died in our place. We are baptized unto Him as the new Leader.

Is this the Spirit's baptism? I think not. The Spirit does not baptize unto death but into the one new Body. It is establishment into the mystical Christ. Our baptism with water is a baptism unto Christ's death.

The apostle goes further, "Therefore we are buried with him by baptism [unto] death: that like as Christ was raised up from the dead by the glory of the Father, even so we also should walk in newness of life" (Rom. 6:4). In my baptism I confess that I have died to the old life as a man in Adam under the dominion of sin. I am through with all that. Now let me prove the reality of this by living the life of a resurrected man—a man linked up with Christ on the other side of death—as I walk in newness of life. Thus all thought of living in sin is rejected, all antinomianism refuted. My new life is to answer to the confession made in my baptism.

I am to realize practically my identification with Christ. I have been planted together with Him in the similitude of His death—that is, in baptism—I shall be (one with Him) also in the similitude of His resurrection. I do not live under sin's domination. I live unto God as He does who is my new Head.

Logically he continues, "Knowing this, that our old man is crucified with him, that the body of sin might be destroyed [or, rendered powerless], that henceforth we should not serve sin, for he that is dead is freed [or, justified] from sin" (vv. 6–7).

My old man is not merely my old nature. It is rather all that I was as a man in the flesh, the "man of old," the unsaved man with all his habits and desires. That man was crucified with Christ. When Jesus died, I (as a man after the flesh) died too. I was seen by God on that cross with His blessed Son.

How many people were crucified on Calvary? There were the thieves, there was Christ Himself—three! But are these all? Paul says in Galatians 2:20, "I am crucified with Christ." He was there, too—so that makes four. And each believer can say, "Our old man is crucified with Him." So untold millions were seen by God as hanging there upon that cross with Christ. And this was not merely that our sins were being dealt with, but that we ourselves as sinners, as children of Adam's fallen race, might be removed from under the eye of God and our old standing come to an end forever.

But we who were crucified with Him now live with Him. So the apostle continues in Galatians 2:20: "Nevertheless I live; yet, not I, but Christ liveth in me: and the life which I now live in the flesh [that is, in this body] I live by the faith of the Son of God, who loved me, and gave Himself for me." And so here. The body of sin is thus annulled, as the body of Pharaoh, all the power of Egypt, was annulled so far as Israel was concerned. Sin is not my master now. In Christ I live unto God. I am no longer to be a slave unto sin. I am righteously free (justified) from sin's authority.

Now he shows the practical effect of all this precious truth. We have died with Christ. We have faith that we shall also live with Him. *Then*—in heaven—sin will have no authority over us. Nor should we own its authority here by yielding ourselves to it. We know that the risen Christ will never die again. Death's authority (and sin brings forth death) is forever abolished. "In that he died, he died unto sin once [for all]" (Rom. 6:10) unto sin as our old master (not His—upon Him never came the yoke; He was ever free from sin), and now in resurrection He lives only unto God. And we are one with Him. Therefore, we, too, are henceforth to live unto God alone. This involves practical deliverance from the power or authority of sin.

It certainly never was the mind of God that His blood-redeemed people should be left under the power of the carnal nature, unable to walk in the liberty of free men in Christ. But practical deliverance is not found by fighting with the old master, *sin* in the flesh, but by the daily recognition of the truth we have just been considering.

And so we are told to count as true what God considers to be true that we died with Christ to all the claims of Pharaoh-Sin, and we are now free to walk in newness of life as one with Christ risen. "Likewise *reckon* ye also yourselves to be dead indeed unto sin, but alive unto God through Jesus Christ our Lord" (v. 11). This word *reckon* is one of the keywords of the chapter. It means, literally, "count as true." God says I died with Christ. I am to count it true. God says I live unto Him. I count it true. As faith reckons on all this I find the claims of sin are annulled. There is no other method of deliverance than that which begins with this reckoning. Reason may argue, "But you do not feel dead!" What have feelings to do with it? It is a judicial fact. Christ's death is my death. Therefore, I reckon myself to have died unto sin's dominion.

The next verse follows in logical sequence. "Let not sin therefore reign in your mortal body, that ye should obey it in the lusts thereof" (v. 12). I feel an impulse rising within demanding that I yield to a certain sinful desire. But if on the alert I say at once, "No, I have died to that. It is no longer to dominate my will. I belong to Christ. I am to live unto Him." As faith lays hold of this the power of lust is broken.

It involves watchfulness and constant recognition of my union with Christ. As in times past I was in the habit of yielding the physical members as instruments of unrighteousness controlled by sin. Now I am to definitely and unreservedly yield myself unto God as one alive from that death into which I went with Christ, and as a natural result all my physical members are His to be used as instruments to work out righteousness for the glory of God whose grace has saved me. The word translated "instruments" is really "weapons," or "armor," as in Romans 13:2; 2 Corinthians 6:7; and 10:4. My talents, my physical members, all my powers are now to be used in the conflict as weapons for God. I am His soldier to be unreservedly at His disposal.

Because I am not saved by any legal principle but by free grace alone, sin is no longer to hold sway over my life. Christ risen is the Captain of my salvation whose behests are to control me in all things.

Nature might reason in a contrary way and tell me that inasmuch as I am under grace not law it matters little how I behave, and I am, therefore, free to sin since my works have nothing to do with my salvation. But as a regenerated man I do not want liberty to sin. I want power for holiness. If I habitually yield myself unto sin to obey its behests voluntarily, I show that I am still sin's servant, and the end of that service is death. But as a renewed man I desire to obey the One whose I now am and whom I serve. So he says, "God be thanked, that ye were the slaves of sin, but ye have obeyed from the heart that form of doctrine which was delivered unto you. Being then made free from sin [that is, by God's judicial act on the cross], ye became the servants of righteousness" (vv.17–18).

He speaks in a figure, illustrating his theme by personifying *sin* and *righteousness* that our weak human minds may understand, and he repeats his exhortation, or rather what had been stated doctrinally he now repeats as a command: "For as ye have yielded your members [slaves] to uncleanness and to iniquity unto iniquity [in the old life before our identification with Christ]; even so now yield your members servants [bondmen] to righteousness unto holiness" (v. 19). When slaves of sin, righteousness was not our recognized master. We can only hang our heads in shame as we think of the fruit of that evil relationship, the end of which would have been death, both physical and eternal.

Therefore, now that we are judicially delivered from sin's dominion and have become bondmen to God, our lives should be abounding in fruit unto holiness and the end everlasting life. We have everlasting life now as a present possession, but here it is the end that is in view when we are at home in that scene where Christ who is our life has gone.

He concludes this section with the solemn yet precious statement: "For the wages of sin is death; but the gift of God is eternal life through Jesus Christ our Lord" (v. 23). Sin is in one respect a faithful master. His pay day is sure. His wages are death. Note, it is not divine judgment that is in view for the moment, but sin's wages. Death is the wages of sin, but "after this the judgment" (Heb. 9:27). Penalty has yet to be faced at the judgment bar of God. Through error to see this many have taken up with the error that physical death involves cessation of being and is both wages and penalty. Scripture clearly tells of divine judgment after sin's wages have been paid.

On the other hand, eternal life is a free gift—the gift of God. None can earn it. It is given to all who trust in Christ as the Savior of sinners. It is ours now, who believe the gospel. We shall enjoy it in all its fullness at the "end."

The seventh chapter takes up another phase of things that would be particularly hard for the Jewish believer to comprehend. It raises and answers the question, "What is the rule of life for the yielded believer?" The Jew would naturally say, "The law given at Sinai." The apostle's answer is "Christ risen!" Alas, how many Gentile believers have missed the point here as well as those who came out of Judaism.

That it is his Jewish-Christian brethren who are primarily before him is clear from the opening verse. "Know ye not, brethren, (for I speak to them that know the law,) how that the law hath dominion over a man as long as he liveth?" (Rom. 7:1). Now it is unthinkable that he is using the term "the law" here in any different sense to that which he has had in mind as he has used it over and over again in the former chapters. The law, here, means the law of Moses, and it means nothing else. It means that which was the heart of the law of Moses, the ten words given on Sinai. And his argument here is that the law has dominion over men until death ends its authority or ends their relationship to it. But he has just been showing us in the clearest possible way that we have died with Christ. Therefore. we died not only unto sin, but we have died to the law as a rule of life. Is this then to leave us lawless? Not at all. For we are now, as he shows elsewhere (1 Cor. 9:21), "under law to Christ", or "en-lawed," that is, "legitimately subject" to Christ our new Head. He is Husband as well as Head, even as Ephesians 5 so clearly shows.

This truth is illustrated in a very convincing way in verses 2–3, and the application is made in verse 4. A woman married to a husband is legally bound to him in that relationship until death severs the tie. If she marries another while her husband is living she becomes an adulteress. But when the first husband is dead, she is free to marry another with no blame attaching to her for so doing.

Even so, death has ended the relationship of the believer to the law, not the death of the law but our death with Christ, which has brought the old order to an end. We are now free to be married to another, even to the risen Christ in order that we might bring forth fruit unto God.

The somewhat weird and amazing conception has been drawn from the apostle's illustration that the first husband is not the law at all but "our old man." This is utterly illogical and untenable, for, as we have seen, the old man is myself as a man in the flesh. I was not married to myself! Such a suggestion is the very height of absurdity. The Jewish believer was once linked with the legal covenant. It was proposed as a means of producing fruit for God. It only stirred up all that was evil in the heart. Death has dissolved the former relationship. The one who once looked to the law for fruit now looks to Christ risen and, as the heart is occupied with Him, that is produced in the life in which God can delight.

He says, "When we were in the flesh [that is, in the natural state, as unsaved men], the motions of sins, which were by the law, did work in our members to bring forth fruit unto death" (v. 5). This clearly establishes the position taken above. The law was the husband, the active agent through whom we hoped to bring forth fruit unto God. But instead of that, we brought forth fruit unto death. All our travail and suffering in the hope of producing righteousness ended in disappointment—the child was still-born.

"But now we are delivered from the law, [having died to that relationship] wherein we were held [note the marginal reading]; that we might serve in newness of spirit, and not in the oldness of the letter" (v. 6). In the illustration the first husband dies and the woman is free to be married to another. In the application he does not say the law has died, but the point he makes is that death (and for us it is Christ's death) has ended the relationship in which we stood toward it. So there is after all no real disagreement. In either case, the former condition is ended by death. The law, as we have seen, was addressed to man in the flesh, and this was our former state, but now all is changed. We are no longer in the flesh, but (as the next chapter will show us) in the Spirit, and so in a new state to which the law in no sense applies.

Again the old question comes to the fore: If all this be true, shall we sin then? Are we to be lawless because not under law? By no means. The law must simply be recognized as having a special ministry but not as the rule of the new life. It is a great detector of sin. Paul could say, "I had not known sin, but by the law" (v. 7).

That is, he had not detected the evil nature within—so correct was his outward deportment—had not the law said, "Thou shalt not covet" (v. 7). The sin nature rebelled against this and wrought in him all manner of covetousness, or unsatisfied desire. Observe carefully how conclusively this proves that it was the Ten Commandments he has had in view throughout. To say it is the ceremonial law alone to which we have died is absurd in view of this statement. Where is the word found that forbids covetousness? In the Ten Commandments. Therefore "the law" means the divine ordinances engraved on tables of stone.

Apart from the law sin was dead, that is, inert and unrecognized. Sins there were even before the law was given, but sin—the nature—was not recognized until the law provoked it.

He says, "I was alive without the law once: but when the commandment came, . . . which was ordained [or proposed] to life, I found it to be unto death. For sin, taking occasion by the commandment, deceived me, and by it slew me" (vv. 9–11). In other words it is as though he said, "I was blissfully unconscious of my true moral condition before God as a sinner until the force of the commandment forbidding covetousness came home to me. I had not realized that evil desire was in itself sinful, providing the desire was not carried out. But the law made this manifest. I struggled to keep down all unlawful desire, but sin—an evil principle within—was too strong for repression. It circumvented me, deceived me, and so by violation of the commandment brought me consciously under sentence of death." This is exactly what the law was intended to do, as he shows in the epistle to the Galatians as well as here. "The law . . . was added because of [or, with a view to] transgressions" (Gal. 3:19). That is, the law served to give to sin the specific character of transgression, thus deepening the sense of guilt and unworthiness.

Therefore, he concludes, "The law is holy, and the commandment holy, and just, and good" (Rom. 7:12). The fault is not in the law but in me.

Well, then, he asks, was this holy law made death to me? Not at all, but it detected that in him which could only result in death—namely, sin, which in order that it might be made manifest in all its hideousness was brought fully to light by the law, thus "working death" in him by that which he owns to be in itself good. And so sin, by means of the legal enactment, is made exceedingly sinful.

Verses 14–25 have been taken by many as the legitimate experience of a Christian throughout all his life. Others have thought that it could not be the conflict of a real Christian at all, but that Paul was describing the conflict between the higher and lower desires of the natural man, particularly of an unconverted Jew under law. But both views are clearly contrary to the argument of this part of the epistle.

As to the latter interpretation, it should be remembered that in this entire section of the epistle the question is the deliverance of a believer from the power of sin and not of an unbeliever from his sins. Moreover, no unsaved man can honestly say, "I delight in the law of God after the inward man" (v. 22). It is only those who possess the new nature who can so speak. And as to this being the normal experience of one already saved, I shall attempt to show as we go on with the study of chapters 7 and 8 that there is an orderly progression from the bewilderment of chapter 7 to the intelligence and walk in the Spirit of chapter 8. All Christians doubtless know something of the state depicted in verses 14–25 of chapter 7, but once out of it no one need ever go through it again. It is not merely the conflict between the two natures. If it were, one might indeed be back in the same unhappy experience again and again. It gives us the exercises of a quickened soul under law who has not yet learned the way of deliverance. This once learned, one is free from the law forever. I have said earlier in the address that primarily here we have a believing Jew struggling to obtain holiness by using the law as a rule of life and resolutely attempting to compel his old nature to be subject to it. In Christendom now the average Gentile believer goes through the same experience, for legality is commonly taught almost everywhere.

Therefore, when one is converted it is but natural to reason that now one has been born of God it is only a matter of determination and persistent endeavor to subject oneself to the law, and one will achieve a life of holiness. And God Himself permits the test to be made in order that His people may learn experimentally that the flesh in the believer is no better than the flesh in an unbeliever. When he ceases from self-effort he finds deliverance through the Spirit by occupation with the risen Christ.

Paul writes in the first person singular, not necessarily as depicting a lengthy experience of his own (though he may have gone through it), but in order that each reader may enter into it sympathetically and understandingly for himself.

The law is spiritual, that is, it is of God, it is holy and supernatural. But I am carnal, even though a believer. I am more or less dominated by the flesh. In 1 Corinthians 2–3 we have distinguished for us the natural man—that is, the unsaved man, the carnal man—who is a child of God undelivered, and the spiritual man, the Christian who lives and walks in the Spirit.

Here the carnal man is sold under sin, that is he is subject to the power of the evil nature to which he has died in Christ, a blessed truth indeed, but one which has not yet been apprehended in faith. Consequently, he continually finds himself going contrary to the deepest desires of his divinely-implanted new nature. He practices things he does not want to do. He fails to carry out his determinations for good. The sins he commits he hates. The good he loves he has not the strength to perform. But this proves to him that there is a something within him which is to be distinguished from his real self as a child of God. He has the fleshly nature still, though born of God. He knows the law is good. He wants to keep it, and slowly the consciousness dawns upon him that it is not really himself as united to Christ who fails. It is sin, dwelling in him, which is exercising control (vv. 14–17).

So he learns the weakness and unprofitableness of the flesh. "I know," he says, "that in me (that is, in my flesh) dwelleth no good thing" (v. 18). He wants to do good, but he lacks the power to perform aright. Still he gives up slowly the effort to force the flesh to behave itself and to be subject to the law.

But the good he would do, he does not, and the evil he would not do, he does. This but establishes him in the conclusion already come to, that, "It is no more I that do it, but sin that dwelleth in me" (v. 20). A law, or principle of action, then, has been discovered. He goes with the good and does the evil. According to the inward man he delights in the law of God, but this does not produce the holiness he expected. He must learn to delight in Christ risen to reach the goal of his desires! This he reaches later, but in meantime he is occupied with the discovery of the two natures with their different desires and activities. He detects "another law," a principle, in his members (that is, the members of the body through which the carnal mind works) that wars against the law of his renewed mind taking him captive to the sin principle that is inseparable from his physical members so long as he is in this life. This principle he calls "the law of sin and death" (8:2). Were it not for this principle or controlling power, there would be no danger of perverting or misusing any human desire or propensity.

Almost convinced that the struggle must go on during the entire course of his earthly existence, he cries in anguish, "Oh, wretched man that I am! who shall deliver me from this body of death?" (7:24). He is like a living man chained to a polluted, because corrupt, corpse and unable to snap the chains. He cannot make the corpse clean and subject, no matter how he tries. It is the cry of hopelessness so far as self-effort is concerned. He is brought to the end of human resources. In a moment he gets a vision by faith of the risen Christ. He alone is the Deliverer from Sin's power, as well as the Savior from the penalty of guilt. "I thank God," he cries, "through Jesus Christ our Lord!" (v. 25). He has found the way out. Not the law but Christ in glory is the rule of life for the Christian.

But the actual entering into this is reserved for the next section. Meantime, he confesses, "So then with the mind [that is, the renewed mind] I myself [the real man as God sees him] serve the law of God, but with the flesh the law of sin" (v. 25). Such an experience cannot be the Christian ideal. The next chapter which we take up separately shows the way out of this perplexing and unsatisfactory state.

If I am addressing any believer who is even now in the agonizing throes of this terrific struggle, endeavoring to subject the flesh to the holy law of God, let me urge you to accept God's own verdict on the flesh and acknowledge the impossibility of ever making it behave itself. Do not fight with it. It will overthrow you every time. Turn away from it; cease from it altogether. Look away from self and law to Christ risen.

Israel of old wanted to find a short cut through Edom, type of the flesh, but the children of Esau came out armed to contest their way. The command of God was to turn away and "compass the land of Edom" (Num. 21:4). And so with us. It is as we turn altogether from self-occupation we find deliverance and victory in Christ by the Holy Spirit.

THE TRIUMPH OF GRACE

Romans 8

It has always seemed to me a great pity that in editing our Bibles and dividing the text into chapters and verses the break was permitted to come where it does between chapters seven and eight. I am persuaded that many souls have failed to see the connection just because of this. We get in the habit of reading by chapters, instead of by subjects. Properly, the first four verses of chapter 8 should be joined right on to chapter 7, thus linking with the expression of hope, "I thank God through Jesus Christ our Lord" (7:25).

These opening verses form a summing up of all the truth previously unfolded in this part of the epistle beginning with Romans 5:12. It is, of course, hardly necessary for me to point out and emphasize what is now familiar to every careful student of the original text: that the last part of verse 1 is an interpolation (which properly belongs to verse 4), obscuring the sense of the great truth enunciated in the opening words: "There is therefore now no condemnation to them which are in Christ Jesus." This magnificent statement requires no qualifying clause. It does not depend on our walk. It is true of all who are in Christ and to be in Him means to be of the new creation. A glance at the RV or any critical translation will show that what I am pointing out is sustained by all the editors. It was man's innate aversion to sovereign grace, I am certain, that brought these qualifying words into the text of the common version. It seemed too much to believe that freedom from condemnation depended on being in Christ Jesus and not upon our walking after the Spirit. So it was easy to lift the words from verse 4 into verse 1. But in verse 4 they have their proper place for there the question of state is to the fore. In verse 1 it is the question of standing that is under consideration.

What unspeakable relief it is to the bewildered, troubled soul, oppressed with a sense of his own unworthiness, and distressed because of frequent failures to live up to his own highest resolves, when he learns that God sees him in Christ Jesus, and as thus seen he is free from all condemnation. He may exclaim, "But I *feel* so condemned." This, however, is not the question. It is not how I feel but it is what God says. He sees me in Christ risen, forever beyond the reach of condemnation.

A prisoner before the bar, hard of hearing and dull of sight, might imagine his doom was being pronounced at the very moment that the judge was giving a verdict of full acquittal. Neither blindness nor deafness would alter this fact. And though we are often slow to hear, and our spiritual vision is most defective, the blessed fact remains that God has pronounced the believer free from condemnation whether he fully rises to the glorious fact or not.

Oh, doubting one, look away then altogether from self and state, look away from frames and feelings to Christ risen, now forever beyond the cross where your sins once put Him, and see yourself in Him, exalted there at God's right hand. He would not be there if the sin question was not settled to the divine satisfaction. The fact that He is there and that you are seen by God in Him is the fullest possible testimony to your freedom from all condemnation.

> Oh, the peace forever flowing
>   From God's thoughts of His own Son,
> Oh, the peace of simply knowing
>   On the cross that was all done.
>
> Peace with God is Christ in glory,
>   God is light and God is love,
> Jesus died to tell the story,
>   Foes to bring to God above.

We are brought to God "in Christ Jesus," and so all question of judgment is forever settled. It can never be raised again.

This leaves the soul at liberty to be occupied with pleasing God not as a means of escaping the divine displeasure but out of love to Him who has brought us to Himself in peace. What the law, with all its stern and solemn warnings and threatenings could not accomplish (that is, produce a life of holiness, because of the weakness and unreliability of the flesh), is now realized in the power of the new life by the Spirit. A clearer reading of verse two would probably be, "The Spirit's law (which is life in Christ Jesus) hath delivered me from the law of sin and death." That is, the Spirit's law of life in Christ Jesus received at new birth is put in contrast to the Law of sin and death against which the believer struggles in vain, as long as he wrestles in his own strength. Victory comes through turning from self to Christ risen. The Spirit's law brings blessing because it gives power to him who had it not before. It is an altogether new principle: life (not in or of ourselves, but) in Christ Jesus. This new life is imparted to the believer, and in the power of this new life he is called to walk. "It is God [who] worketh in [us both the willing and the doing] of his good pleasure" (Phil. 2:13). The law demanded righteousness from a man whose nature was utterly corrupt and perverted, and which could only bring forth corrupt fruit. The Holy Spirit has produced a new nature in the man in Christ, and linked with this new life are new affections and desires so that he gladly responds to the will of the Lord as revealed in His Word. Thus the righteousness of the law, the good in practice that the law required, is actually produced in the man who walks not after the flesh, not as under the power of the old nature, but after the Spirit, or in subjection to the Spirit, who has come to take possession of us for Christ.

In verses 5–27 he proceeds to unfold a wide and soul-uplifting range of truth in connection with the indwelling of the Holy Spirit, who is the only true Vicar of Christ on earth. And first we are reminded that there are two exactly opposite principles to be considered, or two utterly opposed standards of life. They who are after the flesh, that is, the unsaved, are dominated by the fleshly nature— "they . . . mind the things of the flesh" (Rom. 8:5). In these terse words the entire life of the natural man is summed up. In blessed contrast to this they who are after the Spirit, that is those who are born of the Word and the Spirit of God, saved men and women, characteristically mind the things of the Spirit. Parenthetically he explains "[the minding of the flesh] is death" (v. 6), that is its only legitimate result. But "[the minding of the Spirit] is life and peace" (v. 6). He who is thus Spirit-controlled is lifted onto a new plain where death has no place and conflict is not known.

It is not that the flesh is, or ever will be, in any sense improved. The flesh in the oldest and godliest Christian is as incorrigibly evil as the flesh in the vilest sinner. "The carnal mind [or, mind of the flesh] is enmity against God: for it is not subject to the law of God, neither indeed can be" (v. 7). All efforts to reform or purify it are in vain. The law only demonstrates its incurable wickedness. And this explains why the natural man is so utterly unprofitable. "They that are in the flesh cannot please God" (v. 8). It is not, of course, that man, as such, does not know right from wrong or, knowing it, is powerless to do right. To say so would be to declare that man is not a responsible creature but is simply the victim of a hard cruel fatalism. But knowing the evil and approving the good the natural man inclines toward the wrong and fails to do the right, because he is dominated by sin in the flesh, to which he yields his members as instruments of unrighteousness as we have seen in chapter 6. As he is powerless to change his nature, he therefore cannot really please God.

But it is otherwise with the believer. He is no longer in the flesh since born of God. He is now in the Spirit, and the Spirit of God dwells in him. "If so be" (v. 9) does not imply that there are Christians who are not indwelt by the Spirit but has the force of "since," that is, since the Spirit of God dwells in you, you are no longer in the flesh. That is, characteristically, as being of the family of the first man and under the dominion of the old nature. If anyone whether professing to be a believer or not is devoid of the Spirit of Christ, "he is none of his" (v. 9), or "not of Him." It is not merely the disposition of Christ that is in view, but the Spirit of Christ is the Holy Spirit whom Christ has sent into the world and who indwells all His redeemed ones in this dispensation of grace. But this, of course," produces a Christlike disposition in the one so indwelt.

But if Christ (by the Spirit) be thus in us, He alone is the source of our power for holiness. We shall get no help from the body. "The body is dead because of sin" (v. 10). It is to be considered as though lifeless and inert so far as ability to produce fruit for God is concerned. All must be of the Spirit. "The Spirit is life because of righteousness" (v. 10).

This is not to ignore or undervalue the body. It, too, has been purchased by the blood of Christ, and we have the promise that "if the Spirit of him that raised up Jesus from the dead dwell in you, he that raised up Christ from the dead shall also quicken your mortal bodies by his Spirit that dwelleth in you" (v. 11). It is idle to say, as some have done, that this is a present quickening, when the previous verse has told us the very opposite. "The body is dead because of sin"—not actually, of course, but judicially. Therefore we are not to expect anything of it. A strong body does not necessarily mean a strong saint, nor a feeble body a feeble believer. Natural strength may even seem to be a hindrance to spiritual progress if the truth we have been considering be unknown, while feebleness of nature's power may seem to make holiness easier in practice. So monks and ascetics of various kinds have sought to grow in grace by punishing and starving the body. But we are told in Colossians 2 that all this is vain and futile so far as checking fleshly indulgence is concerned.

But the body is for the Lord, and the same Holy Spirit who raised up Jesus from the dead will eventually raise us up by giving resurrection life to these mortal bodies. He is speaking of the body of the living believer who has the new life now in a body subject to death. It shall put on immortality at the Lord's return. Since God has claimed us for this, we owe nothing to the flesh. We are not its debtors to do its service. To do so would only mean to die (it is the great fact to which he calls attention that "sin, when it is finished, bringeth forth death" [James 1:15]). But, if through the power of the indwelling Spirit we put to death the deeds of the body, we shall truly live. The body is viewed as the vehicle through which the flesh acts. It incites the natural appetite to lawless indulgence. The Spirit-led man must be on his guard against this. He has to put to death these unlawful desires. In Colossians 3:5 we read, "Mortify therefore your members which are upon the earth; fornication, uncleanness, inordinate affection, evil concupiscence, and covetousness which is idolatry" (Col. 3:5). Having been crucified with Christ we are now in faith to mortify by self-judgment the deeds of the body. "We which live are always delivered unto death for Jesus' sake" (2 Cor. 4:11).

To walk in the flesh is to do contrary to the whole principle of Christianity, for "as many as are led [controlled] by the Spirit of God, they are the sons of God" (Rom. 8:14). It is by this life in the Spirit's power we mortify the deeds of the body and manifest our new life and relationship. This is not a Spirit of bondage, of legality, filling us with fear and dread, but the Spirit of adoption, of son-acknowledgment, whereby we instinctively lift our hearts to God in the cry of the conscious child, "Abba, Father" (v. 15). Adoption is to be distinguished from new birth. We are children by birth but sons by adoption. In the full sense we have not yet received the adoption. It will all be consummated, as verse 23 shows, at the Lord's return. When a Roman father publicly acknowledged his child as his son and heir, legally in the forum, this ceremony was called "the adoption!" All born in his family were children. Only those adopted were recognized as sons. So we have been born again by the Word of God and thus are children, as were all believers from Abel down. But as indwelt by the Spirit we are adopted sons, and this will be fully manifested in the most public way when we are changed into our Savior's image at His coming again.

The child cry, "Abba, Father," is most suggestive. The one term is Hebrew in the text, the other Greek. For those who are in Christ, the middle wall is broken down. All are one in Him. Together we cry, "Abba, Father." Our Lord Himself used the double term in Gethsemane (see Mark 14:36). Someone has aptly suggested that "Abba" is a word for baby lips, whereas the Greek *pateer,* or the English equivalent, Father, is a word for the more mature. But young and old join together in approaching the Father by the Spirit.

He Himself bears testimony *with* our human spirit that we are God's children. We received His witness *to* us as given in His Word (Heb. 10:15). Thus, we have the witness *in* us, the Word hidden in our hearts (1 John 5:10), and now the Spirit Himself takes up His abode within and leads us into the enjoyment of heavenly things. In the text it is "the Spirit itself." The Greek demands this because the word *Spirit* is a neuter noun. But according to English idiom it is correct to use the personal pronoun. He communes with our spirits; He illumines, instructs, and guides through the Word.

> Whoso hath felt the Spirit of the Highest,
>   Cannot confound, nor doubt Him, nor deny;
> Nay, with one voice, O World, though thou deniest,
>   Stand then on that side, for on this am I.

"The fellowship of the Spirit" (Phil 2:1) is a wonderfully real thing, known and enjoyed by those who live and walk in Him.

If children of God, it naturally follows that we are his heirs, and thus we are joint-heirs with Christ. We share in all His acquired glories, and so we shall eventually be "glorified together" (Rom. 8:17).

In verses 18–27 the apostle contrasts our present state with the coming glory. Even though thus indwelt by the Spirit we are called to a path of suffering and sorrow as we follow the steps of Him who was, on earth, the Man of Sorrows. But all we can possibly suffer here is as nothing compared to the glory soon to be manifested.

All creation is expectantly waiting for the full revelation of the true estate of the sons of God, when it too shall share in that glorious liberty. It was made subject to vanity, not of its own will but through the failure of its federal head, yet subjected not forever, but in hope of final restoration, and in that day it shall be delivered from the "bondage of corruption" and made to share in "the liberty of the glory of the sons of God" (v. 21, author's translation). Creation does not share in the liberty of grace. It shall have its part in the liberty of glory, the kingdom age of millennial blessing. Until then the minor note is heard in all creation's sounds—groaning and travailing in birth pangs through all the present age, waiting for the regeneration. We ourselves, though we have received the salvation of our souls and have the first-fruits of the Spirit (enjoying a foretaste now of what shall soon be ours in all its fullness), we groan in unison with the groaning creation as we wait expectantly for our acknowledged adoption when we shall receive the redemption of our bodies and be fully like Himself.

In this hope we have been saved and in its power we live. We walk by faith, not by sight. If already seen, hope would fade away, but in this hope we patiently wait for the Lord.

Meantime, often tried to the utmost, we do not know even what we should pray for as we ought. But the indwelling Spirit, knowing the mind of God fully, makes intercession within us according to the will of God, though not in audible words but with unutterable groanings. "Once we groaned in bondage, now we groan in grace," as another has well said, and this very groaning is in itself a testimony to the changed conditions brought about by our union with Christ. The Spirit's groanings are in harmony with our own sighs and tears, and the great Heart-Searcher hears and answers in wisdom infinite and love unchanging.

And so we go on in peace amid tribulation, assured in our hearts that, "All things work together for good to them [who] love God, . . . who are the called according to his purpose" (v. 28). This introduces the closing part of the chapter and of this great doctrinal division of our epistle, which is a summing up of all we have gone over, and a masterly conclusion to the opening up of "the righteousness of God as revealed in the gospel." It breaks into two subsections.

In verses 28–34 we have "God for us." In verses 35–39, "No separation."

We have a glorious chain of five links in verses 29–30, reaching from eternity in the past to eternity in the future—foreknown, predestinated, called, justified, glorified! Every link was forged in heaven and not one can ever be broken. This blessed portion is not for theologians to wrangle over but for saints to rejoice in. Foreknown before we ever trod this globe, we have been predestinated to become fully like our blessed Lord—"conformed to the image of [God's] Son," that He, who was from all eternity the *only Begotten,* might be "the firstborn among many brethren" (v. 29). So we have been called by grace divine, justified by faith on the basis of accomplished redemption, and our glorification is as certain as the foreknowledge of God.

What shall we say to all of this? If God is thus so manifestly for us—not against us as once our troubled hearts and guilty consciences made us believe— what power can be against us? Who can successfully combat the divine will?

In giving Christ, God showed us that (as a brother beloved has said), "He loved us better than we loved our sins." If He did not spare "his own Son, but delivered him up for us all, how shall he not with him also freely give us all things?" (v. 32).

The next two verses, 33–34, should probably all be thrown into question form, as in several critical translations: "Who shall lay any thing to the charge of God's elect? Shall God, who justifieth? Who shall condemn? Shall Christ who died, yea, rather, who is risen again, who is even at the right hand of God, who also maketh intercession for us?"

There is no answer possible. Every voice is silenced. Every accusation is hushed. Our standing in Christ is complete, and our justification unchangeable.

And so in the closing verses, 35–39, the apostle triumphantly challenges any possible circumstance, or personal being in this life or the next, to attempt to separate the believer "from the love of God, which is in Christ Jesus." (v. 39). No experience however hard or difficult can do it. Even though exposed as sheep to the slaughter, yet death but ushers us into the presence of the Lord. In all circumstances we more than conquer, we triumph in Christ.

And so, as he began with this portion with "no condemnation," he ends with "no separation."

> I am persuaded, that neither death, nor life, nor angels, nor principalities, nor powers, nor things present, nor things to come [and what is there that is neither present nor to come?], nor height, nor depth, nor any other [created thing], shall be able to separate us from the love of God, which is in Christ Jesus our Lord! (vv. 38–39)

Blessed, wondrous consummation of the most marvelous theme it was ever given to man to make known to his fellows! May our souls enter ever more deeply into it, and find increasing joy and spiritual strength as we contemplate it.

> No condemnation; blessed is the word!
> No separation; forever with the Lord,
> By His blood He bought us, cleansed our every stain;
> With rapture now we'll praise Him.
> The Lamb for sinners slain.
> —J. Denham Smith

PART 2

DISPENSATIONAL

*The Righteousness of God Harmonized
with His Dispensational Ways*

Romans 9–11

GOD'S PAST DEALINGS WITH ISRAEL IN ELECTING GRACE

Romans 9

Having carried us all the way from the distance and bondage and condemnation of Romans 1–3 to the glorious freedom and justification and eternal union with Christ of Romans 8, the apostle now turns to consider another phase of things altogether. He well knew that many of his readers would be pious, godly Jews who had accepted Christ as their Messiah and their Savior, but who were passing through a time of great perplexity and bewilderment as they saw their own nation apparently hardened into opposition against the gospel and sinners of the Gentiles turning to the Lord. They were aware that the prophets predicted a great work of God among the Gentiles, but they had always been accustomed to think of this as following upon the full restoration and blessing of Israel, and, indeed, as flowing *from* it. Israel should blossom and bud and fill the face of the whole earth with fruit. The Gentiles should come to *her* light and find happiness in subjection to her. Now all the prophecies on which they had based their expectations seemed to have failed of fulfillment.

How could Paul reconcile his proclamation of free grace to the Gentiles everywhere apart from their submission to the rights connected with the old covenant?

In the three chapters that are now to occupy us, the apostle meets this question, and that in a masterly way, showing how the righteousness of God is harmonized with His dispensational ways. This part of the epistle may be separated into three subdivisions. Chapter 9 gives us God's *past* dealings with Israel in electing grace; chapter 10, God's *present* dealings with Israel in governmental discipline; and chapter 11, God's *future* dealings with Israel in fulfillment of prophecy.

Opening our Bibles, then, to chapter 9, who can fail to be touched by his earnest words in regard to his brethren after the flesh? He insists that he loves them tenderly, that his heart is constantly burdened because of them. No one could possibly love them more than he did. They, perhaps, thought him estranged from them because of his commission to give the gospel to the nations. But it is very evident, both here and throughout the latter part of the book of Acts, that though he magnified his office as the apostle to the Gentiles, there was always a great tugging at his heart to get to his own people and bear testimony to them. His ministry was ever to the Jew first and then to the Greek.

There is a difference of opinion among men of piety and scholarship as to the exact meaning of verse 3. Did it mean to say that there were times when he had actually wished, if it were possible, to save his brethren by being himself accursed from Christ—that he would have been willing to submit to this? Or is he simply saying that he understands thoroughly the feeling of the most earnest Jew, who in his mistaken zeal detests the Christ, because he himself had at one time actually desired to be accursed from Christ as standing with his brethren after the flesh? If we accept the latter view, we see in this verse simply an expression of the intensity of his feelings as an unconverted Jew. If, as the present lecturer is inclined to do, we accept the former explanation, then we put him on the same platform with Moses who cried, "If it be possible, blot me out of Thy book, only let the people live." But whichever view we finally accept, our sense of his deep interest in his people becomes intensified as we read.

He enumerates in verses 4–5 the great blessings that belong to Israel. He says that to them pertain "the adoption [literally, the son-placing], and the glory, and the covenants, and the giving of the law, and the [ritual] service . . . , and the promises; whose are the fathers, and of whom as concerning the flesh Christ came, who is over all, God blessed for ever. Amen."

Consider these blessings in their order:

First, the son-placing. God had owned the nation of Israel as His son. It is not the New Testament truth of individual adoption as we have it in the epistle to the Ephesians and as we have already considered it in Romans 8. In fact, it is not individual here at all, but national. God could say of Israel, "Out of Egypt have

I called my son" (Matt. 2:15); and, again, "You only have I known of all nations that be upon the earth" (Amos 3:2, author's translation). They were His, and He owned them as such.

Second, the glory. Glory is manifested excellence. And through them God would manifest the excellence of His great name. They were His witnesses.

Third, the covenants. Observe that all the covenants pertain to Israel; that is, the Abrahamic covenant, the Mosaic covenant, the Davidic covenant, and the new covenant. All belonged to them. Believers from among the Gentiles come under the blessings of the new covenant, because it is a covenant of pure grace. But God has Israel and Judah in view when He says through the prophet, "I will make a new covenant with the house of Israel, and with the house of Judah" (Jer. 31:31; see also Heb. 8:8). When our Lord instituted the memorial supper, He said, "This cup is the new covenant in My blood, which is shed for you for the remission of sins" (see Luke 22:20; Matt. 26:28). The blood of the covenant has already been poured out, but the new covenant has not yet actually been made, though it shall be eventually with the earthly people. Meantime, redeemed Gentiles come under all the spiritual blessings of that covenant and, indeed, all the others in a manner far beyond anything that Old Testament prophets ever could have anticipated.

Fourth, the giving of the law. We have already seen that the law was given to Israel. It addressed itself to Israel. It was never given to Gentiles as such, though all men become responsible in regard to its provisions when it is made known to them.

Fifth, the ritual service. God ordained a ritual service of marvelous meaning and wondrous beauty in connection with both the tabernacle and the temple of old, but there is no hint of ritualistic practices of any kind for the church of God as such. In fact, we are warned against them in unmistakable terms in Colossians 2.

Sixth, the promises. The reference, of course, is to the many promises of temporal blessing under Messiah's reign in the kingdom age.

Seventh, the fathers, Abraham, Isaac, and Jacob, the patriarchs, these belonged to the earthly people. The heavenly people have no genealogical list to consult; they are cut off entirely from earthly lineage. The church was chosen in Christ before the foundation of the world. But in Israel we see the descendants of the fathers, though, as the chapter goes on to the show, they are not all reckoned of Israel who are of Israel after the flesh.

Of this people Christ came, born of a virgin—a real man in a true body of flesh and blood with a rational spirit and soul. Nevertheless, as to the mystery of His person, God over all, blessed forever.

To the faithful Jew who had banked upon the promises of God to Israel, it would appear that in large measure these promises had failed. Otherwise, why would Israel nationally be set to one side and the Gentiles be in the place of blessing? But the apostle now proceeds to show that God has ever acted on the principle of sovereign grace. All the special privileges that Israel had enjoyed were to be attributed to this principle. God took them out from among the nations as an elect people, separating them to Himself. But He ever had in mind a *regenerated* people as the people of the promise. Not all who were born of Israel's blood belonged to Israel, as recognized by God. Neither because of the natural seed of Abraham were they necessarily children of promise. In electing grace God had said to Abraham, "In Isaac shall thy seed be called" (Gen. 21:12). He chose to pass over Ishmael, the man born after the flesh, and take up Isaac, whose birth was miraculous. In this He illustrates the principle that "they which are the children of the flesh, these are not the children of God: but the children of the promise are counted for the seed" (Rom. 9:8). What a staggering blow is this to the pretensions of those who boast so loudly in our day of what they call the *universal fatherhood of God and brotherhood of man.* The children of the flesh, we are distinctly told, are *not* the children of God. And in this statement we have emphasized the same truth that our Lord declared to Nicodemus, "Except a man be born again, he cannot see the kingdom of God" (John 3:3).

Isaac was the child of promise. God said, "At this time will I come, and Sarah shall have a son" (Rom. 9:9). Naturally, it would have been impossible for the promise to be fulfilled, but God wrought in resurrection power, quickening the dead bodies of Isaac's parents, and the word came true.

Then again, in the case of the children of Isaac and Rebecca, we see the same principle of electing grace illustrated. We are told that:

> (For the children being not yet born, neither having done any good or evil, that the purpose of God according to election might stand, not of works, but of him that calleth;) it was said unto her, The elder shall serve the younger. As it is written, Jacob have I loved, but Esau have I hated. (vv. 11–13)

What a tremendous amount of needless controversy has raged about these verses! Yet how plain and simple they are, viewed in the light of God's dispensational dealings. There is no question here of predestination to heaven or reprobation to hell. In fact, eternal issues do not really come in throughout this chapter, although, of course, they naturally follow as the result of the use or abuse of

God-given privileges. But we are not told here, nor anywhere else, that before children are born it is God's purpose to send one to heaven and another to hell—to save one by grace, notwithstanding all his evil works, and to condemn the other to perdition, notwithstanding all his yearnings for something higher and nobler than he has yet found. The passage has to do entirely with privilege here on earth. It was the purpose of God that Jacob should be the father of the nation of Israel and that *through* him the promised Seed, our Lord Jesus Christ, should come into the world. He had also predetermined that Esau should be a man of the wilderness—the father of a nation of nomads, as the Edomites have ever been. It is this that is involved in the prenatal decree: "The elder shall serve the younger" (Gen. 25:23; Rom. 9:12). And be it observed that it was not before the children were born, neither had done any good or evil, that God said, "Jacob have I loved, but Esau have I hated" (Rom. 9:13). These words are quoted from the very last book of the Old Testament. We find them in Malachi 1:2–3. Let me read them:

> I have loved you, saith the LORD. Yet ye say, Wherein hast thou loved us? Was not Esau Jacob's brother? saith the LORD: yet I loved Jacob, and I hated Esau, and laid his mountains and his heritage waste for the dragons of the wilderness.

Observe what is in question: God is pleading with the sons of Jacob to serve and obey Him on the ground that He is doubly entitled to their obedience, first, because He is their Creator, and, second, because of the privileges, the earthly blessings, He has given them. Comparatively speaking, He has loved Jacob, and hated Esau. That is, He gave to Jacob a beautiful fatherland, well-watered, productive, delightful for situation. He gave them, too, a holy law, pastors, shepherd-kings to guide them, prophets to instruct them, a ritual system full and expressive to lead their hearts out in worship and praise. All these things were denied to Edom. They were the children of the desert. We do not read that a prophet was ever sent to them, though they were not left without some knowledge of God. Esau received instruction from the lips of his parents, but for a morsel of bread he sold his birthright. And his descendants have ever been characterized by the same independent lawless spirit. Dispensationally, Jacob was loved; Esau hated. There is no reference to the individual as such. "God so loved the world," and therefore every child of Jacob or of Esau may be saved who will. But no one can dispute the fact that Jacob and his descendants enjoyed earthly privileges, and spiritual, too, that Esau and his children had never known.

Is God unrighteous in thus distinguishing between nations? Is He unrighteous, for instance, today in giving to the peoples of northern Europe and of America privileges that the inhabitants of central Africa and inland South America have never known? By no means. He is sovereign. He distributes the nations of men upon the earth as seems good to Himself. Though He takes up one nation in special grace and passes by another, that does not in the slightest degree hinder any individual in any nation from turning to God in repentance. If any men anywhere under the sun, in any circumstances whatever, look up to God, no matter how deep their ignorance, confessing their sin and crying out for mercy, it is written, "Whosoever shall call upon the name of the Lord shall be saved" (Rom. 10:13).

Paul quotes the word of God to Moses: "I will have mercy on whom I *will* have mercy, and I will have compassion on whom I *will* have compassion" (Rom. 9:15).

Observe, you do not get the negative. He does not say, "I will condemn whom I will condemn, or I will reprobate to eternal destruction whom I will reprobate." There is no such thought in the mind of God, who "desires not the death of the sinner, but that all should turn to Him and live." When were these words spoken to Moses? Turn back to Exodus 33:19. Read the entire passage and note the occasion on which God used them. Israel had forfeited all claim to blessing on the ground of law. They had made a calf of gold and bowed down before it, even while Moses was in the mount receiving the tables of the covenant. Thus they had violated the first two commandments before they were brought into the camp, after having declared but a few days before, "All that the LORD hath said will we do, and be obedient" (Exod. 24:7). *Because* of this, God was about to blot them out from the face of the earth, but Moses, the mediator, pleaded their cause in His presence. He even offered, as we have seen, to die in their stead, if that might turn aside the fierce anger of the Lord.

But now observe the wonders of sovereign grace: God took refuge in His own inherent right to suspend judgment, if it pleased Him. And so He exclaims, "I . . . will be gracious to whom I *will* be gracious, and will show mercy on whom I *will* show mercy" (Exod. 33:19). He spared the people, thus making them a wondrous witness to His grace. Apart from this sovereign grace no one would ever be saved, because *all* men have forfeited title to life through sin. Israel, nationally, owed all their blessing to God's mercy and compassion, when in righteousness they would have been cut off from the land of the living. If it pleased God now to take up the Gentiles and show mercy to them, what ground had Israel to complain?

So, then, exclaims the apostle, "It is not of him that willeth, nor of him that runneth, but of God that showeth mercy" (Rom. 9:16). He is not setting aside the will of man. He is not declaring that no responsibility to run in the way of righteousness rests upon man. But he is declaring that, apart from the sovereign mercy of God, no man would ever will to be saved or run in the way of His commandments.

He turns next to speak of Pharaoh, for it is evident that one cannot logically accept the truth already demonstrated without recognizing the fact that God *does* give some up to destruction and leave them to perish in their sins. Pharaoh was a Gentile, the oppressor of Israel. To him God sent His servants demanding submission. In his pride and haughtiness, in his brazenness and wickedness, he exclaimed, "Who is the LORD, that I should obey his voice?" (Exod. 5:2). He dares to challenge the Almighty, and God condescends to accept the challenge. He says:

> Even for this same purpose have I raised thee up, that I might show my power in thee, and that my name might be declared throughout all the earth. (Rom. 9:17)

He is not speaking here of a helpless babe. The words have no reference to the birth of Pharaoh. They have to do exclusively with the outstanding position that God gave him in order that he might be a lesson to all succeeding generations of the folly of fighting against God. The Greeks used to say, "Whom the gods would destroy, they first make mad." It was a principle that even the heathen could plainly discern. We see the same principle still: an Alexander, a Caesar, a Napoleon, a Kaiser permitted to climb to the very summit, almost, of human ambition, only to be hurled ignominiously into the depths of execration at last

And so God demonstrates that He has "mercy on whom he *will* have mercy, and whom he will he hardeneth" (v. 18). He is the moral governor of the universe and He "worketh all things [according to] the counsel of his own will" (Eph. 1:11). "None can stay his hand, or say unto God, What doest thou?" (Dan. 4:35). If men dare to rush ruthlessly upon the thick bosses of the Almighty, they must experience His righteous wrath.

Beginning with verse 19 and going on to the end of the chapter, the apostle undertakes to meet the objection of the fatalist. The man who says, "Well, granting all you've been saying, then God's decrees are irresistible and I myself am but an automaton, moved about at His will, absolutely without responsibility. Why does He find fault? What ground can there be for judgment of a creature who can never will nor run but as God Himself directs? To resist His will is impossible. Where, then, does moral responsibility come in?"

Such objections to the doctrine of the Divine Sovereignty have been raised from the earliest days. But, inasmuch as we have already seen that the apostle simply has in view privilege here on earth, those objections fall to the ground. The privileged Jew may fail utterly to appreciate the blessings lavished upon him and so come under divine condemnation, while the ignorant barbarian, bereft of all the blessings of civilization and enlightenment, may, nevertheless, have an exercised conscience that will lead him into the presence of God. At any rate, it is the height of impiety for puny man to sit in judgment upon God. It is as though the vessel wrought upon the wheel should turn to the potter and ask, indignantly, "Why hast thou made me thus?" (v. 20). Clearly, he who has the intelligence to form vessels out of clay has the right to make them of such shape or size or for such use as he deems best. Of the very same lump of clay he may make one vessel unto honor, to be displayed upon the sideboard to admiring throngs, and another unto dishonor, for use in a scullery and altogether without beauty or attractiveness.

If God, the great Former of all willing to manifest both His anger and His power, endures with much long-suffering vessels that call down His indignation because having a will, which the work of the potter has not, they deliberately fit themselves for destruction, shall anyone find fault if He manifests the riches of His glory in His dealings with other vessels of mercy which He has had in view for the glory of His Son from eternity? And such vessels of mercy are the called of God, whether Jews by birth or Gentiles, also. Passage after passage from the Old Testament is called into requisition to show that this is nothing new in God's ways with men, and that the prophets have foreseen just such a setting aside of Israel and taking up of the Gentiles as has already taken place. Hosea testified that God has said, "I will call them my people, which were not my people; and her beloved, which was not beloved. And it shall come to pass, that in the place where it was said unto them, Ye are not my people; they shall be called the children of the living God" (vv. 25–26). Israel forfeited all title to be called His people.

During the present dispensation, when grace is going out to the Gentiles, they would be set to one side *nationally*, as by-and-by the same grace that is now being shown to the nations will be manifested again to them, and they shall once more be called the children of the living God. Isaiah prophesied that although the number of the children of Israel should be as the sands of the sea, yet of this vast throng only a remnant should be saved, and that in the day of the Lord's indignation, when He would be executing His judgment upon the earth. The same prophet saw the sin of the people as the sin of the cities of the plain, and exclaimed, "Except the Lord of hosts hath left us a seed, we should be as Sodom, and be made like unto Gomorrah" (Isa. 1:9, author's translation).

What then, is the conclusion? Simply that the unrighteous Gentiles have, through grace, attained to a righteousness which is of faith. They followed not after righteousness, but God in righteousness pursued after them and made known His gospel, that they might believe and be saved. Israel, on the other hand, to whom He had given a law of righteousness, was even more guilty than the Gentiles, for they refused to follow it. Therefore, they missed that righteousness which the law would have inculcated.

Why did they miss it? Because they failed to realize that it is only to be obtained by faith, and that no man, by his own power, can ever keep that Holy and perfect law. When God sent His Son into the world, who is the embodiment of all perfection and in whom the law was fulfilled perfectly, they knew Him not but stumbled over the stumbling stone of a lowly Christ when they were expecting a triumphant King. They realized not their need of one who could accomplish righteousness on their behalf, because they lacked faith. And so they fulfilled the Scripture in condemning Him. But, nevertheless, wherever He is individually received by faith, He saves the soul that trusts Him, though the nation has stumbled and fallen. According as it is written, "Behold, I lay in Zion a stumblingstone and rock of offense: and whosoever believeth on him shall not be ashamed" (Rom. 9:33). When He came in grace the first time, Israel refused Him. But "the stone that the builders rejected is made the head of the corner" (Matt. 21:42, author's translation). When He comes again He will be as the stone falling in judgment upon the Gentiles, whereas Israel then repentant and regenerated will see in Him the chief cornerstone.

GOD'S PRESENT DEALINGS WITH ISRAEL IN GOVERNMENTAL DISCIPLINE

Romans 10

Having, as we have seen, vindicated in a masterly way the righteousness of God in setting aside Israel nationally because of unbelief and taking up the Gentiles during the present dispensation of grace, the apostle now goes on to show that this deflection of the nation as such does not in any wise involve the rejection of the individual Israelite. The nation as such is no longer looked upon as in covenant relationship with God, nor will it be until it comes under the new covenant at the beginning of the Millennium when "a nation shall be born in a day." But the same promises apply to any individual member of the house of Israel as to any individual Gentile.

In the first three verses the apostle expresses his yearning desire and prayer for his kinsmen. He longs and prays that they may be saved. For though Abraham's seed after the flesh, they are "lost sheep," and need to be sought and found by the Good Shepherd just as truly as those "other sheep" of the Gentiles. But the pitiable thing is that, although lost, they do not realize their true condition.

Filled with a mistaken zeal for God, marked by an outward adherence to Judaism as a divinely-established system, they are earnestly trying to serve the God of their fathers, but not according to knowledge. That is, they have refused the fuller revelation He has given of Himself, His mind, and His will through Christ Jesus. "For they being ignorant of God's righteousness, and going about to establish their own righteousness, have not submitted themselves unto the righteousness of God" (Rom. 10:3).

The term "God's righteousness" is used here somewhat differently to the general expression, the "righteousness of God." We have seen heretofore that the righteousness of God is used in two ways. First, it is God's consistency with Himself, as one has expressed it, and thereby becomes the great sheet-anchor of the soul because in the gospel God has revealed how He can be just and the Justifier of those who put faith in Christ. The sin question has been settled in a righteous way, as God's nature demanded that it should be before He could deal in grace with guilty men. The second aspect is that of imputation. God imputes righteousness to all who believe. Therefore Christ, and Christ Himself, is the righteousness of the believer. We are thus made, or constituted, the righteousness of God in Him according as it is written in the book of the prophet Jeremiah: "This is his name whereby he shall be called, The Lord our Righteousness *[Jehovah Tsid-kenu]*" (23:6).

But in these three verses where the apostle says, "They being ignorant of God's righteousness" (Rom. 10:3), it seems plain that he simply means that they are ignorant of how righteous God really is; therefore, they go about attempting to establish a righteousness of their own. No man would think of doing this, if he realized for a moment the transcendent character of the divine righteousness. The utter impossibility of producing a righteousness of works suitable for a God of such infinite righteousness would cause the soul to shrink back in acknowledgement of his own helplessness. It is when men reach this place that they are ready to submit themselves unto that righteousness of God which has been revealed in the gospel. When I learn that I am absolutely without righteousness in myself—that is, without such a righteousness as is suited to a righteous God—then I am glad to avail myself of that righteousness that He Himself proclaims in the gospel and in which He clothes me when I trust in Christ. "For Christ is the end [i.e., the object for the consummation] of the law for righteousness to every one that believeth" (v. 4). The law proposed a righteousness that I could not furnish. Christ has met every requirement of that holy law; He has died under its penalty. He has risen from the dead and is Himself the righteousness which all need.

In the verses that follow, the apostle contrasts *legal* righteousness or a "by works righteousness" with this "in *faith* righteousness." He cites from Moses, who describes legal righteousness in the solemn words, "The man which doeth those things shall live by them" (v. 5; see Lev. 18:5). This is law in its very essence, "Do and live." But no man ever yet did that which entitled him to life, for if a man should "keep the whole law, and yet offend in one point, he is guilty of all" (James 2:10)—that is, he is a lawbreaker. He has not necessarily violated every commandment. But a thief is as truly a lawbreaker as a murderer. And the law having been violated, even once, man's title to life thereunder is forfeited.

Now the righteousness which is of faith depends upon testimony that God has given. Again the apostle quotes from Moses, who in Deuteronomy 30:12–14 presses upon the people the fact that God has given testimony that man is responsible to believe. The testimony there, of course, was the revelation from Sinai. But the apostle takes up Moses' words and, in a wonderful way under the guidance of the Spirit, applies them to Christ. "Say not in thine heart, Who shall ascend into heaven? (that is, to bring Christ down from above:) Or, Who shall descend into the deep? (that is, to bring up Christ again from the dead.)" (Rom. 10:6–7). Christ has already come down. He has died. God has raised Him from the dead. And upon this depends the entire gospel testimony.

Therefore, he goes on to say, "The word is nigh thee, even in thy mouth, and in thy heart: that is, the word of faith, which we preach" (v. 8). The gospel has been proclaimed. They have heard it and are familiar with its terms. The question is: Do they believe it and confess the Christ it proclaims as their Lord? For in verses 9–10 he epitomizes the whole matter in words that have been used of God through the centuries to bring assurance to thousands of precious souls, "That if thou shalt confess with thy mouth the Lord Jesus [or, literally, Jesus as Lord], and shalt believe in thine heart that God hath raised him from the dead, thou shalt be saved. For with the heart man believeth unto righteousness; and with the mouth confession is made unto salvation." The heart is simply another term for the real man. The apostle is not trying to draw a fine distinction, as some preachers do, between believing with the head and believing with the heart. He does not occupy us with the *nature* of belief; he *does* occupy us with the *object* of faith. We believe the message that God has given concerning Christ. If we believe at all, we believe with the heart. Otherwise, we do not really trust. "With the heart" man believes. The confession here is not, of course, necessarily the same thing as where our Lord says, "Whosoever . . . shall confess me before men, him will I confess also before my Father which is in heaven" (Matt. 10:32). This is rather the soul's confession to God Himself that he takes Jesus as Lord.

He then cites another Old Testament Scripture from the book of the prophet Isaiah (28:16), which declares that "Whosoever believeth on him shall not be ashamed" (Rom. 10:11). In this way he proves that the universality of the present gospel faith is in no wise in conflict with the revealed Word of God as given to the Jew of old. "Whosoever" includes the whole world. Already he has established the fact in chapter 3 that there is no difference between Jew and Gentile, so far as sin is concerned. Now he gives the other side of the "no difference" doctrine. "The same Lord over all is rich unto all that call upon him. For whosoever shall call upon the name of the Lord shall be saved" (vv. 12–13). To call upon the name of the Lord is, of course, to invoke His name in faith. His name speaks of what He is. He who calls upon the name of the Lord puts his trust in Him, as it is written, "The name of the LORD is a strong tower; the righteous runneth into it, and is safe" (Prov. 18:10).

The Jew had been accustomed to think of himself as the chosen of the Lord, and as the one to whom was committed the testimony of the one true and living God. Therefore, the objector naturally asks, and Paul puts the very words in his mouth, "How then shall they call on him in whom they have not believed?" (Rom. 10:14a). And he follows this question with another: "And how shall they believe in him of whom they have not heard?" (v. 14b). And this again with a third question: "How shall they hear without a preacher?" (v. 14c). Nor are the objections ended with this, for again he says: "And how shall they preach, except they be sent? as it is written, How beautiful are the feet of them that preach the gospel of peace, and bring glad tidings of good things!" (v. 15). The Jew believed in God. He had heard of Him. To him preachers had proclaimed the message, and these preachers had been sent of God. But who authorized anyone to overleap the Jewish bounds and go with the gospel of peace to the Gentiles?

In reply to the objector, Paul reminds him that Israel who had all these privileges had not responded as might have been expected—not all had obeyed the gospel. And this, too, was foreseen by the Old Testament prophets. Isaiah sadly asked, "Lord, who hath believed our report?" (v. 16), indicating that many who heard would refuse to accept this message. But then the objector answers, "You admit, Paul, that 'faith cometh by hearing, and hearing by the word [or the report] of God' (v. 17)." "Yes," he replies, "but have they not heard? Is there any people so utterly dark and ignorant that the Word of God in some form has not come to them, thus putting them into responsibility?" (see v. 18). Psalm 19 testifies that the voice of God may be heard in His creation: the sun, the moon, the stars—all the marvels of this wonderful universe—testify to the reality of a *personal* Creator. And so the psalmist says, "Their sound went into all the earth, and their words unto the ends of the world" (v. 18).

It is not a new thing, then, for God to speak to Gentiles. All that is new about it is that He is now speaking more fully, more clearly than He ever spoke before. He is now proclaiming in unmistakable terms an offer of salvation to all who trust His Word. And did not Israel know that God was going to take up the peoples of the nations? They *should* have known, for Moses himself said: "I will provoke you to jealousy by them that are no people, and by a foolish nation I will anger you" (v. 19). And Isaiah, with uncompromising boldness, declares: "I was found of them that sought me not; I was made manifest unto them that asked not after me" (v. 20). Surely words like these could only apply to the heathen of the Gentile world. And as for Israel, with all their privileges, concerning them God had said: "All day long I have stretched forth my hands unto a disobedient and gainsaying people" (v. 21).

The subject is continued in the opening verses of the next chapter, in which, as we shall see, the apostle shows how God is getting His election, even out of Israel, during the present dispensation. But we will consider the entire chapter in one address, and so I forbear further comment now, save to insist that the gist of the present portion is evidently this: during the present dispensation, when grace is going out to the nations beyond the bounds of the Jewish race, this does not involve the utter rejection of Israelites, but it does imply the end of special privilege. They may be saved if they will, but on exactly the same terms as the despised Gentile. The middle wall of partition is broken down, but grace is offered through Jesus Christ to all who own their guilt and confess His name.

GOD'S FUTURE DEALINGS WITH ISRAEL IN FULFILLMENT OF THE PROPHETIC SCRIPTURES

Romans 11

This eleventh chapter is most illuminating in regard to God's dispensational plan. We have already seen how His past dealings with Israel proved His righteousness in acting toward the Gentiles as He now does, despite the covenant made with the earthly people. Then in chapter 10 we have seen that although the nation as such is set to one side, this does not in any way hinder the individual Israelite from turning to God and finding that same salvation which He, in His sovereignty, is proclaiming through His servants to the Gentiles.

In the first part of our present chapter, verses 1–6, the subject of chapter 10 is continued and brought to a conclusion. The question is asked: "Hath God cast away his people?" (11:1). By no means. Paul's own experiences proved that this was not the case, for he was an Israelite of the natural seed of Abraham and of the tribe of Benjamin. Yet he had been laid hold of by the Spirit of God and brought to a saving knowledge of the Lord Jesus Christ. And what was true of him *might* be true of any other. What had really happened was simply the fulfillment of the words of the prophet Elijah in a wider sense than when he spoke in Ahab's day. The nation had rejected every testimony sent to it. As a people they had killed the prophets and defiled Jehovah's altar. But as in Elijah's day, God had reserved seven thousand to Himself who had not bowed the knee to the image of Baal, so "at this present time also there is a remnant according to the election of grace" (v. 5). God rejects the nation, but grace goes out to the individual.

The great thing, however, for Israel to understand is that, if saved at all, they are saved exactly as Gentiles are saved, and that is by grace. Grace, as we have seen, is unmerited favor. Yea, we may put it even stronger: it is favor against merit. This precludes all thought of work. If merit of any sort is taken into consideration, then it is no more grace. On the other hand, if salvation be of works, this leaves no place whatever for grace, because it would take from work its meritorious character. The two principles—salvation by grace and salvation by works—are diametrically opposed one to the other. There can be no admixture of law and grace; they are mutually destructive principles.

Beginning with verse 7, the apostle now undertakes to show God's secret purpose in connection with Israel in the coming day. What the nation sought, it has failed to obtain, but the election (that is, those who are content to be saved by grace) *do* obtain it. As to the rest, they are judicially blinded. Again he quotes from the Old Testament to show that this is in full accord with the prophetic Word. As Isaiah wrote, "God hath given them the spirit of slumber, eyes that they should not see, and ears that they should not hear" (v. 8), and He shows that this is true unto this day. David, too, had written: "Let their table be made a snare, and a trap, and a stumblingblock, and a recompense unto them: let their eyes be darkened, that they may not see, and bow down their back always" (vv. 9–10). These terrible imprecations were fulfilled when the representatives of the nation deliberately rejected Christ and called down judgment upon the heads of their descendants when they cried in Pilate's judgment hall, "His blood be on us, and on our children" (Matt. 27:25). Rejecting Messiah, God rejected them.

And many Christians have taken it for granted that He is through with them as a nation forever. This, the apostle now shows, is far from the truth. He asks, "Have they stumbled that they should fall?" (Rom. 11:11)—that is, utterly fall, fall without any hope or possibility of recovering. The answer again is, "By no means." God has overruled their present defection to make known His riches of grace toward the Gentiles, and this, in turn, will be used eventually to provoke Israel to jealousy and to turn them back to the God of their fathers and to the Christ whom they have rejected. This recovery will be a means of untold blessing to that part of the world which has not yet come to a saving knowledge of the gospel. With holy enthusiasm he exclaims: "Now if the [defection] of them be the riches of the world, and the diminishing of them the riches of the Gentiles; how much more their fulness?" (v. 12). It is well to note the use he makes of this word *fullness,* as we shall come upon it lower down in the chapter. The fullness of Israel will be the conversion of Israel—the fulfillment of God's purpose regarding them.

Paul was the apostle to the Gentiles, and as such, he magnified his office. But he would not have the Gentiles for a moment think that he had lost his interest in Israel. Rather, he would see them stirred to emulation that many might be saved from among them as they saw the grace of God going out to the Gentiles. On the other hand, he would not have the Gentile glory over the Jew because the latter was set aside and the former enjoyed the blessings that the Jew would have had, had he been ready to receive them. He continues his argument by introducing a parable, which brings out most vividly the divine plan. He says: "For if the casting away of them be the reconciling of the world, what shall the receiving of them be, but life from the dead?" (v. 15). That is, if—as they wander among all the nations a disappointed and weary people under the ban of the God of their fathers—the message of grace is going out to the Gentiles and an election from them are receiving the message, what will it mean to the world as a whole when Israel *nationally* will turn back to the Lord and become in very truth a holy people—His witnesses to all nations?

"For if the firstfruit be holy, the lump is also holy: and if the root be holy, so are the branches" (v. 16). If the regenerated remnant in Israel be indeed a people set apart to God, so eventually will the nation be to which they belong. And if the root of the covenant olive tree be holy (that is, Abraham, who believed God, and it was counted to him for righteousness), so are all those who are really linked with him by faith. They were natural branches in the olive tree—Israelites by birth but not by grace, who were broken off. And in order that the promises of God to Abraham should not fail, "In thy seed shall all the nations of the earth be blessed" (Gen. 22:18; 26:4), the branches of the wild olive tree—the Gentiles—were grafted in among the remnant of Israel. Thus Jew and Gentile believing together partake of the root and fatness of the olive tree. But now the grave danger is lest the Gentile should rest on mere outward privileges and, while linked with the children of the promise, should fail to appreciate for themselves the gospel of God and so prove unreal. In that case, God will have to deal with the Gentiles as He had dealt with the Jews. And so we get the solemn warning: "Boast not against the branches. But if thou boast, thou bearest not the root, but the root thee" (Rom. 11:18). Some might say, "Well, but 'the [natural] branches were broken off, that I [a Gentile] might be grafted in" (v. 19). The answer is clear and distinct: "Because of unbelief they were broken off, and thou standest by faith" (v. 20). Therefore the admonition, "Be not highminded, but fear: for if God spared not the natural branches, take heed lest he also spare not thee" (vv. 20–21).

Do we need to pause to ask whether the Gentiles have valued their privileges? Is it not patent to every observing spiritually-minded person that conditions in Christendom are as bad today as they ever were in Israel? Do we not see apostasy from the truth everywhere prevalent? Are not the characteristic features of the last days, as depicted in 2 Timothy 3, everywhere manifest? If so, may we not well be warned that the time is near when the unfruitful branches will be torn out of the olive tree and the natural branches, at last turning back to God, be grafted in again to their own olive tree?

In these dispensational ways we see manifested that goodness and severity of God, which has already been so clearly brought out in the ninth chapter. On those who fell, who refused to believe the testimony, severity. But toward ignorant and unworthy Gentiles, goodness, but this goodness only to be continued toward them if they continue to appreciate it. Otherwise, they, too, shall be cut off. Who can doubt that the day of the cutting off is near at hand, when the true church having been caught up to be with the Lord, judgment will be meted out to unfaithful Christendom, and then God will turn back in grace to Israel, if they abide not still in unbelief, and they shall be regrafted into their own olive tree, according to the power of the God of resurrection?

I recall an article by a well-known "higher critic," which I read some years ago, in which he was ridiculing the idea of the apostle Paul's inspiration because of his apparent ignorance of one of the first principles of horticulture: "Paul," said he, "was actually so ignorant of the art of grafting that he speaks of grafting wild branches into a good tree, evidently not aware of the fact that it is customary to graft good branches into a wild tree." It is clear that the reverend critic had never carefully read the apostle's own words, as given in the next verse, or he would not have been caught in such a trap. Paul clearly indicates that his illustration is one which he well knew to be opposed to that which was ordinarily done. He says: "For if thou wert cut out of the olive tree which is wild by nature, and wert grafted *contrary* to nature into a good olive tree: how much more shall these, which be the natural branches, be grafted into their own olive tree?" (v. 24).

No, Paul was not ignorant of horticulture, nor was the Holy Spirit ignorant, who was guiding him and inspiring him as he wrote. That which is not customary to man is often in full accord with the divine plan, as here.

And so, in verses 25–32, we see just what must take place before this regrafting,

and what will follow afterward. "I would not, brethren, that ye should be ignorant of this mystery, lest ye should be wise in your own conceits; that blindness
in part has happened to Israel, until the fullness of the Gentiles be come in. And
so all Israel shall be saved" (vv. 25–26).

This, then, is one of the secret things hidden in the mind of God until the
due time for its revelation: Israel will be blinded in part, but, thank God, only in
part, until the present work of God among the Gentiles be completed. Here we
have the second use of this word *fullness*. "The fulness of the Gentiles" is the
completion of the work among the nations that has been going on ever since
Israel's rejection. This "fullness," as we know from other Scripture passages, will
come in when our Lord calls His church to be with Himself, in accordance with
1 Thessalonians 4 and 1 Corinthians 15. It is then that "all Israel shall be saved."
We are not to understand by the term "all Israel" everyone of Israel's blood, for
we have already learned that "they are not all Israel, [who] are of Israel: . . . but
the children of the promise are counted for the seed" (9:6, 8). So the remnant
will be the true Israel in that glorious day when "there shall come out of Zion the
Deliverer, and shall turn away ungodliness from Jacob," for God has said, "this is
my covenant unto them, when I shall take away their sins" (11:26–27).

So then, the apostle concludes, they are enemies of the gospel for the present
time, but through their enmity grace goes out to the Gentiles. Nevertheless,
according to the divine plan, they are still beloved for the fathers' sakes, for
God's gifts and calling He never retracts. The promises made to the patriarchs
and to David shall and *must* be fulfilled. Study carefully psalm 89 in this connection. And just as the Gentiles who in time past had not believed God but have
now obtained mercy through the Jews' unbelief, so, in like manner, when the
Gentiles prove unbelieving and are set to one side, Israel will obtain mercy when
they turn back in faith to God.

Whether Jew or Gentile, all alike are saved on the same principle, "For God
hath concluded them all in unbelief, that he might have mercy upon all" (v. 32).

The last four verses are in the nature of a Doxology. The apostle's heart is
filled with worship, praise, and admiration as the full blaze of the divine plan
fills the horizon of his soul. He exclaims: "O the depth of the riches both of the
wisdom and knowledge of God! how unsearchable are his judgments, and his
ways past finding out!" (v. 33).

Apart from revelation, none could have known His mind, just as no created
being could ever have been His counselor. No one ever earned grace by first giving
to Him in order that blessing might be recompensed, but everything is *"of* him,
and *through* him, and *to* him, . . . to whom be glory for ever. Amen." (v. 36).

PART 3

PRACTICAL

*Divine Righteousness Producing
Practical Righteousness in the Believer*

Romans 12–16

The Walk of the Christian in Relation to His Fellow Believers and to Men of the World

Romans 12

We come now to consider the practical bearing of all this precious truth, which the Spirit of God has been unfolding before our astonished eyes. In this last part of the epistle we learn what the effect should be upon the believer who has laid hold, by faith, of the truth of the gospel. We may divide this third part, roughly, as follows: subdivision 1, Romans 12:1–15:7, God's good and acceptable and perfect will unfolded; subdivision 2, Romans 15:8–33, which divides into two parts the conclusion of the matter and his own service; subdivision 3, Romans 16:1–24, salutations and warning. Verses 25–27 form an appendix to the entire epistle.

The first two verses of chapter 12 are the introduction to this entire practical part of the letter, based upon the revelation given in chapters 1–8. For we may very properly consider chapters 9–11 as a great parenthesis, occasioned because of the necessity of clearing the mind of the believing Jew in regard to the ways of God.

The opening words necessarily link with the closing part of chapter 8: "I beseech you, therefore, brethren" (12:1). The "therefore" refers clearly to the magnificent summing up of Christian standing and eternal blessing in the eighth chapter. Because you are in Christ free from all condemnation; because you are indwelt by the Holy Spirit; because you are sons by adoption, because you are eternally linked up with Christ; because you are the elect of God, predestined to be conformed to the image of His Son; because you are beyond all possibility of condemnation, since Christ has died and been raised again and sits at God's right hand; because no charge can ever be laid against the believer that God will hear; because there is no separation from the love of God for those who are in Christ Jesus—"I beseech you [to] present your bodies a living sacrifice, holy, acceptable unto God, which is your [intelligent] service!" (v. 1). Christ gave Himself for us—a sacrifice in death. Like the firstborn in Egypt, redeemed by the blood of the lamb, you are now to be devoted to Him.

As the Levites were afterward presented to God to live sacrificial lives in place of the firstborn, so each believer is called upon to recognize the Lord's claims upon him and to present, or yield, his body as a living sacrifice, set apart and acceptable unto God, because of the price that has been paid for his redemption (see Num. 8:11–21; Dan. 3:28). How much do we really know of this experimentally? We who once yielded our members to the service of sin and Satan are now called upon to yield ourselves wholly unto God as those who are alive from the dead. This will involve sacrifice all the way, the denial of self, and the constant recognition of the divine claims upon us.

The second verse makes clearer the meaning involved: "Be not conformed to this world: but be ye transformed by the renewing of your mind, that ye may prove what is that good, and acceptable, and perfect, will of God."

The cross of Christ has come in between the believer and the world. To conform himself to the ways of this present evil age is to be unfaithful to the One whom the world has rejected but whom we have owned as Lord and Savior. "I would give the world to have your experience," said a young woman on one occasion to a devoted Christian lady. "My dear," was the reply, "that's exactly what it cost me. I gave the world for it." The loyal heart exclaims with gladness, not grudgingly,

> Take the world, but give me Jesus;
>   All earth's joys are but in name;
> But His love abideth ever,
>   Through eternal years the same.

Moved by the "expulsive power of a new affection," it becomes easy for the soul to say with Paul: "God forbid that I should glory, save in the cross of the Lord Jesus Christ, [by which] the world is crucified unto me, and I unto the world" (Gal. 6:14). We are not to suppose that nonconformity to the world necessarily involves awkwardness of behavior, peculiarity of dress, or boorishness in manner. But the entire world system is summed up in three terms: (1) the lust of the flesh; (2) the lust of the eye; and (3) the pride of life, or the ostentation of living. Therefore, nonconformity to the world implies holding the body and its appetites in subjection to the Spirit of God, subjecting the imagination to the mind of Christ, and walking in lowliness of spirit through a scene where self-confidence and boasting are the order of the day.

In 2 Corinthians 3:18 we read that, "We all, beholding as in a glass the glory of the unveiled face of the Lord, are changed [or transformed] into the same image by the Spirit of the Lord " (literal rendering).

And so here we are commanded to be transformed by the renewing of our minds. That is, as the mind is occupied with Christ and the affections set on things above, we become like Him who has won our hearts for Himself. Walking in loving obedience, we prove the blessedness of the "good, and acceptable, and perfect, will of God" (Rom. 12:2). Through the rest of the chapter we have God's good will in regard to our relations, particularly to fellow believers; in chapter 13, the will of God for the believer in relation to human government and society in general; in chapter 14 and the first seven verses of chapter 15, the will of God in regard to the believer's relation to those who are weak in the faith.

We note, then, that the believer is here looked upon as a member of the body of Christ, and this, while speaking of wondrous privilege, nevertheless involves grave responsibility. It might be well to point out here that the body of Christ is looked at in two very distinct aspects in the epistles. In Ephesians and Colossians we have the body in its dispensational aspect, embracing all believers from Pentecost to the return of the Lord for His church. Looked at in this way, Christ alone is the Head, and all are united to Him, whether as to their actual condition they be numbered among the living or the dead. But in 1 Corinthians 12 and here in Romans 12, the body is looked upon as something manifested on the earth, and, therefore, the apostle speaks of eyes and ears, and so forth, as in the body here below. The absurd deduction has been drawn from this that the *church* of the book of Acts and of the early epistles of Paul is not at all the same thing as the church of the prison epistles. This view is pure assumption, based upon a farfetched dispensationalism that destroys a sense of Christian responsibility to a very large degree wherever it is fully embraced. In Corinthians, and in Romans, too, the body of Christ is viewed on earth. Inasmuch as there are those set in the church who speak and act for the Head in heaven, it is quite in keeping to use the figures of the eyes, ears, and so on. "[If] one member suffer, all the members suffer with it" (1Cor. 12:26) could not be said of saints in heaven. Their sufferings are forever over. But as long as there is a suffering saint on earth, every other member of the body of Christ shares with him in his affliction.

I remember well, as a boy, gazing with rapt admiration upon a regiment of Highlanders as they marched through the streets of my native city, Toronto, Canada, and I was thrilled when I was told that that regiment had fought in the battle of Waterloo. It was quite a disappointment to me afterward to learn that not one man of them all had been in that great battle. I was gazing on the regiment as then constituted, and the battle of Waterloo had taken place many years before. But it was the same regiment, just with new recruits taking the places constantly of those who passed away. So it is with the body of Christ on earth. Believers die and depart to be with Christ and join the choir invisible above. Others take their places here below, and thus the church continues from century to century.

Now as a member of Christ's body I need to realize that I am not to act independently of other members, nor am I to think of myself as exalted above the rest but to think soberly as one to whom God has dealt a measure of faith, as He also has to every other Christian. As there are many members in the human body and no two members have the same office, so believers, though many, together constitute one body in Christ and are all members one of another. But our gifts differ, and each one is to use whatever gifts may be given to him according to the grace that God supplies. If he have the gift of prophecy, he is to speak according to the proportion of faith. If his place be characteristically that of service, let him serve in subjection to the Lord. If he be a teacher, let him teach in lowly grace. If an exhorter, let him seek to stir up his brethren, but in the love of Christ. If he be one to whom God has entrusted earthly treasure that he may give generously to relieve the need of his brethren or to further the work of the gospel, let him distribute with simplicity not ostentatiously as drawing attention to himself or his gifts. If he be fitted to rule in the assembly of God let him be a diligent pastor or shepherd of the flock. If it be given him to show mercy to the needy or undeserving, let it be with cheerfulness.

Above all things, let *love* be genuine without pretense or hypocrisy, abhorring that which is evil but cleaving to that which is good.

How much we need the simple exhortations of verse 10: "Be kindly affectioned one to another with brotherly love; in honour preferring one another."

Elsewhere he writes: "Be ye kind one to another" (Eph. 4:32). How rare a virtue true kindness is! How often pretended zeal for truth or for church position dries up the milk of human kindness! And yet this is one of the truest Christian virtues. Dr. Griffith Thomas used to tell of an old Scotch pastor who frequently said to his congregation: "Remember, if you are not very kind, you are not very spiritual." And yet how often people imagine that there is something even incongruous between spirituality and kindness! How differently would Christians speak of one another and act toward one another if these admonitions were but kept in view.

The first part of the eleventh verse is better translated, "Not remiss in zeal." It is not to be taken as a mere exhortation to careful business methods, but whatever one has to do should be done zealously, with spiritual fervor, as serving the Lord.

It is hardly necessary to take up each verse in detail. The exhortations are too plain to be misunderstood. In verse 16, however, it may be as well to point out that the apostle is not really inculcating condescension, as though of higher beings to those of less worth, but what he really says is: "Mind not high things, but go along with the lowly." The last five verses possibly have the world in view rather than fellow Christians, and yet it is unhappily true that even in all dealings with fellow believers the same admonitions are needed. It is not always possible to live peaceably, even with fellow saints, let alone with men of the world. Therefore, the word, *"If possible,* as much lieth in you, live peaceably with all men" (v. 18). Some have had difficulty over the meaning of the expression, "Give place unto wrath," in verse 19. What I understand the apostle to say is this: "Do not attempt to avenge yourselves, but leave room for the judgment of God. If wrath must be meted out, let Him do it, not yourself." For it is written: "Vengeance is mine: I will repay, saith the Lord" (v. 19).

Savonarola said, "A Christian's life consists in doing good and suffering evil." It is not for him to take matters into his own hands, but rather to act upon verses 20–21 in simple confidence that God will not suffer any trial to come upon him through others which will not eventually work out for good.

This is not natural, but it is possible to the man who walks in the Spirit. A young nobleman complained to Francis of Assisi of a thief. "The rascal," he cried, "has stolen my boots." "Run after him quickly," exclaimed Francis, "and give him your socks." This was the spirit of the Lord Jesus "who, when he was reviled, reviled not again" (1 Peter 2:23), and for hatred ever gave love.

No one can fail to see how like are these exhortations to the teaching of our blessed Lord in the so-called Sermon on the Mount. Yet the difference is immense. For there His words were the acid test of discipleship while waiting for the coming of the kingdom which is yet to be displayed. But here we have exhortation to walk in accord with the new nature that we possess as children of God. It is not in order that we "may be the children of [our] Father in heaven" (Matt. 5:45). It is the manifestation of the Spirit's work in those who belong to the new creation.

The Will of God as to the Believer's Relation to Government and to Society, and the Closing Sections

Romans 13–16

The position of the Christian in this world is necessarily, under the present order of things, a peculiarly difficult and almost anomalous one. He is a citizen of another world, passing as a stranger and a pilgrim through a strange land. Presumably loyal in heart to the rightful King, who earth rejected and counted worthy only of a malefactor's cross, he finds himself called upon to walk in a godly and circumspect way in a scene of which Satan, the usurper, is the prince and god. Yet he is not to be an anarchist nor is he to flaunt the present order of things. His rule ever should be: "We [must] obey God rather than men" (Acts 5:29). Nevertheless, he is not to be found in opposition to human government, even though the administrators of that government may be men of the most unrighteous type.

As we come to the study of this thirteenth chapter, it is well for us to remember that he who sat upon the throne of empire when Paul gave this instruction concerning obedience to the powers that be was one of the vilest beasts in human form whoever occupied a throne. This ruler was a sensuous, sensual brute, who ripped up the body of his own mother in order that he might see the womb that bore him. He was an evil, blatant egotist of most despicable character, whose cruelties and injustices beggar all description. And yet God in His providence permitted this demon-controlled wretch to wear the diadem of the greatest empire the world had yet known. Paul himself designates him elsewhere as a savage beast when he writes to the young preacher Timothy, "God delivered me out of the mouth of the lion" (see 2 Tim. 4:17).

While the powers of the emperor were more or less circumscribed by the laws and the Senate, nevertheless his rule was one that could not but spell ruin and disaster for many of the early Christians. What faith was required on their part to obey the instruction given by the Spirit of God in the first seven verses of this chapter! And if under such government Christians were called upon to be obedient, surely there is no place for sedition or rebellion under any government. "The potsherds of the earth may strive with the potsherds of the earth" (Isa. 45:9, author's translation) and one government may be overthrown by another, but whichever government is established in power at a given time, the Christian is to be subject to it. He has the resource of prayer if its edicts are tyrannous and unjust, but he is not to rise in rebellion against it. This is a hard saying for some of us, I know, but if any be in doubt let him read carefully the verses now before us. "Let every soul be subject unto the higher powers. For there is no power but of God: the powers that be are ordained of God" (Rom. 13:1).

This is not to seek to establish the doctrine of the divine right of kings, but it simply means this: that God, who sets up one man and puts down another for His own infinitely wise purpose, ordains that certain forms of government or certain rulers shall be in the place of authority at a given time. As the book of Daniel tells us, He sets over the nations the basest of men at times as a punishment for their wickedness. But in any case, there could be no authority if not providentially permitted and therefore recognized by Himself.

To resist this authority, the second verse shows us, is to resist a divine ordinance. But it would certainly be farfetched to say that they that resist shall receive to themselves damnation, if by "damnation" we mean everlasting punishment. The word here as in 1 Corinthians 11 means *judgment,* but not in the sense of eternal judgment necessarily. Rulers are not a terror to good works but to the evil. Even a Nero respected such as walked in obedience to the law. The reason he persecuted the Christians was that they were reported to be opposed to existing institutions. He, then, who would not be afraid of those in authority is called upon to walk in obedience to the law—to do good—and thus his righteousness will be recognized. After all, the ruler is the minister of God to each one for good. But he who does evil, violating the institutions of the realm, may well fear, for into the magistrate's hand has been committed by God Himself the sword, which he does not bear in vain. He is set by God to be His minister in the government of the world and to execute judgment upon those who act in a criminal way.

So, then, the Christian is called upon to be subject to government, not only to avoid condemnation, but also that he may himself maintain a good conscience toward God. Let him pay tribute, even though at times the demands may seem to be unrighteous, rendering to all their dues, paying his taxes honorably, and thus showing that he desires in all things to be subject to the government.

It will be observed that all the instruction we have here puts the Christian in the place of subjection and not of authority. But, if in the providence of God, he be born to the purple, or put in the place of authority, he, too, is to be bound by the Word of God as here set forth.

The balance of the chapter has to do with the Christian's relation to society in general, and that in view of the coming of the Lord and the soon-closing up of the present dispensation. He is to maintain the attitude not of a debtor but a giver—to owe no man anything but rather to let love flow out freely to all. For every moral precept of the second table of the law, which sets forth man's duty to his neighbor, is summed up in the words: "Thou shalt love thy neighbour as thyself." He who thus loves could, by no possibility, ever be guilty of adultery, murder, theft, lying, or covetousness. It is impossible that love should be manifested in such ways as these. "Love worketh no ill to his neighbour: therefore love is the fulfilling of the law" (Rom. 13:10). It is in this way that the righteous requirement of the law is fulfilled in us who walk not after the flesh but after the Spirit, as we have already seen in looking at Romans 8:1–4.

Every passing day brings the dispensation of grace nearer to its end and hastens the return of the Lord. It is not for the Christian, then, to be sleeping among the dead but to be fully awake to his responsibilities and privileges, realizing that the salvation for which we wait—the redemption of the body—is nearer now than when we believed. The night when Satan's sway bears rule over the earth has nearly drawn to its close. Already the light of day begins to dawn. It is not, therefore, for those who have been saved by grace to have aught to do with works of darkness but rather, as soldiers, to have on the armor of light standing for that which is of God, living incorruptly as in the full light of day, not in debauchery or wantonness of any kind, neither in strife and envying, but having put on the Lord Jesus Christ, having confessed themselves as one with Him, to take the place of death with Him in a practical sense, thus making no provision for the indulgence of the lust of the flesh.

It was these two closing verses of this thirteenth chapter that spoke so loudly to the heart of Augustine of Hippo when, after years of distress, he was fearful to confess Christ openly, even when intellectually convinced that he should be a Christian lest he would find himself unable to hold his carnal nature in subjection, and so might bring grave discredit upon the cause with which he thought of identifying himself. But as he read the words: "Let us walk honestly, as in the day; not in rioting and drunkenness, not in chambering and wantonness, not in strife and envying. But put ye on the Lord Jesus Christ, and make not provision for the flesh, to fulfil the lusts thereof" (vv. 13–14), the Spirit of God opened his eyes to see that the power for victory was not in himself but in the fact that he was identified with a crucified and risen Savior.

As he gazed by faith upon His blessed face and the Holy Spirit showed him something of the truth of union with Christ, he entered into the assurance of salvation and realized victory over sin. When in an unexpected way he came face to face with one of the beautiful but wanton companions of his former days, he turned and ran. She followed, crying, "Austin, Austin, why do you run? It is only I." He replied as he sped on his way, "I run, because it is not I!" Thus he made no provision for the flesh.

In chapter 14 and the first seven verses of chapter 15 the Holy Spirit emphasizes the believer's responsibilities toward his weaker brethren. He is to walk charitably toward those who have less light than himself.

The weak in faith, that is, those whose uninstructed consciences cause them to be in trouble as to things indifferent, are to be received and owned as in this full Christian position and not to be judged for their questionings or doubtful thoughts. The principle is a most far-reaching one, and indicates the breadth of Christian charity that should prevail over the spirit of legality into which it is so easy to fall. Light is not the ground of reception to Christian privileges, but life. All those who are children of God are to be recognized as fellow members of the body and, unless living in evident wickedness, to be accorded their blood-bought place in the Christian company. Wickedness and weakness are not to be confounded. The wicked person is to be put away (see 1 Cor. 5), but the weak brother is to be received and protected.

Of course, it is not reception into fellowship that is here in view. The one who was weak in faith was already inside. He must not be looked upon coldly and judged for his doubtful thoughts (see margin), but received cordially and his weak conscience carefully considered. It might be one who is still under law as to things clean and unclean or one who has difficulty regarding holy days. In the former case, the brother who is strong in the liberty that is in Christ believes he may, as a Christian, eat all things, raising no questions as to their ceremonial cleanness. The weak brother is so afraid of defilement he subsists on a vegetable diet rather than possibly partake of what has been offered to idols or is not "Kosher"—that is, clean according to Levitical law.

The one who is "strong" must not look with contempt upon his overscrupulous brother. On the other hand, the weak one is forbidden to accuse the stronger of insincerity or inconsistency.

Or, if it be a question of days and one brother with a legal conscience possibly still holds to the sanctity of the Jewish Sabbath, while another sees all days as now alike and to be devoted to the glory of God, each must seek to act as before Him and be "fully persuaded in his own mind" (14:5).

Who has given one servant to regulate another? Both are accountable to one Master, and He recognizes integrity of heart and will uphold His own. Where there is sincerity and it is the glory of the Lord that each has in view, both must endeavor to act as in His presence. There can be no question but that the principle here enunciated if firmly held would make for fuller fellowship among saints and save from many heart-burnings.

We do not live for ourselves. Whether we will or no, we are constantly affecting others for good or ill. Let us then recognize our individual responsibility to the Lord, whose we are and whom we are to serve, whether in life or in death. "For to this end Christ both died, and rose, . . . that he might be Lord both of the dead and living" (v. 9). The words, *"and revived,"* are a needless interpolation omitted from all critical versions.

At the judgment seat of God (according to the best reading), where Christ Himself is the Arbiter, all will come out, and He will show what was in accord with His mind. Until then we can afford to wait, realizing that we must all give account of ourselves to Him. In view of this, "Let us not . . . judge one another any more" (v. 13), but let there be individual self-judgment, each one striving so to walk as not to put any occasion to fall in a weak brother's way.

Even where one is clear that his own behavior is consistent with Christian liberty, let him not flaunt that liberty before the weak lest he "destroy [one] for whom Christ died" (v. 15; see also 1 Cor. 8:11). It is of course the ruin of his testimony that is in view. Emboldened by the example of the strong one, he may venture to go beyond the dictates of conscience and so bring himself under a sense of condemnation, or he may become discouraged, thinking others inconsistent, and so drift from the Christian company.

After all, questions of meats and drinks are but of minor importance. "For the kingdom of God is not meat and drink"—that is, has not to do with temporalities as have all merely human kingdoms—but it is spiritual in character and has to do with "righteousness, and peace, and joy in the Holy [Spirit]" (v. 17). Where one is exercised as to these things (even though mistaken as to others), he serves Christ and is acceptable to God and approved of men.

Every right-thinking person appreciates sincerity. "Let us therefore follow after the things that make for peace, and things wherewith one may edify another" (v. 19).

It is far better to abstain from ought that would trouble the conscience of a weak brother than to turn him aside by insisting on liberty, and so be responsible for his failure and the breakdown of his discipleship.

If one has faith that he can safely do what another condemns, let him have it to himself before God and not flaunt it flagrantly before the weak. But let him be sure he is not self-condemned while he professes to be clear. For he who persists in a certain course concerning which he is not really at ease before God does not truly act in faith, and so is condemned (not "damned" of course—for this word properly refers to eternal judgment), because "whatsoever is not of faith is sin" (v. 23). That is to say, if I act contrary to what I believe to be right, even though there be nothing morally wrong in my behavior, I am really sinning against conscience and thus against God.

He sums it all up in the first seven verses of chapter 15. The strong should bear the burdens of the weak—as sympathetically entering into their difficulties—and not insist on liberty to please themselves. Rather let each one have his neighbor's good in view, seeking his building up and not carelessly destroying his faith by ruthlessly insisting on his own personal liberty. True liberty will be manifested by refraining from what would stumble a weaker one.

In this Christ is the great example. He who need never have yielded to any legal enactment voluntarily submitted to every precept of the law, and even went far beyond it, pleasing not Himself (as when He paid the temple tax, giving as His reason, "Lest we should [stumble] them" [Matt. 17:27]), thus taking upon Himself the reproaches of those who reproached God. His outward behavior was as blameless as His inward life, yet men reviled Him as they reviled God.

Verse 4 stresses the importance of Old Testament Scripture. "Whatsoever things were written aforetime were written for our learning, that we through patience and comfort of the scriptures might have hope." Link with this 1 Corinthians

10:6, 11. "All Scripture is not about me, but all Scripture is for me," is a quotation well worth remembering.

He closes this section by praying that "the God of patience and consolation" (v. 5) may give the saints to be of one mind toward each other, with Christ whose blessed example he has cited, that all may unitedly glorify God, even the Father of our Lord Jesus Christ. Mind and mouth must be in agreement if this be so. And so he exhorts them to receive one another as Christ also received us to the glory of God. If Christ could take us up in grace—whether weak or strong—and make us meet for the glory, surely we can be cordial and Christlike in our fellowship one with another. Again, I repeat, it is not the question of receiving into the Christian company that is in view here, but the recognition of those already inside.

Properly speaking, the epistle as such—the treatise on the righteousness of God—is brought to a conclusion in verses 8–13. All that comes afterward is more in the nature of postscript and appendix.

What has really been demonstrated in this very full treatise? "Now I say that Jesus Christ was a minister of the circumcision for the truth of God, to confirm the promises made unto the fathers: and that the Gentiles might glorify God for His mercy" (vv. 8–9). That is, he has shown throughout that our Lord came in full accord with the Old Testament promises. He entered into the sheepfold by the door (as John's gospel tells us in chap. 10) and was the divinely appointed minister to the Jews, come to confirm the covenanted promises. Though the nation rejected Him, this does not invalidate His ministry, but it opens the door of mercy to the Gentiles in a wider way than ever, though in full accord with the Jewish Scriptures. And so he cites passage after passage to clinch the truth already taught so clearly, that it was foreknown and predetermined that the Gentiles should hear the gospel and be given the same opportunity to be saved that the Jew enjoyed. That this "mercy" actually transcends anything revealed in past ages we know since "the revelation of the mystery" (16:25), to which he alludes in the last verses of the next chapter.

But his point here is that it is not contrary to the predictions of the prophets, but entirely consistent with what God had been pleased to make known beforehand. And so he brings this masterly unfolding of the gospel and its result to a close by saying, "Now the God of hope fill you with all joy and peace in believing, that ye may abound in hope, through the power of the Holy [Spirit]" (15:13). In believing what? Why, simply in believing the great truths set forth in the epistle—the tremendous verities of our most holy faith—setting before us man's ruin by sin and his redemption through Christ Jesus. When we believe this, we are filled with joy and peace as we look on in hope to the consummation of it all at our Lord's return, meantime walking before God in the power of the indwelling Spirit who alone makes these precious things real to us.

The balance of the chapter takes on a distinctly personal character as the apostle takes the saints at Rome into his confidence and tells them of his exercises regarding them and his purpose to visit them. From the reports that had come to him he was persuaded that they were already in a very healthy spiritual state, "full of goodness, filled with all knowledge, and able also to admonish one another" (v. 14). So he had no thought of going to them as a regulator, but he felt that he had a ministry, committed to him by God, that would be profitable for them. Besides, Rome was part of that great Gentile world into which he had been sent and to which his ministry specially applied, "that the offering up of the Gentiles might be acceptable, being sanctified by the Holy [Spirit]" (v. 16). Israel was no longer the one separate nation, but the gospel was for all alike.

It was therefore to be expected that he should visit them whenever the way was opened, and as it seemed to him that his mission to those in Asia Minor and eastern Europe was now in large measure fulfilled, he purposed shortly going westward as far as to Spain and hoped to visit them on the way. Meantime, he was going up to Jerusalem to carry an offering from the saints of Macedonia and Achaia to the needy believers of Judea. As soon as this was accomplished he hoped to leave for Spain, visiting them en route. What a mercy that the near future was sealed to him. How little he realized what he must soon be called upon to suffer for Christ's name's sake. "Man proposes, but God disposes." And He had quite other plans for His devoted servant—though they included a visit to Rome, but in chains!

Sure that in God's due time he would get to them and "come in the fulness of the blessing of the gospel of Christ" (v. 29), he beseeches them to pray for the success of his mission to his own countrymen and that he might be delivered from the unbelieving Jews. The prayer was answered, but in how different a manner to what he anticipated!

Chapter 16 consists largely of salutations to saints known to him now dwelling in Rome and from others who were in his company. The first two verses are in the nature of a letter of commendation for Phoebe a deaconess of the assembly in Cenchrea, a town just south of Corinth in Achaia (see Acts 18:18). She would doubtless be well-known to Aquila and Priscilla (who are mentioned by name—in inverse order—in the next verse). But he does not leave her to depend upon her friends' recollections of the past, but by this letter assures the saints of her present standing in the church.

Priscilla and Aquila were to him as members of his own family—so intimate had been their association. He cannot forget how they had put themselves in jeopardy for his sake. It was in their house that one of the assemblies in Rome met. Another of the saints from Achaia was there also, Epaenetus, firstfruits of his mission to Corinth.

As we go over the long list and note the delicate touches, the tender recollections, the slight differences in commendation, we feel we are drawn very close to these early believers and would like to know more of their history and experiences. We are interested in learning that there were relatives of his, Andronicus and Junia, who, he says, were "in Christ before me" (v. 7), and we wonder if their prayers for their brilliant young kinsman may not have had much to do with his remarkable conversion.

Another kinsman is mentioned in verse 11, Herodion by name, but whether converted before or after him we are not told.

There is a very human touch in the thirteenth verse: "Salute Rufus chosen in the Lord, and his mother and mine." Somewhere on his journeys this Christian matron, though unnamed, had mothered the devoted and self-denying servant of Christ, and he remembered with a peculiar gratitude her care for him.

All the names are of interest. We shall be glad to meet them all "in that day" and learn more of their devotion to the Lord and their sufferings for His name's sake, though we cannot linger over the record here.

Before sending messages from his associates he puts in a warning word against false teachers in verses 17–18: "Now I beseech you, brethren, mark them which cause divisions and offenses contrary to the doctrine which ye have learned; and avoid them. For they that are such serve not our Lord Jesus Christ, but their own belly; and by good words and fair speeches deceive the hearts of the simple." The evildoers here referred to are not Christian teachers, even though in error. They are ungodly men who, as Jude tells us, have crept in from the outside. They are not servants of Christ but tools of the Devil, brought in from the world to corrupt and divide the people of God. It is a fearfully wicked thing to apply such words to real Christians who, however mistaken they may be, love the Lord and yearn over His people, desiring their blessing. In Philippians 3:18–19 we learn more of those "who serve their own belly," that is, who live only for self-gratification: "Many walk, of whom I have told you often, and now tell you even weeping, that they are the enemies of the cross of Christ: whose end is destruction, whose God is their belly, and whose glory is in their shame, who mind earthly things." These are identical with the wretched division makers of our present chapter. Let us be exceedingly careful how we charge true servants of Christ with being of this unholy number, even though we may feel that truth compels us to take issue with them as to some things they do or teach.

Though he warns the Roman saints of the danger of listening to men of this type he lets them know that he has only heard good things of them, but he is jealous that they should maintain their excellent record. Alas, how soon did this very church open its doors to just such false teachers as he warned them against, and so by the seventh century you have the Papacy itself enthroned in Rome!

He would have us simple concerning evil and wise unto what is good, not occupied with error but with truth. That truth will triumph soon when the God of peace shall bruise Satan under the feet of the saints.

The closing salutations from Paul and his companions are given in verses 21–24. Timothy and Luke were with him. We now learn for the first time that Jason was a near relative (see Acts 17:5–9), which accounts in measure for his reception of and devotion to Paul upon the visit to Thessalonica. Sosipater, also a kinsman, is linked with him.

Tertius, the scribe who acted as Paul's amanuensis, adds his greeting. Apart from this we should never have known the name of the actual writer of the letter.

Was the "Gaius mine host" of verse 23, the same as the Gaius who received the traveling brethren and was commended by John for his Christian hospitality in his third epistle? We do not know, but he was at least a man of the same spirit. Of Erastus we have heard elsewhere (Acts 19:22; 2 Tim. 4:20), but Quartus is not mentioned in any other passage. Both the names Tertius and Quartus would indicate that those who bore them were probably slaves at one time—their names just meaning the third and the fourth respectively. Slaves were often named simply by number.

The benediction of verse 24 concludes the epistle and marks it as genuinely Pauline (see 2 Thess. 3:17–18). "Grace" was his secret mark, so to speak, that attested his authorship. Significantly enough it is found in Hebrews 13:25 and in no other epistles save in his.

Verses 25–27 are an appendix, in which he links his precious unfolding of the gospel with that "mystery," which it was his special province to make known among the Gentiles and which is unfolded so fully in Ephesians 3 and several other Scripture passages.

> Now to him that is of power to establish you according to my gospel, and the preaching of Jesus Christ, according to the revelation of the mystery, which was kept secret since the [ages] began, but now is made manifest, and by [prophetic writings], according to the commandment

of the everlasting God, made known to all nations for the obedience of faith: to God only wise, be glory through Jesus Christ for ever. Amen. (vv. 25–27).

To Paul was committed a twofold ministry—that of the gospel (as linked with a glorified Christ) and that of the church—the mystery hid in God from before the creation of the world but now revealed by the Spirit. See this double ministry as set forth in Colossians 1:23–29 and Ephesians 3:1–12.

"The mystery" was not something of difficult, mysterious character, but a sacred secret never known to mankind until in due time opened up by the Holy Spirit through the apostle Paul and by him communicated to all nations for the obedience of faith. It was not hid in the Scripture to be brought to light eventually, but we are distinctly told it was hid in God until such time as He chose to manifest it. This was not until Israel had been given every opportunity to receive Christ both in incarnation and resurrection. When they definitely refused Him, God made known what had been in His heart from eternity—that from all nations, Jews and Gentiles, He would redeem and take out an elect company who would, by the Spirit's baptism, be formed into one body to be associated with Christ in the most intimate relationship (likened in Eph. 5 to that of husband and wife, or head and body), not only now but through all the ages to come.

This great mystery of Christ and the church has now been manifested and made known by prophetic writings—not as translated here "by the scriptures of the prophets." But the meaning clearly is, made known by the writings of inspired men, New Testament prophets, in this day of gospel light and testimony.

Nor is it just a beautiful and wonderful theory or system of doctrine to be held in the intellect. It involves present identification with Christ in His rejection and, hence, is made known to all nations for the obedience of faith. It is not developed in the epistle to the Romans, for here the great theme, as we have seen, is the Righteousness of God as revealed in the gospel. But it is touched on here in order to link the unfolding of the gospel in this letter with the revelation of the mystery, as given in the prison epistles particularly. This is not to say that we have new and higher truth in Ephesians and Colossians, for instance, than in Romans and earlier letters. All form part of one whole and constitute that body of teaching everywhere proclaimed by the apostle through his long years of ministry, but not all committed to writing at one time. The "mystery" of Romans 16:25 is the same as that of the later epistles, and ever formed an integral part of his messages. It would not be necessary to say this were there not some today who would divorce completely Paul's ministry in Acts from that which he embodied in the last of his letters written after the rejection of his message by the Jews in Rome as recorded in Acts 28. The appendix to the Roman letter is the complete denial of this. It is here added to manifest the unity of his ministry of the gospel and the church, though twofold in character.

And with this we conclude our present somewhat cursory study, trusting that our review of the epistle has not been in vain but will be for increased profit and blessing as we wait for God's Son from heaven.

To God only wise be glory through Jesus Christ for ever. Amen.

LECTURES ON THE EPISTLE TO THE
GALATIANS

PREFACE

The messages that follow were given in the Moody Church, Chicago, as a series and are published in the hope that they may prove helpful to some who have been confused regarding law and grace.

They are not intended for the learned, or for theologians, but for the common people, who value plain unfoldings of the Word of God.

H. A. IRONSIDE

PART 1

PERSONAL

Galatians 1–2

INTRODUCTION

Galatians 1:1–5

Paul, an apostle, (not of men, neither by man, but by Jesus Christ, and God the Father, who raised him from the dead;) and all the brethren which are with me, unto the churches of Galatia: grace be to you and peace from God the Father, and from our Lord Jesus Christ, who gave himself for our sins, that he might deliver us from this present evil world, according to the will of God and our Father: to whom be glory for ever and ever. Amen. (vv. 1–5)

The epistle to the Galatians links very intimately with that to the Romans. There seem to be good reasons for believing that both of these letters were written at about the same time, probably from Corinth while Paul was ministering in that great city. In Romans we have the fullest, the most complete opening up of the gospel of the grace of God that we get anywhere in the New Testament. In the letter to the Galatians we have that glorious gospel message defended against those who were seeking to substitute legality for grace. There are many expressions in the two letters that are very similar. Both, as also the epistle to the Hebrews, are based upon one Old Testament text found in chapter 2 of the book of Habakkuk: "The just shall live by his faith." May I repeat what I have mentioned in my *Lectures on Romans* and also my *Notes on Hebrews?* In the epistle to the Romans the emphasis is put upon the first two words. How shall men be just with God? The answer is, *"The just* shall live by faith." But if one has been justified by faith, how is he maintained in that place before God? The answer is given in the epistle to the Galatians, and here the emphasis is upon the next two words, "The just *shall live* by faith." But what is that power by which men are made just and by which they live? The epistle to the Hebrews answers that by putting the emphasis upon the last two words of the same text, "The just shall live *by faith."* So we may see that these three letters really constitute a very remarkable trio, and in spite of all that many scholars have written to the contrary, personally I am absolutely convinced that the three are from the same human hand, that of the apostle Paul. I have given my reasons for this view in my book on the Hebrews, so I need not go into that here.

Now something of the reasons for the writing of this letter. Paul had labored in Galatia on two distinct occasions. A third time he was minded to go there, but the Spirit of God plainly indicated that it was not His will and led him elsewhere, eventually over to Europe. In chapters 13 and 14 of Acts we read of Paul's ministry in Antioch of Pisidia, in Iconium, in Lystra, and in Derbe. While Antioch is said to be in Pisidia and these other three cities are located in Lycaonia, according to the best records we have, both the provinces of Pisidia and Lycaonia were united to Galatia at this time, so that these were really the cities of Galatia where Paul labored and where God wrought so mightily. The inhabitants of Galatia are the same people racially as the ancient inhabitants of Ireland, Wales, and the Highlands of Scotland, also of France and northern Spain, the Gauls. Galatia is really the country of the Gauls, and those deep emotional feelings that characterize the races I have mentioned—the mystical Scots; the warmhearted Welsh; the volatile French; and the brilliant, energetic Irish—were manifested in these Gauls of old. They spread from Galatia over into western Europe and settled France and northern Spain, and then came over to the British Isles. As many of us are somewhat linked with these different groups that we have mentioned, we should have a special interest in the epistle to the Galatians, which, by the way, is the death blow to so-called British-Israelism. The Gauls were Gentiles, not Israelites.

When Paul first went in among them they were all idolaters, but through the ministry of the Word he was used to bring many of them to a saving knowledge of the Lord Jesus Christ, and they became deeply devoted to the man who had led them to know the Lord Jesus Christ as their Savior. It was a wonderful thing to them to be brought out of the darkness of heathenism into the glorious light and liberty of the gospel. But sometimes when people accept the gospel message with great delight and enthusiasm, they have to go through very severe testings afterward, and so it proved in the case of the Galatians. After Paul had left them there came down from Judea certain men claiming to be sent out by James and the apostolic band at Jerusalem, who told the Galatians that unless they kept the law of Moses, observed the covenant of circumcision, and the different holy days of the Jewish economy and the appointed seasons, they could not be saved. This so stirred the apostle Paul when he learned of it that he sought on a second visit to deliver these people from that legality. But some way or another there is something about error when once it grips the minds of people that makes it assume an importance in their minds that the truth itself never had. That is a singular thing. One may be going on with the truth of God in a calm, easy way, and then he gets hold of something erroneous, and he pushes that thing to the very limit. We have often seen this demonstrated.

I refer here only to false teaching. I do not know the names of the men who came into Galatia to seek to turn the Galatians away from the truth of the gospel as set forth by the apostle Paul, but I do know what their teaching was. They were substituting law for grace, they were turning the hearts and minds of these earnest Christians away from their glorious liberty in Christ, and bringing them into bondage to legal rites and ceremonies. In order to do this it was necessary for them to try to shake the confidence of the people in their great teacher who had led them to Christ, the apostle Paul himself, and so they called in question his authority. Their attack was directed against his apostleship, nor did they hesitate to impugn his integrity.

They wormed their way into the confidence of the believers by undermining their faith in the man who had led them to Christ, hoping thereby that they would break down their reliance upon the gospel of the grace of God and substitute legal observances in its place.

When Paul heard this he was deeply grieved. With him, doctrine was not simply a matter of views. It was not a question of maintaining his own position at all costs. He realized that men are sanctified by the truth of God, and that on the other hand they are demoralized by error, and so to him it was a matter of extreme importance that his converts should cling to that truth which edifies and leads on in the ways that be in Christ. When this news of their defection came to him he sat down and wrote this letter. He did not do what he generally did. We have no other instance in the New Testament, so far as I know, of Paul writing a letter with his own hand. Ordinarily he dictated his letters to a secretary who wrote for him. They had a form of shorthand in those days, and copies have come down to us, so that we may see how they worked. And then these letters were properly prepared and sent out by his different amanuenses. But on this occasion he was so stirred, so deeply moved, that apparently he could not wait for an amanuensis. Instead, he called for parchment, pen, and ink, and sat down and with nervous hand wrote this entire letter. He says at the close of it, "You see with what large characters I have written you with mine own hand." That is the correct translation of his words. Paul evidently had something the matter with his eyes, and so could not see very well, and like a partially blind person he took his pen and with large, nervous characters filled up the parchment, and it looked like a long letter. He then hurried it off to Galatia, hoping it would be used of God to recover these people from the errors into which they had fallen. In some respects it is the most interesting of all his letters, for it is so self-revealing. It is as though he opens a window into his own heart that we may look into the very soul of the man and see the motives that dominated and controlled him. The letter itself is simple in structure. Instead of breaking it up into a great many small sections, I look at it as having three great divisions.

- Part 1: Personal (Gal. 1–2)
- Part 2: Doctrinal (Gal. 3–4)
- Part 3: Practical (Gal. 5–6)

If we once have these firmly fixed in our minds, we shall never forget them. The subject of the letter is "Law and Grace." The way the apostle unfolds it is this: chapters 1 and 2 are personal. In these chapters he is largely dealing with his own personal experiences. He shows how he, at one time a rigid, legalistic Jew, had been brought into the knowledge of the grace of God, and how he had had to defend that position against legalists. Chapters 3 and 4 are doctrinal. In these chapters, the very heart of the letter, he opens up, as in the epistle to the Romans, the great truth of salvation by grace alone. Chapters 5 and 6 are practical. They show us the moral and ethical considerations that result from a knowledge of salvation by free grace. These divisions are very simple.

We turn now to consider the introduction to the letter in the personal portion. The first three verses constitute the apostolic salutation: "Paul, an apostle." Go over the other letters, and you will find that he never refers to himself as "apostle" unless writing to some people where his apostleship has been called in question, or where he has some great doctrine to unfold that people are not likely to accept unless they realize that he had a definite commission to make it known. He evidently prefers to speak of himself as "the servant of Jesus Christ," and that word "servant" means a bondman, one bought and paid for. Paul loved to think of that. He had been bought and paid for by the precious blood of Christ, and so he was Christ's bondman. But on this occasion he saw the necessity of emphasizing his apostleship because great truths were in question, and they were so intimately linked with his personal commission from God that it was necessary to stress the fact that he was a definitely appointed messenger. The word *apostle,* after all, really means "messenger," or "minister," but is used in a professional sense in connection with the twelve who were the apostles particularly to the Jews, though also to the Gentiles, and then of Paul himself, who was preeminently the apostle to the Gentiles, and yet always went first to the Jews in every place where he labored.

Paul was an apostle, "not of men, neither by man." I think he had special reason for writing like this. His detractors said, "Where did he get his apostleship? Where did he get his commission? Not from Peter, not from John. Where did he get his authority?" Oh, he says, I glory in the fact that I did not get anything from man. What I have received I received directly from heaven. I am not an apostle of men nor by means of man. It was not men originally having authority who conferred authority upon me, it was not a school, or a bishop, or a board of bishops, at Jerusalem, that conferred this authority on me. "Not *of* men, neither *by* man." Even though God appointed me, my authority was not conferred of man. St. Jerome says, "Really there are four classes of ministry in the professing Christian church. First, there are those sent neither from men, nor through men, but directly from God." And then he points out that this was true of the prophets of the Old Testament dispensation. They were not commissioned by men, neither authorized by men, but they were commissioned directly from God, and of course this is true of the apostle Paul. "Then secondly," Jerome says, "there are those who get their commissions from God and through man, as for instance a man feels distinctly called of God to preach, and he is examined by his brethren and they are satisfied that he is called to preach, and so commend him to the work, perhaps by the laying on of hands. And so he is a servant of God, a minister of God, from God and through man. Then in the third class there are those who have their commissions from man, but not from God. These are the men who have chosen the Christian ministry as a profession; perhaps they never have been born again, but having chosen the ministry as a profession they apply to the bishop, or presbytery, or church, to ordain them." But as Spurgeon said, "Ordination can do nothing for a man who has not received his call from God. It is simply a matter of laying empty hands on an empty head." The man goes out heralded as a minister, but he is not God's minister. And then Jerome says, "There is a fourth class. There are men who pose as Christ's ministers, and have received their authority neither from God nor from man, but they are simply free-lances. You have to take their own word for it that they are definitely appointed. Nobody else has been able to recognize any evidence of it." Paul was in the first class. He had received his commission directly from God, and no man had anything to do with even confirming it. But what about the saints at Antioch laying hands on him when he and Barnabas were to preach to the Gentiles? you may ask. That was not a human confirmation of his apostleship because he went there as an apostle of the Lord.

How did Paul get his commission? He tells us in chapter 26 of the book of Acts. When he fell stricken on the Damascus road the risen Christ appeared to him, and said to him, "I am Jesus whom thou persecutest. But rise, and stand upon thy feet: for I have appeared unto thee for this purpose, to make thee a minister and a witness both of these things which thou hast seen, and of those things in the which I will appear unto thee; delivering thee from the people, and from the Gentiles, unto whom now I send thee, to open their eyes, and to turn them from darkness to light, and from the power of Satan unto God, that they may receive forgiveness of sins, and inheritance among them which are sanctified by faith that is in me" (vv. 15–18). Paul says that is where he got his commission. "Whereupon, O King Agrippa, I was not disobedient unto the heavenly vision" (v. 19), but in accord with his divinely-given instructions he went forth to teach at "Damascus, and at Jerusalem, and throughout all the coasts of Judea, and then to the Gentiles, that they should repent and turn to God, and do works meet for repentance" (v. 20). So Paul was an apostle "not of men, neither by man, but by Jesus Christ, and God the Father, who raised him from the dead."

I think he had special reason for emphasizing the resurrection. There were those who said, "Paul cannot be an apostle, because he never saw the Lord Jesus. He was not one of the twelve, he was not instructed by Christ. How then can he rightly appropriate to himself the name of an apostle?" He says, "Have not I seen Jesus Christ? I saw Him as none of the rest did. I saw Him in the glory as the risen One, and heard His voice from heaven, and received my commission from His lips." That is why in one place he calls his message the "glorious gospel of the blessed God." That might be translated, "The gospel of the glory of the happy God." God is so happy now that the sin question has been settled and He can send the message of His grace into all the world, and it is "the gospel of the glory of the happy God" because it is from the glory.

And then Paul links others with himself. He was not alone but was always glad to recognize his fellow workers, and so says, "All the brethren which are with me, unto the churches of Galatia: grace be to you and peace from God the Father, and from our Lord Jesus Christ." "Grace" was the Greek greeting; "Peace" was the Hebrew greeting. Paul glories in the fact that the middle wall of partition between Jew and Gentile has been broken down in the new creation, and so brings these two greetings together. How beautifully they fit with the Christian revelation. It is not the grace that saves, but the grace that keeps. It is not peace *with* God, which was made by the blood of His cross and which was theirs already, but the peace *of* God which they were so liable to forfeit if they got out of communion with Him.

Then in verses 4 and 5 he goes on to emphasize the work of our Lord Jesus. Let us consider these words very thoughtfully, very tenderly, very meditatively. "Our Lord Jesus Christ, who gave himself for our sins." Oh, that we might never forget what Christ has suffered for our sakes! "Who gave himself." To whom does the pronoun refer? The One who was the Eternal Son of the Father, who was with the Father before all worlds, and yet who stooped in infinite grace to become Man. As Man He did not cease to be God; He was God and Man in one glorious Person, and therefore abounding in merit so that He could pay the mighty debt that we owed to God. He settled the sin question for us as no one else could. The little hymn says:

> No angel could our place have taken,
> Highest of the high though he;
> The loved One, on the cross forsaken,
> Was one of the Godhead Three!

Of all men it is written, "None of them can by any means redeem his brother, nor give to God a ransom for him: (for the redemption of their soul is [too costly, let it alone] for ever)" (Ps. 49:7–8). But here is One who became Man to redeem our soul: "The Son of man came not to be ministered unto, but to minister, and to give his life a ransom for many" (Matt. 20:28).

"Who gave himself." Think of it! When we call to mind our own sinfulness, the corruption of our hearts, the wickedness of our lips, when we think of what our sins deserve and how utterly helpless we were to deliver ourselves from the justly deserved judgment, and then we think of Him, the Holy One, the Just One,

The Sovereign of the skies,
Who stooped to man's estate and dust
That guilty worms might rise,

how our hearts ought to go out to Him in love and worship. I think it was hard for Paul to keep the tears back when he wrote this, "Who gave himself for our sins." We would like to forget those sins, and yet it is well sometimes that we should remember the hole of the pit from which we were dug, for our sins will be the black background that will display the glorious jewel of divine grace for all eternity. Not only that He might save us from eternal judgment, not only that we might never be lost in that dark, dark pit of woe of which Scripture speaks so solemnly and seriously, but that even here we may be altogether for Himself, "that he might deliver us from this present evil world." Man has made it wicked by his sinfulness, his disloyalty to God, but we who are saved are to be delivered from it, that we might be set apart to God.

"According to the will of God and our Father." In these words he sums up the purpose of our Lord's coming into the world. He came to die for our sins that we might be delivered from the power of sin and be altogether for Himself. "To whom be glory for ever and ever. Amen." This forms the salutation, and the introduction follows.

NO OTHER GOSPEL

Galatians 1:6–9

I marvel that ye are so soon removed from him that called you into the grace of Christ unto another gospel: which is not another; but there be some that trouble you, and would pervert the gospel of Christ. But though we, or an angel from heaven, preach any other gospel unto you than that which we have preached unto you, let him be accursed. As we said before, so say I now again, if any man preach any other gospel unto you than that ye have received, let him be accursed. (vv. 6–9)

Those are very strong words, and I can quite understand that some people may have difficulty in reconciling them with the grace that is in Christ Jesus. Twice the apostle pronounces a curse upon those who preach any other gospel than that which he himself had proclaimed to these Galatians when they were poor sinners, and which had been used of God to lead them to the Lord Jesus Christ. Some might ask, Is this the attitude of the Christian minister, to go about cursing people who do not agree with him? No, and it certainly was not Paul's attitude. Why, then, does he use such strong language? It is not that he himself is invoking a curse upon anyone, but he is declaring, by the inspiration of the Holy Spirit of God, that divine judgment must fall upon any one who seeks to pervert the gospel of Christ or to turn people away from that gospel. In other words, the apostle Paul realizes the fact that the gospel is God's only message to lost man, and that to pervert that gospel, to offer people something else in place of it, for a man to attempt to foist upon them an imitation gospel is to put in jeopardy the souls of those who listen to him. Our Lord Jesus Christ emphasized this when He pointed out that those men who taught people to trust in their own efforts for salvation were blind leaders of the blind, and that eventually both leader and led would fall into the ditch. It is a very serious thing to mislead men along spiritual lines; it is a terrible thing to give wrong direction when souls are seeking the way to heaven.

I remember reading a story of a woman who with her little babe was on a train going up through one of the eastern states. It was a very wintry day. Outside a terrific storm was blowing, snow was falling, and sleet covered everything. The train made its way along slowly because of the ice on the tracks and the snowplow went ahead to clear the way. The woman seemed very nervous. She was to get off at a small station where she would be met by some friends, and she said to the conductor, "You will be sure and let me know the right station, won't you?"

"Certainly," he said, "just remain here until I tell you the right station."

She sat rather nervously and again spoke to the conductor, "You won't forget me?"

"No, just trust me. I will tell you when to get off."

A commercial man sat across the aisle, and he leaned over and said, "Pardon me, but I see you are rather nervous about getting off at your station. I know this road well. Your station is the first stop after such-and-such a city. These conductors are very forgetful; they have a great many things to attend to, and he may overlook your request, but I will see that you get off all right. I will help you with your baggage."

"Oh, thank you," she said. And she leaned back greatly relieved.

By-and-by the name of the city she mentioned was called, and he leaned over and said, "The next stop will be yours."

As they drew near to the station she looked around anxiously for the conductor, but he did not come. "You see," said the man, "he has forgotten you. I will get you off," and he helped her with her baggage, and as the conductor had not come to open the door, he opened it, and when the train stopped he stepped off, lifted her bag, helped her off, and in a moment the train moved on.

A few minutes later the conductor came and looking all about said, "Why, that is strange! There was a woman here who wanted to get off at this station. I wonder where she is."

The commercial man spoke up and said, "Yes, you forgot her, but I saw that she got off all right."

"Got off where?" the conductor asked.

"When the train stopped."

"But that was not a station! That was an emergency stop! I was looking after that woman. Why, man, you have put her off in a wild country district in the midst of all this storm where there will be nobody to meet her!"

There was only one thing to do, and although it was a rather dangerous thing, they had to reverse the engine and go back a number of miles, and then they went out to look for the woman. They searched and searched, and finally somebody stumbled upon her, and there she was frozen on the ground with her little dead babe in her arms. She was the victim of wrong information.

If it is such a serious thing to give people wrong information in regard to temporal things, what about the man who misleads men and women in regard to the great question of the salvation of their immortal souls? If men believe a false gospel, if they put their trust in something that is contrary to the Word of God, their loss will be not for time only but for eternity. And that is why the apostle Paul, speaking by the inspiration of the Holy Spirit, uses such strong language in regard to the wickedness, the awfulness of misleading souls as to eternal things. These Galatians were living in their sins, they were living in idolatry, in the darkness of pagan superstition, when Paul came to them and preached the glorious gospel that tells how "Christ died for our sins . . . and that he was buried, and that he rose again the third day according to the scriptures" (1 Cor. 15:3–4). They were saved, for you know the gospel of the grace of God works. It is wonderful when you see a man who has been living in all kinds of sin, and God by the Holy Spirit brings him to repentance and leads him to believe the gospel; everything changes, old habits fall off like withered leaves, a new life is his. He has power to overcome sin, he has hope of heaven, and he has assurance of salvation. That is what God's gospel gives.

These Galatians, after Paul had been used to bring them into the liberty of grace, were being misled by false teachers, men who had come down from Judea, who professed to be Christians but had never been delivered from legality. They said to these young Christians, "You have only a smattering of the gospel; you need to add to this message that you have received, the teaching of the law of Moses, 'Except ye be circumcised after the manner of Moses, ye cannot be saved'" (Acts 15:1). Thus they threw them back on self-effort, turning their eyes away from Christ and fixing them upon themselves and their ability to keep the law. Paul says, "This thing will ruin men who depend upon their own self-efforts to get to heaven; they will miss the gates of pearl." No matter how earnest they are, if they depend upon their own works they will never be partakers of the inheritance of the saints in light. So far as these Galatians who were really born again were concerned, this false doctrine could not be the means of their eternal perdition, yet it would rob them of the joy and gladness that the Christian ought to have. How could any one have peace who believed that salvation depended on his own efforts? How could he be certain that he had paid enough attention to the demands of the law or ritual? It is the gospel of the grace of God which believed gives men full assurance. And so the apostle Paul was very indignant to find people bringing in something else instead of the gospel of the grace of God, and he is surprised that these Galatians who rejoiced in the liberty of Christ should be so ready to go back to the bondage of law.

"I marvel," he says, "that ye are so soon removed from him that called you into the grace of Christ unto another gospel." He marvels that they should so soon be turned aside from the message of grace. What is grace? It is God's free, unmerited favor to those who have merited the very opposite. These Galatians, like ourselves, had merited eternal judgment, they deserved to be shut away from the presence of God forever, as you and I deserve to be, but through the preaching of grace they had been brought to see that God has a righteousness which He offers freely to unrighteous sinners who put their faith in His blessed Son. But now, occupied with legal ceremonies, laws, rules, and regulations, they had lost the joy of grace and had become taken up with self-effort. Paul says, "I cannot understand it," and yet after all, it is very natural for these poor hearts of ours. How often you see people who seem to be wonderfully converted, and then they lose it all as they get occupied with all kinds of questions, rules, ceremonies, and ritual. God would have each heart occupied with His blessed Son, "in whom are hid all the treasures of wisdom and knowledge" (Col. 2:3).

"I marvel that ye are so soon removed from him that called you into the grace of Christ unto another gospel." In our King James Version we read, "Another gospel," and then verse 7 continues, "Which is not another." That sounds like a contradiction, but there are two different Greek words used here. The first is the word *heteron,* something contrary to sound teaching, something different. The apostle says, "I marvel that ye are so soon removed from him that called you into the grace of Christ [to a *different*] gospel." This mixture of law and grace is not God's gospel, not something to be added to what you have already received, not something to complete the gospel message; it is opposed to that, it is a heterodox message, one opposed to sound teaching. There is only one gospel.

Go through the Book from Genesis to Revelation and there is only one gospel—that first preached in the Garden of Eden when the message went forth that the Seed of the woman should bruise Satan's head. That was the gospel, salvation through the coming Christ, the Son of God born of a woman. It is the same gospel preached to Abraham. We read in this Book that the gospel was before preached to Abraham. God took him out one night and said, "Look at the stars; count them."

And Abraham said, "I cannot count them." He said, "Look at the dust of the earth, and count the dust."

Abraham said, "I cannot count it." "Well, think of the sand at the seashore; count the grains of sand." And Abraham said, "I cannot count them."

And God answered, "In thy seed shall all the nations of the earth be blessed" (Gen. 22:18). "And I will make thy seed as the dust of the earth" (Gen. 13:16). Abraham might have said, "Impossible! My seed! I have no child, and I am already a man advanced in years, and my wife is an elderly woman. Impossible!" But God had given the word, "In thy seed [which is Christ] shall all the nations of the earth be blessed." That was the gospel—all nations to be blessed through Christ, the Seed of Abraham. And "Abraham believed God, and it was counted unto him for righteousness" (Rom. 4:3). He was justified by faith because he believed the gospel. It is the same gospel that we find running through the book of Psalms. David, stained with sin, the twin sins of adultery and murder, cries, "Thou desirest not sacrifice; else would I give it: thou delightest not in burnt offering. The sacrifices of God are a broken spirit: a broken and a contrite heart, O God, thou wilt not despise" (Ps. 51:16–17). "Purge me with hyssop, and I shall be clean: wash me, and I shall be whiter than snow" (Ps. 51:7). And there is only one way a poor sinner can be purged, and that is by the precious blood of the Lord Jesus Christ. David looked on in faith to the Christ, the Son of God, and his hope was in this one gospel.

It is the gospel that Isaiah proclaimed when he looked down through the ages and cried, "He was wounded for our transgressions, he was bruised for our iniquities: the chastisement of our peace was upon him; and with his stripes we are healed" (Isa. 53:5). It was the gospel that Jeremiah preached when he said, "This is his name whereby he shall be called, THE LORD OUR RIGHTEOUSNESS" (Jer. 23:6). It was the gospel of Zechariah, "Awake, O sword, against my shepherd, and against the man that is my fellow, saith the LORD of hosts: smite the shepherd, and the sheep shall be scattered" (Zech. 13:7).

This was the gospel that John the Baptist preached. He came preaching the gospel of the kingdom, and as he pointed to Jesus he said, "Behold the Lamb of God, which taketh away the sin of the world" (John 1:29). And this was the gospel that Jesus Himself proclaimed when He said, "For God so loved the world, that he gave his only begotten Son, that whosoever believeth in him should not perish, but have everlasting life" (John 3:16). This was Peter's gospel when he spoke of Jesus, saying, "To him give all the prophets witness, that through his name whosoever believeth in him shall receive remission of sins" (Acts 10:43). This was the gospel of the apostle John who said, "If we walk in the light, as he is in the light, we have fellowship one with another, and the blood of Jesus Christ his Son cleanseth us from all sin" (1 John 1:7). This was the gospel of the apostle James who said, "Of his own will begat he us with the word of truth" (James 1:18). This is the gospel that they will celebrate through all the ages to come as millions and millions of redeemed sing their song of praise, "Unto him that loveth us, and loosed us from our sins in his own blood" (Rev. 1:5 RV). And this was Paul's gospel when he declared, "Through this man is preached unto you the forgiveness of sins: and by him all that believe are justified from all things" (Acts 13:38–39). One gospel! And there is no other!

I have often felt sorry when I have heard some of my brethren whom I have learned to love in the truth, and with whom I hold a great deal in common, try to explain some apparent differences throughout the gospel centuries and talk as though there are a number of different gospels. Some say when Christ was on earth and in the early part of the book of Acts, they preached the gospel of the kingdom but did not know the grace of God. I wonder whether they remember the words of John 3:16 and John 1:29, and recollect that it was the Lord who said, "Verily, verily, I say unto you, He that heareth my word, and believeth on him that sent me, hath everlasting life, and shall not come into condemnation; but is passed from death unto life" (John 5:24). How short our memories are sometimes, if we say that Jesus was not preaching grace when here on earth when Scripture says, "The law was given by Moses, but grace and truth came by Jesus Christ" (John 1:17). Can we say that Peter and his fellow apostles in the early part of Acts were not preaching grace when it was Peter who declared, "To him give all the prophets witness, that through his name whosoever believeth in him shall receive remission of sins" (Acts 10:43). There is only one gospel!

They say there is one gospel of the kingdom, another gospel of the grace of God, then there is the gospel of the glory, and some day there will be the ever-lasting gospel, and that these are all different gospels. If such statements were true, these words of Paul would fall to the ground, "If any man preach any other gospel unto you than that ye have received, let him be accursed." Someone wrote me that she was surprised that a man who ought to know better should talk about there being only one gospel. "Why," she said, "even Dr. C. I. Scofield would teach you better, because in his Bible he shows that there are four gospels." I want to read you what Dr. Scofield says, in his notes on Revelation 14:6:

This great theme may be summarized as follows:
  1. In itself the word gospel means good news.
  2. Four *forms* of the gospel are to be distinguished:

(1) The gospel of the kingdom. This is the good news that God purposes to set up on the earth, in fulfilment of the Davidic Covenant, a kingdom, political, spiritual, Israelitish, universal, over which God's Son, David's heir, shall be King, and which shall be, for one thousand years, the manifestation of the righteousness of God in human affairs.

Two *preachings* of this gospel are mentioned, one past, beginning with the ministry of John the Baptist, continued by our Lord and His disciples, and ending with the Jewish rejection of the King. The other is yet future, during the great tribulation, and immediately preceding the coming of the King in glory.

(2) The gospel of the grace of God. This is the good news that Jesus Christ, the rejected King, has died on the cross for the sins of the world, that He was raised from the dead for our justification, and that by Him all that believe are justified from all things. This form of the gospel is described in many ways. It is the gospel "of God" because it originates in His love; "of Christ" because it flows from His sacrifice, and because He is the alone Object of gospel faith; of "the grace of God" because it saves those whom the law curses; of "the glory" because it concerns Him who is in the glory, and who is bringing the many sons to glory; of "our salvation" because it is the "power of God unto salvation to every one that believeth"; of "the uncircumcision" because it saves wholly apart from forms and ordinances; of "peace" because through Christ it makes peace between the sinner and God, and imparts inward peace.

(3) The everlasting gospel. This is to be preached to the earth-dwellers at the very end of the great tribulation and immediately preceding the judgment of the nations. It is neither the gospel of the kingdom, nor of grace. Though its burden is judgment, not salvation, it is good news to Israel and to those who, during the tribulation, have been saved.

(4) That which Paul calls, "my gospel." This is the gospel of the grace

of God in its fullest development, but includes the revelation of the result of that gospel in the outcalling of the Church, her relationships, position, privileges, and responsibility. It is the distinctive truth of Ephesians and Colossians, but interpenetrates all of Paul's writings.

These words are very clear. There is only one gospel, and that is God's good news concerning His Son; but it takes on different aspects at different times according to the circumstances and conditions in which men are found. In Old Testament times they looked on to the coming of the Savior, but they proclaimed salvation through His atoning death. In the days of John the Baptist stress was laid upon the coming kingdom, and the King was to lay down His life. In the days of the Lord's ministry on earth He presented Himself as King, but was rejected and went to the cross, for He Himself declared that He "came not to be ministered unto, but to minister, and to give his life a ransom for many" (Matt. 20:28). During the early chapters of the book of Acts we find this gospel proclaimed to Jews and Gentiles alike, offering free salvation to all who turn to God in repentance, but when God raised up the apostle Paul, He gave him a clearer vision of the gospel than any one had yet had. He showed that not only are men forgiven through faith in our Lord Jesus Christ, but that they are justified from all things, and stand in Christ before God as part of a new creation. This is a fuller revelation of the good tidings, but the same gospel.

By-and-by, during the days of the great tribulation, the everlasting gospel will be proclaimed, telling men that the once-rejected Christ shall come again to set up His glorious kingdom, but even in that day men will be taught that salvation is through His precious blood, for as the result of that preaching a great multitude will be brought out of all kindreds and tongues who have "washed their robes, and made them white in the blood of the Lamb" (Rev. 7:14).

Yes, there is only one gospel and if any one comes preaching any other gospel, telling you there is any other way of salvation save through the atoning work of the Lord Jesus, it is a heterodox gospel. Some such had come to Galatia and perverted the gospel of Christ, and it is this that led Paul in the intensity of his zeal for that gospel to exclaim, as guided by the Holy Spirit who inspired him, "Though we, or an angel from heaven, preach any other gospel unto you than that which we have preached unto you, let him be [Anathema]" (let him be devoted to judgment), if he is substituting anything for the precious gospel of the grace of God. Notice, if the angel who proclaims the everlasting gospel in the days of the great tribulation preaches any other gospel than that of salvation through faith in Christ alone, that angel comes under the curse, for Paul says,

"Though . . . an angel from heaven, preach any other gospel unto you than that which we have preached unto you, let him be accursed."

Out West I often met disciples of Joseph Smith, and when I got them in a corner with the Word of God and they could not wiggle out, they would say, "Well, we have what you do not have. An angel came to Joseph Smith and gave him the book of Mormon." And so they reasoned that the Bible is not enough, because an angel had revealed something different. I do not believe in the prophet Joseph Smith, and I do not believe that an angel ever appeared to him, unless it was in a nightmare. But if he did, then that angel was from the pit and he is under the curse, because, "Though . . . an angel from heaven, preach any other gospel unto you than that which we have preached unto you, let him be accursed." People may say, "But Paul, you are all worked up, you are losing your temper." You know, if you become very fervent for the truth, folks say you are losing your temper. If you say strong things in defense of the truth, they will declare you are unkind; but men will use very fervent language about politics and other things, and yet no one questions their loss of temper, but they think we should be very calm when people tear the Bible to pieces! If anything calls for fervent and intense feelings it is the defense of the gospel against false teaching.

Lest any one should say, "Well, Paul, you would not have written that if you had been calmer; you would not have used such strong language," Paul repeats himself in verse 9, and says, "As we said before, so say I now again, If any man preach any other gospel unto you than that ye have received, let him be [Anathema]." That is cool enough. He is not speaking now as one wrought up. He has had time to think it over and has weighed his words carefully. Yes, on sober, second thought he again insists on what he declared before, that the divine judgment hangs over any man who seeks to mislead lost humanity by telling them of any other way of salvation save through the precious atoning blood of the Lord Jesus Christ.

In closing I put the question to you: On what are *you* resting your hope for eternity? Are you resting on the Lord Jesus Christ? Are you trusting the gospel of the grace of God? "By grace are ye saved through faith; and that not of yourselves: it is the gift of God" (Eph. 2:8).

PAUL'S CONVERSION AND APOSTLESHIP

Galatians 1:10–24

For do I now persuade men, or God? or do I seek to please men? for if I yet pleased men, I should not be the servant of Christ. But I certify you, brethren, that the gospel which was preached of me is not after man. For I neither received it of man, neither was I taught it, but by the revelation of Jesus Christ. For ye have heard of my conversation in time past in the Jews' religion, how that beyond measure I persecuted the church of God, and wasted it: and profited in the Jews' religion above many my equals in mine own nation, being more exceedingly zealous of the traditions of my fathers. But when it pleased God, who separated me from my mother's womb, and called me by his grace, to reveal his Son in me, that I might preach him among the heathen; immediately I conferred not with flesh and blood: neither went I up to Jerusalem to them which were apostles before me; but I went into Arabia, and returned again unto Damascus. Then after three years I went up to Jerusalem to see Peter, and abode with him fifteen days. But other of the apostles saw I none, save James the Lord's brother. Now the things which I write unto you, behold, before God, I lie not. Afterwards I came into the regions of Syria and Cilicia; and was unknown by face unto the churches of Judaea which were in Christ: but they had heard only, that he which persecuted us in times past now preacheth the faith which once he destroyed. And they glorified God in me. (vv. 10–24)

The apostle Paul in this section is obliged to defend his apostleship. There is something pitiable about that. He had come to these Galatians when they were heathen, when they were idolaters, and had been God's messenger to them. Through him they had been brought to the Lord Jesus Christ. But they had fallen under the influence of false teachers, and now looked down upon the man who had led them to Christ; they despised his ministry and felt they were far better informed than he. This is not the only time in the history of the church that such things have happened. Often we see young converts happy and radiant in the knowledge of sins forgiven, until under the influence of false teachers they look with contempt upon those who presented the gospel to them.

In the first place, Paul undertakes to show how he became the apostle to the Gentiles. In verse 10 he says, "For do I now persuade men, or God?" What does he mean by that? Do I seek the approval of men or of God? Manifestly, of God. The apostle Paul was not a timeserver, he was not seeking simply to please men who in a little while would have to stand before God in judgment, if they died in their sins. His express purpose was to do the will of the One who had saved him and commissioned him to preach the gospel of His grace. So he says, "I am not attempting to seek the approval of men, but of God. I do not seek to please men," that is, I am not trying to get their approbation. It is true that in another verse he says, "Let every one of us please his neighbour for his good to edification" (Rom. 15:2), but there is no contradiction there. It is right and proper to seek in every way I can to please and help my friend, my neighbor, my brother; but on the other hand, when I attempt to preach the Word of God, I am to do it "not as pleasing men, but God, which trieth our hearts" (1 Thess. 2:4). The preacher who speaks with man's approval as his object is untrue to the commission given to him. "If I yet pleased men, I should not be the servant of Christ." He would simply be making himself the servant of men.

"But I certify you, brethren, that the gospel which was preached of me is not after man. For I neither received it of man, neither was I taught it, but by the revelation of Jesus Christ." The gospel differs from every human religious system. In some of our universities they study what is called, "The Science of

Comparative Religions." The study of comparative religions is both very interesting and informative, if you consider, for instance, the great religions of the
pagan world such as Buddhism, Brahmanism, Islam. They have much in common, and much in which they stand in contrast one to another. But when you
take Christianity and put it in with these religions, you make a mistake; Christianity is not simply a religion, it is a divine revelation. Paul says, "I did not get
my gospel from men. No man communicated it to me. I received it directly
from heaven." Of course we do not all get it in this way, as a direct revelation, as
Paul did, and yet, in every instance, if a man is brought to understand the truth
of the gospel, it is because the Holy Spirit, who is the Spirit of wisdom and
revelation in the knowledge of Christ, opens that man's heart and mind and
understanding to comprehend the truth. Otherwise he would not receive it.
"The natural man receiveth not the things of the Spirit of God: for they are
foolishness unto him: neither can he know them, because they are spiritually
discerned" (1 Cor. 2:14), and of course the natural man is not pleased with this
divine revelation. Men are pleased when the preacher glosses over their sins,
when he makes excuses for their wrongdoings, when he panders to their weak-
nesses or flatters them as they attempt to work out a righteousness of their own.
But when a man preaches the gospel of the grace of God and insists upon man's
utterly lost and ruined condition, declares that he is unable to do one thing to
save himself, but must be saved through the atoning death of the Lord Jesus
Christ, there is nothing about that to please the natural man. It is divine grace
that opens the heart to receive that revelation. That was the revelation that came
to Paul.

There was a time when the apostle hated Christianity, when he did all in his
power to destroy the infant church, and now he says to these Galatians, "Ye have
heard of my conversation [that is, my behavior] in time past in the Jews' religion, how that beyond measure I persecuted the church of God, and wasted it."
Twice here he uses the expression, "The Jews' religion" (vv. 13–14). The original
word simply means Judaism, and is not to be confounded with the word used in
the epistle of James, "Pure religion and undefiled before God and the Father is
this, to visit the fatherless and widows in their affliction, and to keep himself
unspotted from the world" (James 1:27). There "religion" is used in a proper
sense, and we who are saved should be characterized by that; but as the apostle
uses the word here it is something entirely different. The two English words,
"Jews' religion," are translated from the one Greek word which means "Judaism." Paul hoped through that to save his soul and gain favor with God, until
through a divine revelation he had an altogether different conception of things.

As long as he believed in Judaism he "persecuted the church of God, and wasted it." One of the pitiable things that has occurred since is that members of the professed church of God have turned around to persecute the people of Judaism. Strange, this seems, when Jesus says, "Do good to them that hate you, and pray for them which despitefully use you, and persecute you" (Matt. 5:44).

Paul hated Christianity. He persecuted Christians and tried to root up Christianity from the earth, and says that he "profited in the Jews' religion above many my equals in mine own nation, being more exceedingly zealous of the traditions of my fathers." He could say, "After the most straitest sect of our religion I lived a Pharisee" (Acts 26:5). Judaism was dearer than life to him. He thought it was the only truth, that all men, if they would know God at all, must find Him through Judaism. He was exceedingly zealous of the traditions of the fathers, not only of what was written in the Bible, in the law of Moses, what the prophets had declared, but added to that the great body of such traditions as have come down to the Jews of the present day in the Talmud. He would have lived and died an advocate of Judaism if it had not been for the miracle of grace. How did it happen that this Jew who could see nothing good in Christianity turned about and became its greatest exponent? There is no way of accounting for it except through the matchless sovereign grace of God. Something took place in that man's heart and life that changed his entire viewpoint, that made him the protagonist who devoted over thirty years of his life to making Christ known to Jews and Gentiles. He tells us what brought about the change: "But when it pleased God, who separated me from my mother's womb, and called me by his grace, to reveal his Son in me, that I might preach him among the heathen; immediately I conferred not with flesh and blood" (vv. 15–16). When the appointed time came, when God in sovereign grace said, as it were, "Arrest that man," and stopped him on the Damascus turnpike, and when Christ in glory appeared to him, Saul of Tarsus was brought to see that he had been fighting against Israel's Messiah and God's blessed Son. Then Christ was not only revealed *to* him, but Christ was revealed *in* him.

We have both the objective and the subjective sides of truth. When I as a poor sinner saw the Lord Jesus suffering, bleeding, dying for me, when I saw that He was "wounded for my transgressions, he was bruised for my iniquities," when I realized that He had been "delivered up for my offenses and raised again for my justification," when I put my heart's trust in Him, when I believed that objective truth, then something took place within me subjectively. Christ came to dwell in my very heart. "Christ in you," says the apostle, "the hope of glory." It pleased God to reveal His Son not only to me but in me. I was brought to know Him in a richer, fuller way than I could know the dearest earthly friend. It was no longer for Paul a matter of one religion against another. Now he had a divine commission to go forth and make known to other men the Christ who had become so real to him. So when this glorious event took place, when through God's sovereign grace he was brought to know the Lord Jesus Christ, he says, "I realized that this glorious understanding was not for me alone but that I might make Him known to others; it pleased God 'to reveal his Son in me, that I might preach him among the heathen.'" When the Lord saved Paul He told him He had that in view.

In Acts 9, in the story of the apostle's conversion, we read that God spoke to Ananias and sent him to see Paul in the street called Straight in Damascus. He did not want to go at first, he was afraid he would be taking his life in his hands; but the Lord said unto him, "Go thy way: for he is a chosen vessel unto me, to bear my name before the Gentiles, and kings, and the children of Israel: for I will show him how great things he must suffer for my name's sake" (Acts 9:15–16). So Ananias went in obedience to the vision and communicated the mind of God to Paul. The Lord had already said, "I have appeared unto thee for this purpose, to make thee a minister and a witness both of these things which thou hast seen, and of those things in the which I will appear unto thee; delivering thee from the people, and from the Gentiles, unto whom now I send thee" (Acts 26:16–17). Preeminently he was the apostle to the Gentiles, but he also had a wonderful ministry for his own people, and all through his life his motto was, "To the Jew first, and also to the Greek" (Rom. 1:16). Into city after city he went hunting out the synagogues or finding individual Jews or groups, telling them of the great change that had come to him and pleading with them to submit to the same wonderful Savior. When they rejected his message, he turned to the Gentiles and preached the gospel to them.

Some of these Galatians questioned whether he really was an apostle, for he never saw the Lord when He was here on earth; he did not get his commission from the twelve. He says, "No, I did not, and I glory in that I am an apostle, not of men, neither by man, but by Jesus Christ. I received my commission from heaven when I saw the risen Christ in glory and He came to make His abode in my heart. He commissioned me to go out and preach His message." "Immediately I conferred not with flesh and blood." They thought he should have gone to Jerusalem to sit down and talk the matter over with the other apostles, and find out whether they endorsed him and were prepared to ordain him to the Christian ministry, or something like that. But he says, "No, I did not seek anyone out, nor confer with any one. My commission was from heaven, to carry it out in dependence upon the living God." So he adds, "Neither went I up to Jerusalem to them which were apostles before me; but I went into Arabia, and returned again unto Damascus" (v. 17). He did not go at the beginning to what they considered the headquarters of the Christian church, Jerusalem, to get authorization. Instead of that he seems to have slipped away. In reading Acts we would not know this, but here he indicates that he went into Arabia Petra, and there in some quiet place, perhaps living in a cave, he spent some time waiting on God that he might have things cleared up in his own mind. He wanted time to think things out, time for God to speak to him, and in which he could speak to God. There the truth in all its fullness, its beauty, its glory, opened up to him. It was not there that he had the revelation of the body of Christ. He received that on the Damascus turnpike when the Lord said to him, "Saul, Saul, why persecutest thou me?" What a revelation was that of the body that all believers on earth constitute! They are so intimately linked with their glorious Head in heaven that one member cannot be touched without affecting their Head. There was a great deal he needed to understand, and so into the wilderness he went.

Have you ever noticed how many of God's beloved servants had their finishing courses in the university of the wilderness? When God wanted to fit Moses to be the leader of His people He sent him to the wilderness. He had gone through all the Egyptian schools, and thought he was ready to be the deliverer of God's people. When he left the university of Egypt he may have said, "Now I am ready to undertake my great lifework." But, immediately, he started killing Egyptians and hiding them in the sand, and God says, "You are not ready yet, Moses; you need a post-graduate course." He was forty years learning the wisdom of Egypt, and forty years forgetting it and learning the wisdom of God, and finally, when he received his post-graduate degree he was sent of God to deliver His people.

Elijah had his time in the wilderness. David had his time there. Oh, those years in the wilderness when hunted by King Saul like a partridge on the mountainside. They were used to help fit him for his great work. And then think of our blessed Lord Himself! He was baptized in the Jordan, presenting Himself there in accordance with the Word of God as the One who was to go to the cross to fulfill all righteousness on behalf of needy sinners, and the Holy Spirit like a dove descended upon Him. He then went into the wilderness for forty days, and prayed and fasted in view of the great ministry upon which He was to enter. Then He passed through that serious temptation of Satan, emerging triumphant, and went forth to preach the gospel of the kingdom. Now here is this man who hated His name, who detested Christianity, but after having had a sight of the risen Christ he goes off into the wilderness for a period of meditation, prayer, and instruction before he commences his great work. Then he says he "returned again unto Damascus," and he preached Christ in the synagogues "that he is the Son of God." If you read carefully in the book of Acts you will see that it was not until after the conversion of Paul that any one preached Christ as the Son of God. I know the expression, "Thy holy Child Jesus," is used, but the better rendering is "Servant." Peter preached Jesus as the Messiah, the Servant, but Paul began the testimony that Jesus was in very truth the Son of God. When the Lord Jesus interrogated Peter, "Whom say ye that I am?" Peter answered, "Thou art the Christ, the Son of the living God" (Matt. 16:15–16). But it was not yet God's time to make that known, for the message was limited, in measure, to the people of Israel in the early part of Acts. But when Saul was converted, without fear of man he preached in those very synagogues that Jesus is the Son of God and he himself now was persecuted bitterly by those who once admired him as the leader in their religious practices.

Three years went by before this man went to Jerusalem. He went from place to place and finally did go there, but not in order to be ordained or recognized as an apostle. In verse 18 he tells us why he went up, "Then after three years I went up to Jerusalem to see Peter, and abode with him fifteen days." The word *see* in the original is very interesting. It is the Greek word from which we get our English word, *history,* the telling of a story, talking things over, and so Paul says that after three years he went up to Jerusalem to relate his history to Peter, to talk things over with him, to tell him what the Lord had done. What a wonderful meeting that was! It would have been wonderful, unnoticed in a corner of the room, to have heard the conversation. Peter who had known the Lord, who had denied the Lord, who had been so wonderfully restored, who preached with such power on the day of Pentecost and was used so mightily to open the door to the Jews and then to the Gentiles, Peter told his story and Paul told his. And when they got through I imagine Peter would say, "Well, Paul, you have the same message I have, but I think the Lord has given you more than He has given to me, and I want to give you the right hand of fellowship. I rejoice in your ministry, and we can go on together proclaiming this glad, glorious gospel." Fifteen days of wonderful fellowship!

As to the rest of the apostles Paul says, "But other of the apostles saw I none, save James the Lord's brother." We are not certain which James he means. He may be the man referred to as James the son of Alphaeus, the cousin of the Lord, who would be spoken of as His brother. My personal opinion is that he is the James who occupies so large a place in the book of Acts—James who was the brother of our Lord Jesus Christ, who did not believe while the Savior was here on earth, but was brought to believe in Him in resurrection, and who led the church of God in Jerusalem. Paul saw him, but from none of them did he get any special endorsement or authorization. He met them on common ground. They were apostles of the Lord Jesus Christ; so was he, by divine appointment.

"Now the things which I write unto you, behold, before God, I lie not." Strange that he should have to say this! Strange that these Galatians, his own converts, should think for a moment that he might be untruthful! But when one gets under the power of false teaching, as a rule he is ready to make all kinds of charges as to the integrity, the honesty of other people. And so it is here, and the apostle has to say, "The things that I am telling you are true. I am not lying."

After returning from Jerusalem he launched out on his great missionary program. "Afterwards I came into the regions of Syria and Cilicia; and was unknown by face unto the churches of Judaea which were in Christ." He had been known among other assemblies in Judaism, Jewish assemblies knew him well, but Christians in Judea, believers who had separated from Judaism, had never seen him. "But they had heard only, that he which persecuted us in times past now preacheth the faith which once he destroyed." And what power there was in that! Here was the man who had gone to all lengths to turn a man away from Christ, even attempted to compel him to blaspheme, threatened him with death if he would not repudiate the gospel of the Lord Jesus Christ. Now this great change has come, and word is going through the churches, "The great persecutor has become an evangelist; he is no longer our enemy, but is preaching to others the same faith that means so much to us." "And they glorified God in me." Truly, Paul's conversion was a divine, sovereign work of grace, and praise and glory redounded to the One who had chosen, commissioned, and sent him forth.

The abundant resultant fruit was to His glory. Nothing gives such power to the ministry of Christ as genuine conversion. I do not understand how any man can presume to be a minister who does not know the reality of a personal conversion and the truth of the gospel.

That gospel has lost none of its power. It can work just as wonderful miracles today for men who will put their trust in the Lord Jesus Christ. Have you trusted Him? Have you believed in Him? Is He your Savior? Do you know what it means to be converted? Can you say, "Thank God, my soul is saved; God has revealed His Son in me"?

THE GOSPEL AS MINISTERED TO JEW AND GENTILE

Galatians 2:1–10

Then fourteen years after I went up again to Jerusalem with Barnabas, and took Titus with me also. And I went up by revelation, and communicated unto them that gospel which I preach among the Gentiles, but privately to them which were of reputation, lest by any means I should run, or had run, in vain. But neither Titus, who was with me, being a Greek, was compelled to be circumcised: and that because of false brethren unawares brought in, who came in privily to spy out our liberty which we have in Christ Jesus, that they might bring us into bondage: to whom we gave place by subjection, no, not for an hour; that the truth of the gospel might continue with you. But of these who seemed to be somewhat, (whatsoever they were, it maketh no matter to me: God accepteth no man's person:) for they who seemed to be somewhat in conference added nothing to me: but contrariwise, when they saw that the gospel of the uncircumcision was committed unto me, as the gospel of the circumcision was unto Peter; (for he that wrought effectually in

Peter to the apostleship of the circumcision, the same was mighty in me toward the Gentiles:) and when James, Cephas, and John, who seemed to be pillars, perceived the grace that was given unto me, they gave to me and Barnabas the right hands of fellowship; that we should go unto the heathen, and they unto the circumcision. Only they would that we should remember the poor; the same which I also was forward to do. (vv. 1–10)

In this second chapter Paul tells of another visit to Jerusalem, a very important one, referred to in Acts 15. "Fourteen years after I went up again to Jerusalem with Barnabas, and took Titus with me also." This was after certain persons came from James to Antioch, where the apostle was laboring, and insisted upon things that are mentioned in this letter—that the Gentile believers must be subjected to Jewish rites and ceremonies, that they must be circumcised, must keep the law of Moses, or they could not be saved. When Paul came in contact with them he waited until he had a definite revelation commanding him to go to Jerusalem. He says, "I went up by revelation." He did not go alone; he took Barnabas with him.

Barnabas had come from Jerusalem to find him in Tarsus, to persuade him to go to Antioch and assist in the ministry there. In the beginning it was Barnabas who was the leader, and Paul was the follower. But as time went on Barnabas took the lower place and Paul came to the front. With Barnabas it was a case of, "He must increase, but I must decrease." We read elsewhere of him, "He was a good man, and full of the Holy Ghost and of faith" (Acts 11:24). Such a man can stand to see someone else honored and himself set to one side. So Barnabas stepped into the background and Paul came to the front. And then Paul says, "And took Titus with me also." Why did he mention that? Because this was a test case. These false brethren who had come down to Galatia had insisted that in Jerusalem and Judea no one would condone the idea that a Gentile could be saved if he did not accept the sign of the Abrahamic covenant and were not circumcised. But Paul says, "I took Titus with me also," and he was a Gentile. He had never submitted to this rite, and Paul had never suggested that he should, and so he took him to Jerusalem, as it were to the headquarters of the legalists.

"And I went up by revelation, and communicated unto them that gospel which I preach among the Gentiles, but privately to them which were of reputation, lest by any means I should run, or had run, in vain." He gave them an outline of the glad tidings that he preached among the Gentiles, but he did this privately "to them that were of reputation." When we go back to Acts 15 we find that Paul called together the apostles who happened to be in Jerusalem, James, Cephas, and John, together with the elders of the church there, and to them he told the story of his ministry, his activities. He outlined for them the contents of the gospel message which he carried to the Gentiles. As they listened they accepted him as one with themselves in the proclamation of the same gospel that they preached, even though that gospel was fuller, was richer, than that to which they had attained, for there were certain things made known to Paul that had not been revealed to them.

A few years before, God had been obliged to give Peter a special revelation in order that he might enter into that wondrous mystery, namely, that Jew and Gentile when saved were now to be recognized as one body in Christ. Peter never uses the term "the body," but he does convey the same thought. Blessing for Jew and Gentile was on the ground of grace, and the Lord revealed that to him on the housetop in Joppa when he had a vision of a sheet descending unto him, "wherein were all manner of fourfooted beasts of the earth, and wild beasts, and creeping things, and fowls of the air" (Acts 10:12). And a voice from heaven said, "Rise, Peter; kill, and eat" (Acts 10:13). But Peter, like a good Jew, said, "Not so, Lord; for I have never eaten any thing that is common or unclean" (Acts 10:14). And the Lord said to him, "What God hath cleansed, that call not thou common" (Acts 10: 15), thus indicating the sanctification of the Gentiles. That prepared Peter for the mission to the house of Cornelius, where he preached Christ and opened the door of the kingdom to the Gentiles, as some time before he had been used to open it to the Jews in Jerusalem. Paul and Barnabas talked with the brethren freely, declaring what God had done, and after much discussion, Peter related God's dealings in grace, and James appealed to Scripture to decide the matter as to the Gentiles. They were in happy agreement. Paul, as we have already noticed, had had a fuller, clearer unfolding than was given to Peter, but it was the same gospel basically, and in order to show that there was no such thought in their minds as to subjecting Gentiles to legal ceremonies, he says, "But neither Titus, who was with me, being a Greek, was compelled to be circumcised." What a tremendous answer that was to these Judaizers who were perverting these Galatians and turning them away from the simplicity of the grace of God. They said, "A man uncircumcised cannot be recognized as in the family of God." Paul says, "I took Titus with me, and talked the matter over with the elders at Jerusalem, and they did not say one word about making Titus submit to circumcision. He was accepted as a fellow Christian just as he was." What an answer to those who were criticizing him and misleading his converts!

"And that because of false brethren unawares brought in, who came in privily to spy out our liberty which we have in Christ Jesus, that they might bring us into bondage: to whom we gave place by subjection, no, not for an hour; that the truth of the gospel might continue with you." To whom does he refer? To these Judaizers who had wormed their way privately into the assembly of the Christians in Galatia. Paul says, "Not even for peace's sake did we submit to them, because we would have been robbing you of your blood-bought heritage in Christ. And so because of our love for you and our realization of the value of the grace of God, we refused even on the ground of Christian love to submit to these men. We never subjected ourselves to them."

And then in the next few verses he tells us an interesting little story about an arrangement made while in Jerusalem as to a division of spheres of labor, an arrangement made in perfect Christian fellowship and happy harmony (vv. 6–10). "But of these who seemed to be somewhat, (whatsoever they were, it maketh no matter to me: God accepteth no man's person:) for they who seemed to be somewhat in conference added nothing to me." He could speak that way, you see, because he had received his revelation directly from heaven. It was the risen, glorified Christ who had appeared to him on the Damascus road, the same blessed Lord who had taught him during those months in Arabia, where he had retired that he might mull things over and get a clear understanding of the wonderful message he was to carry to the Gentile world. Therefore, even though he mingled with the apostles and elders who had been saved years before he knew Christ, he did not stand in awe of them. They might be recognized leaders, but God does not accept any man's person, and they were simply brothers in Christ. They had to be taught of God, and so did he. He does not ask them to confer any authority on him nor give him any special opening up of the truth that he was to proclaim to the Gentiles, though he was glad to sit down on common ground and talk things over in a brotherly way. And they said, "Why, certainly, we recognize the fact that God has raised you up for a special mission, and we have fellowship with you in that." "But contrariwise, when they saw that the gospel of the uncircumcision was committed unto me, as the gospel of the circumcision was unto Peter"; notice the preposition rendered here "of." The Greek word may be rendered "for," and the point was this—they saw that God had given him a special revelation, a special understanding of the gospel for the Gentiles. God had fitted him by early training, and then by enlightenment after conversion, to do a work among the Gentiles which they did not feel they were fitted for. On the other hand, God had fitted Peter to do a special work among the Jews and had used him in a remarkable way on the day of Pentecost, and through the years since God had set His seal upon Peter's ministry to Israel. And so they talked things over, and they said, "It is very evident, Paul, that God has marked you out to carry the message to the Gentiles as Peter is carrying it to the Jews." He says, "For he that wrought effectually in Peter to the apostleship of the circumcision, the same was mighty in me toward the Gentiles."

"And when James, Cephas, and John, who seemed to be pillars [apparently they were the leaders], perceived the grace that was given unto me, they gave to me and Barnabas the right hands of fellowship; that we should go unto the heathen, and they unto the circumcision." Is it not a remarkable thing that men have read into these words the amazing idea that what the apostle Paul is saying here is that as they talked together they found out that there were two gospels?—that Peter and the other apostles chosen by the Lord had one gospel, the gospel of the circumcision, and that Paul and Barnabas had another, the gospel of the Gentiles. And so they were to go on preaching one gospel to the Jews, and Paul and Barnabas were to preach a different gospel altogether to the Gentiles! What amazing ignorance of the divine plan that would lead any one to draw any such conclusion! The apostle has already told us, "Though we, or an angel from heaven, preach any other gospel unto you than that which we have preached unto you, let him be accursed" (1:8). Peter had been among the Galatians preaching to them the same gospel he preached everywhere else. Was he accursed? Angels will proclaim the everlasting gospel in the coming day. Will they be under the curse? Surely not. There is only the one gospel, though it takes on different forms at different times. Peter's gospel was that of a full, free, and eternal salvation through the death, resurrection, and unchanging life of our Lord Jesus Christ, and Paul's gospel was exactly the same. Let us go back and see something as to Peter's gospel and then compare it with Paul's.

On the day of Pentecost we listen to Peter preaching. He says, speaking of our Lord Jesus Christ, that David witnessed concerning Him, "He seeing this before spake of the resurrection of Christ, that his soul was not left in hell, neither his flesh did see corruption. This Jesus hath God raised up, whereof we all are witnesses. Therefore being by the right hand of God exalted, and having received of the Father the promise of the Holy Ghost, he hath shed forth this, which ye now see and hear. . . . Therefore let all the house of Israel know assuredly, that God hath made that same Jesus, whom ye have crucified, both Lord and Christ" (Acts 2:31–33, 36). Does this sound as if there was any difference from the gospel the apostle Paul preached? Surely not. It is the same message of the crucified, risen, and exalted Savior.

What was the effect of this preaching? Remember, this was the gospel that Peter preached. The people cried out, "Men and brethren, what shall we do?"

They did not cry as the Philippian jailer, "Sirs, what must I do to be saved?" (Acts 16:30), but, "Men and brethren, what shall we do?" It was as though they said, "Peter, we have been waiting for years for the coming of the Messiah; we have believed that He was the One who should put away our sins and bring us into everlasting blessing, and now we realize from what you say that He has come and has been crucified and has gone up to God's right hand. Whatever are we to do? Are we hopeless? Are we helpless? We have rejected our Messiah; what shall we do?" And Peter said, "Repent, and be baptized every one of you in the name of Jesus Christ for the remission of sins, and ye shall receive the gift of the Holy Ghost. For the promise is unto you, and to your children, and to all that are afar off, even as many as the Lord our God shall call" (Acts 2:38–39). Peter is saying, "If you believe the message that I have preached to you that there is remission of sins, there is salvation for you; you do not need to go into judgment when the nation goes into judgment. But you must repent." And what is it to repent? It is a complete change of attitude. In other words, change your mind, change your attitude, and be baptized, acknowledging that you receive the Savior that the nation has rejected, and when you do, you stand on new ground altogether. What a fitting message for those Jewish believers! On that day three thousand of them took the step, and by their baptism cut themselves off from the nation that rejected Christ and went over to the side of Christ, and were known as among the children of God.

Let us listen to Peter again.

> Repent ye therefore, and be converted, that your sins may be blotted out, when the times of refreshing shall come from the presence of the Lord; and he shall send Jesus Christ, which before was preached unto you: whom the heaven must receive until the times of restitution of all things, which God hath spoken by the mouth of all his holy prophets since the world began. . . . Unto you first God, having raised up his Son Jesus, sent him to bless you, in turning away every one of you from his iniquities. (Acts 3:19–21, 26)

What is Peter preaching here? The same gospel that Paul preached afterward. He is telling them that the Jewish nation has rejected Christ and is therefore under judgment. And how dire the judgment that has fallen upon that nation! But, he says, if you would be delivered from that, repent, change your attitude, turn again, accept the Christ that the nation is rejecting, and you will be ready to welcome Him when He comes back again. Peter is not yet giving them the revelation of the Rapture, but he is telling them that when Christ appears they as individuals will be ready to welcome Him, even though the nation has to know the power of His judgment.

> Be it known unto you all, and to all the people of Israel, that by the name of Jesus Christ of Nazareth, whom ye crucified, whom God raised from the dead, even by him doth this man stand here before you whole [he had just healed a lame man]. This is the stone which was set at nought of you builders, which is become the head of the corner. Neither is there salvation in any other: for there is none other name under heaven given among men, whereby we must be saved. (Acts 4:10–12)

Is this different from Paul's gospel? It is exactly the same, but Peter is presenting it in a way that the Jewish people, who had all the centuries of instruction behind them, would thoroughly understand.

Now you hear the same man preaching in the house of Cornelius (Acts 10). He tells the story of the life and death and resurrection of Jesus.

> God anointed Jesus of Nazareth with the Holy Ghost and with power: who went about doing good, and healing all that were oppressed of the devil; for God was with him. And we are witnesses of all things which he did both in the land of the Jews, and in Jerusalem; whom they slew and hanged on a tree: him God raised up the third day, and showed him openly; not to all the people, but unto witnesses chosen before of God, even to us, who did eat and drink with him after he rose from the dead. And he commanded us to preach unto the people, and to testify that it is he which was ordained of God to be the Judge of quick and dead. To him give all the prophets witness, that through his name whosoever believeth in him shall receive remission of sins. (Acts 10:38–43)

Is this a different gospel from that which we should preach today? Is this a different gospel from that proclaimed by the apostle Paul? Surely not. It is the same gospel, the gospel of the grace of God, salvation alone through the finished work of our Lord Jesus.

But now turn to the epistle of Peter, which is addressed to Jewish converts, the gospel for the circumcision.

> Forasmuch as ye know that ye were not redeemed with corruptible things, as silver and gold, from your vain conversation received by tradition from your fathers; but with the precious blood of Christ, as of a lamb without blemish and without spot: who verily was foreordained before the foundation of the world, but was manifest in these last times for you. (1 Peter 1:18–20)

This is the gospel that Peter preached to the circumcision. Compare it with that gospel preached by Paul to Jew and Gentile.

> And we declare unto you glad tidings, how that the promise which was made unto the fathers, God hath fulfilled the same unto us their children, in that he hath raised up Jesus again; as it is also written in the second psalm, thou art my Son, this day have I begotten thee. And as concerning that he raised him up from the dead, now no more to return to corruption, he said on this wise, I will give you the sure mercies of David. Wherefore he saith also in another psalm, thou shalt not suffer thine Holy One to see corruption. For David, after he had served his own generation by the will of God, fell on sleep, and was laid unto his fathers, and saw corruption: but he, whom God raised again, saw no corruption. Be it known unto you therefore, men and brethren, that through this man is preached unto you the forgiveness of sins: and by him all that believe are justified from all things, from which ye could not be justified by the law of Moses. (Acts 13:32–39)

Is there anything different here from that which Peter preached? Nothing different, but a fuller unfolding. Peter is never said to have preached justification, but forgiveness and remission. Paul added justification. When God forgives through the risen, glorified Jesus He not only forgives but He justifies. It is impossible for an earthly judge to both forgive and to justify a man. If a man is justified, he does not need to be forgiven. Imagine a man charged with a crime going into court, and after the evidence is all in he is pronounced not guilty, and the judge sets him free. Someone says as he leaves the building, "I want to congratulate you; it was very nice of the judge to forgive you."

"Forgive nothing! He did not forgive me; I am justified. There is nothing to forgive."

You cannot justify a man if he does a wicked thing, but you can forgive. But God not only forgives but justifies the ungodly, because He links the believer with Christ, and we are made "accepted in the beloved" (Eph. 1:6). We stand before God as clear of every charge as if we had never sinned. The two messages are one; but Paul's is a little fuller than that of Peter. One had the message peculiarly adapted to the Jews and the other to the Gentiles, and so they decided on distinct spheres of labor. We have something similar on the mission fields today. The heads of the boards get together, and one says, "Suppose that such-and-such a group of you work in this district, and another in this one." Do you say, "Oh dear, they have four or five different gospels?" Not at all; it is the same gospel. One goes to Nigeria, another to Uganda, another to Tanzania, and others to other sections, but it is the same glorious message. And it is very simple, unless one is trying to read into it things of which the apostles never dreamed. Paul and Peter never had the privilege of studying the modern systems of some of our ultradispensationalists, and so did not have the ideas that some people try to foist upon Christians today.

Verse 10 is interesting: "Only they would that we should remember the poor; the same which I also was forward to do." I wonder whether Paul did not smile as he heard that. They said, "You go to the Gentiles, Paul, but don't forget there are many poor saints here in Judea, and although you do not preach among us, send us a collection from time to time." He did, and thus showed that it was one body and one Spirit, even as they are called in one hope of their calling.

PETER'S DEFECTION AT ANTIOCH

Galatians 2:11–21

But when Peter was come to Antioch, I withstood him to the face, because he was to be blamed. For before that certain came from James, he did eat with the Gentiles: but when they were come, he withdrew and separated himself, fearing them which were of the circumcision. And the other Jews dissembled likewise with him; insomuch that Barnabas also was carried away with their dissimulation. But when I saw that they walked not uprightly according to the truth of the gospel, I said unto Peter before them all, If thou, being a Jew, livest after the manner of Gentiles, and not as do the Jews, why compellest thou the Gentiles to live as do the Jews? We who are Jews by nature, and not sinners of the Gentiles, knowing that a man is not justified by the works of the law, but by the faith of Jesus Christ, even we have believed in Jesus Christ, that we might be justified by the faith of Christ, and not by the works of the law: for by the works of the law shall no flesh be justified. But if, while we seek to be justified by Christ, we ourselves also are found sinners, is therefore Christ the minister of sin? God forbid. For if I build again the things which I destroyed, I make myself a transgressor. For I

150 | GALATIANS

through the law am dead to the law, that I might live unto God. I am crucified with Christ: nevertheless I live; yet not I, but Christ liveth in me: and the life which I now live in the flesh I live by the faith of the Son of God, who loved me, and gave himself for me. I do not frustrate the grace of God: for if righteousness come by the law, then Christ is dead in vain. (vv. 11–21)

This passage suggests a number of interesting considerations. First of all, we are rather astonished perhaps to find Paul and Peter, both inspired men, both commissioned by the Lord Jesus Christ to go out into the world proclaiming His gospel, both apostles, now sharply differing one from the other. It would suggest certainly that the apostle Peter, who is the one at fault, is not the rock upon which the church is built. What a wobbly kind of a rock it would be if he were, for here is the very man to whom the Father gave that wonderful revelation that Christ was the Son of the living God, actually behaving in such a way at Antioch as to bring discredit upon the gospel of the grace of God. If Peter was the first Pope he was a very fallible one, not an infallible. But he himself knew nothing of any such position, for he tells us in the fifth chapter of his first epistle that he was a fellow elder with the rest of the elders in the church of God, not one set in a position of authority over the presbytery, the elders, in God's church. Then too the reading of the Scripture suggests to us the tremendous importance of ever being on the alert lest in some way or another we compromise in regard to God's precious truth.

We have already seen what an important thing that truth was in the eyes of the apostle Paul when he could call down condign judgment on the man, or even the angel, who preaches any other gospel than that divine revelation communicated to him. We know it was not simply because of ill-temper that he wrote in this way but because he realized how important it is to hold "the faith which was once [for all] delivered unto the saints" (Jude 3). That explains his attitude here in regard to Peter, a brother apostle. It had been agreed, as we have seen, at the great council in Jerusalem that Peter was to go to the Jews and Paul to the Gentiles, but as they compared their messages they found that one did not contradict the other, that both taught and believed salvation was through faith alone in the Lord Jesus Christ, and that both recognized the futility of works of law as providing a righteousness for sinful men.

To Antioch, a Gentile city in which there was a large church composed mainly of Gentile believers, where Paul and Barnabas had been laboring for a long time, Peter came for a visit. I suppose he was welcomed with open arms. It must have been a very joyous thing for the apostle Paul to welcome Peter, and to be his fellow laborer in ministering the Word of God to these people of Antioch. At first they had a wonderfully happy time. Together they went in and out of the homes of the believers and sat down at the same tables with Gentile Christians. Peter was once so rigid a Jew that he could not even think of going into the house of a Gentile to have any fellowship whatsoever. What a happy thing it was to see these different believers, some at one time Jews, and others once Gentiles, now members of one body, the body of Christ, enjoying fellowship together, not only at the Lord's table, but also in their homes. For when Paul speaks of eating with Gentiles I take it that it was at their own tables where they could have the sweetest Christian fellowship talking together of the things of God while enjoying the good things that the Lord provides. But unhappily there came in something that hindered, that spoiled that hallowed communion.

Some brethren came from Jerusalem who were of the rigid Pharisaic type, and although they called themselves (and possibly were) Christians, they had never been delivered from legalism. Peter realized that his reputation was at stake. If they should find him eating with Gentile believers and go back to Jerusalem and report this, it might shut the door on him there, and so prudently, as he might have thought, he withdrew from them, he no longer ate with them. If he chose not to eat with the Gentiles, could any one find fault with him for that? If he regarded the prejudices of these brethren might he not be showing a certain amount of Christian courtesy? He felt free to do these things, but not if they distressed these others. But Paul saw deeper than that; he saw that our liberty in Christ actually hung upon the question of whether one would sit down at the dinner table or not with those who had come out from the Gentiles unto the name of our Lord Jesus, and so this controversy. "When Peter was come to Antioch," Paul says, "I withstood him to the face, because he was to be blamed." There is no subserviency on Paul's part here, no recognition of Peter as the head of the church. Paul realized that a divine authority was vested in him, and that he was free to call in question the behavior of Peter himself though he was one of the original twelve. "For before that certain came from James"—James was the leader at Jerusalem—"he did eat with the Gentiles: but when they were come, he withdrew and separated himself, fearing them which were of the circumcision." We read in the Old Testament, "The fear of man bringeth a snare," and here we are rather surprised to find the apostle Peter, some years after Pentecost, afraid of the face of man. It has often been said that Peter before Pentecost was a coward, but when he received the Pentecostal baptism everything was changed. He stood before the people in Jerusalem and drove the truth home to them, "Ye . . . killed the Prince of Life," and he who had denied his Lord because of the fear of man now strikes home the fact that they "denied the Holy One and the Just, and desired a murderer to be granted unto you" (Acts 3:14). The inference has been drawn by some that if one receives the Pentecostal baptism he will never be a coward again, and also that all inbred sin has been then burned out by the refining fire of God. But we do not find anything like that in the Word of God. It is true that under the influence of that Pentecostal baptism Peter did not fear the face of man, but now he had begun to slip. The fact that one has received great spiritual blessing at any particular time gives no guarantee that he will never fear again.

We now find Peter troubled by that same old besetment that had brought him into difficulty before, afraid of what others will say of him, and when he saw these legalists he forgot all about Pentecost, all about the blessing that had come, all about the marvelous revelation that he had when the sheet was let down from heaven and the Lord said, "What God hath cleansed, that call not thou common" (Acts 10:15). He forgot how he himself had stood in Cornelius' household and said, "It is an unlawful thing for a man that is a Jew to . . . come unto one of another nation; but God hath shown me that I should not call any man common or unclean" (Acts 10:28). He forgot that at the council in Jerusalem it was he who stood before them all and after relating the incidents in connection with his visit to Cornelius, exclaimed, "We [we who are Jews by nature] believe that through the grace of the Lord Jesus Christ *we* shall be saved, even as they" (Acts 15:11, emphasis added). That was a wonderful declaration. We might have expected him to say, "We believe that through the grace of the Lord Jesus Christ *they* shall be saved, even as we," that is, "these Gentiles may be saved by grace even as we Jews are saved by grace." But no, he had had a wonderful revelation of the real meaning of Pentecost and this glorious dispensation of the grace of God. What made him forget all this? The scowling looks of these men from Jerusalem. They had heard that he had been exercising a liberty in which they did not believe, and they had come to watch him. He thought, "It will never do for me to go into the houses of the Gentiles to eat while these men are around." So without thinking how he would offend these simple Gentile Christians who had known the Lord only a short time, and in order to please these Jerusalem legalists, he withdrew from the Gentiles as far as intimate fellowship was concerned. He was not alone in this for he was a man of influence and others followed him. "And the other Jews dissembled likewise with him." It looked as though there might be two churches in Antioch very soon, one for the Jews and another for the Gentiles, as though the middle wall of partition had not been broken down.

"The other Jews dissembled likewise with him." And what must have cut

Paul to the quick, his own intimate companion, his fellow worker, the man who had understood so well from the beginning the work that he should do, "Barnabas also was carried away with their dissimulation." How much he puts into those words! Barnabas who knew so much better, Barnabas who had seen how mightily God had wrought among the Gentiles, and who knew that all this old legalistic system had fallen never to be raised again, even Barnabas was carried away with their dissimulation.

"Dissimulation" is rather a fine-sounding word. I wonder why the translators did not translate the Greek word the same as they generally did in other places in the Bible. It may have been that they did not like to use the other word in connection with a man like Barnabas. It is just the ordinary word for hypocrisy. "The other Jews [became hypocrites] likewise with him; insomuch that Barnabas also was carried away with their [hypocrisy]." Peter might have said, "We are doing this to glorify God," but it was nothing of the kind; it was downright hypocrisy in the sight of God. Paul recognized it as what it was, and said, "But when I saw that they walked not uprightly according to the truth of the gospel, I said unto Peter before them all . . ." This was not a clandestine meeting, there was no backbiting. What he had to say he said openly, and he did not seem to spare Peter's feelings. We must ever remember the Word, "Thou shalt in any wise rebuke thy neighbour, and not suffer sin upon him" (Lev. 19:17). Some years afterward he wrote to Timothy, "Them that sin rebuke before all, that others also may fear" (1 Tim. 5:20). There was too much at stake to pass over this lightly. It was too serious a matter to settle quietly with Peter in a corner, for it had been a public scandal, and it called in question the liberty of Gentiles in Christ and so must be settled in a public way. One can imagine the feelings of Peter, noble man of God that he was, and yet he had been carried away with this snare. At first he was startled as he looked at Paul, and then I fancy with bowed head, the blood mantling his face in shame, he realized how guilty he was of seeking to please these legalists who would rob the church of the marvelous gospel of grace. "If thou, being a Jew, livest after the manner of Gentiles, and not as do the Jews, why compellest thou the Gentiles to live as do the Jews?" He has let the cat out of the bag. I think I see those Jewish men look up and say, "What is this? He has been living after the manner of Gentiles?" Yes, they should have known it, for he had a right to do it. God had given all men this liberty and Peter had been exercising it, but now he was bringing himself into bondage. Peter had said, "We Jews know that a man is not justified by the works of the law, but we have to be saved by grace even as the Gentiles, so why insist upon bringing these Gentiles under bondage to Jewish forms and ceremonies?"

Paul went on: "'We who are Jews by nature, and not sinners of the Gentiles, knowing that a man is not justified by the works of the law, but by the faith of Jesus Christ, even we have believed in Jesus Christ, that we might be justified by the faith of Christ, and not by the works of the law: for by the works of the law shall no flesh be justified.' We gave up all confidence in law-keeping as a means of salvation when we turned to Christ, and now, Peter, would you by your behavior say to the Gentile brethren, 'You should come under the bondage of law-keeping, from which we have been delivered in order to be truly justified?'" It was a solemn occasion, for there was an important question at stake, and Paul handled it like the courageous man that he was.

Are you, like so many others, trying to do the best you can in order to obtain God's salvation? Listen then to what He says, "By the works of the law shall no flesh be justified."

> Could my tears forever flow,
>> Could my zeal no languor know,
> These for sin could not atone;
>> Thou must save, and Thou alone.

Some years ago, after listening to me preach on the street corner a man said to me, "I detest this idea that through the death and righteousness of Another I should be saved. I do not want to be indebted to anybody for my salvation. I am not coming to God as a mendicant, but I believe that if a man lives up to the Sermon on the Mount and keeps the Ten Commandments, God does not require any more of him."

I asked, "My friend, have you lived up to the Sermon on the Mount and have you kept the Ten Commandments?"

"Oh," he said, "perhaps not perfectly; but I am doing the best I can."

"But," I replied, "the Word of God says, 'Whosoever shall keep the whole law, and yet offend in one point, he is guilty of all' (James 2:10). And, 'It is written, Cursed is every one that continueth not in *all* things which are written in the book of the law to do them' (Gal. 3:10), and because you have not continued you are under the curse."

That is all the law can do for any poor sinner. It can only condemn, for it demands perfect righteousness from sinful men, a righteousness which no sinful man can ever give, and so when God has shown us in His Word that men are bereft of righteousness, He says, "I have a righteousness for guilty sinners, but they must receive it by faith," and He tells us the wondrous story of the death and resurrection of our Lord Jesus Christ—"[He] was delivered for our offenses" (Rom. 4:25). And having trusted Him shall we *go* back to works of the law?

"If," says Paul, "while we seek to be justified by Christ, we ourselves also are found sinners"—if we who have trusted in Jesus are still sinners seeking a way of salvation—"is therefore Christ the minister of sin?" Moses was the mediator of the law, and it was to be used by God to make sin become exceeding sinful. Is that all Christ is for? Is it simply that His glorious example is to show me how deep is my sin, how lost my condition, and then am I to save myself by my own efforts? Surely not. That would be but to make Christ a minister of sin, but Christ is a minister of righteousness to all who believe. I think verse 17, and possibly verse 18, concludes what Paul says to Peter. "If I build again the things which I destroyed, I make myself a transgressor." We do not have quotation marks in the ancient Greek text, so have no way of knowing exactly where Paul's words to Peter end, but probably he concluded his admonition to Peter with this word.

"For I through the law am dead to the law, that I might live unto God." What does he mean by that? He means that the law condemned me to death, but Christ took my place and became my Substitute. I died in Him. "I through the law died to the law, that I might live unto God." Now I belong to a new creation altogether. And oh, the wonder of that new creation! The old creation fell in its head, Adam, and the new one stands eternally in its Head, the Lord Jesus Christ. We are not trying to work for our salvation, we are saved through the work that He Himself accomplished. We can look back to that cross upon which He hung, the bleeding Victim, in our stead, and we can say in faith, "I am crucified with Christ." It is as though my life had been taken, He took my place; "I am crucified with Christ: nevertheless I live." As I was identified with Him in His death on the cross now I am linked with Him in resurrection life, for He has given me to be a partaker of His own glorious eternal life. "Nevertheless I live; yet not I." It is not the old "I" come back to life again, "but Christ liveth in me." He, the glorious One, is my real life, and that "life which I now live in the flesh," my experience down here as a Christian man in the body, "I live"—not by putting myself under rules and regulations and trying to keep the law of the Ten Commandments but—"by the faith of the Son of God, who loved me, and gave himself for me." As I am occupied with Him, my life will be the kind of life which He approves. "The Son of God, who loved me, and gave himself for me." I wish each of us might say those words over in his heart. Can you say it in your heart? It is not, "The Son of God, who loved *the world,* and gave himself for *the world,*" but, "The Son of God, who loved *me,* and gave himself for me." Only those who trust Him can speak like that. Can you say it from your heart? If you have never said it before you can look up into His face today, and say it for the first time. And so Paul concludes this section, "I do not frustrate the grace of God"—or, I will not set it aside—"for if righteousness come by the law, then Christ is dead in vain." But because righteousness could not be found through legality, through self-effort, Christ gave Himself in grace for needy sinners, and He is Himself the righteousness of all who put their trust in Him.

PART 2

DOCTRINAL

Galatians 3–4

"WHO HATH BEWITCHED YOU?"

Galatians 3:1–9

O foolish Galatians, who hath bewitched you, that ye should not obey the truth, before whose eyes Jesus Christ hath been evidently set forth, crucified among you? This only would I learn of you, Received ye the Spirit by the works of the law, or by the hearing of faith? Are ye so foolish? having begun in the Spirit, are ye now made perfect by the flesh? Have ye suffered so many things in vain? if it be yet in vain. He therefore that ministereth to you the Spirit, and worketh miracles among you, doeth he it by the works of the law, or by the hearing of faith? Even as Abraham believed God, and it was accounted to him for righteousness. Know ye therefore that they which are of faith, the same are the children of Abraham. And the scripture, foreseeing that God would justify the heathen through faith, preached before the gospel unto Abraham, saying, In thee shall all nations be blessed. So then they which be of faith are blessed with faithful Abraham. (vv. 1–9)

We now enter upon the strictly doctrinal part of this epistle. In verse 1 of this chapter the apostle Paul uses very unusual language. What he really means is this, "How is it that you seem to have come under a sort of spell, so that you have lost your grasp of the truth and your hearts and minds have become clouded by error?" Error affects people in that way. It is quite possible for one to have been truly converted and to have begun with a clear, definite knowledge of the saving grace of the Lord Jesus, and then because of failure to follow on to study the Word and to pray over it, to come under the influence of some false system, some unscriptural line of teaching. And so often when people do come under some such influence you find it almost impossible to deliver them. They seem to be under a spell.

Of course the apostle is not saying that one person has the power of bewitching another, but he is using that as an illustration. He says, "These men who have come down from Jerusalem, teaching that you cannot be saved unless you are circumcised and keep the law of Moses, have gotten such an influence over you that you are like people bewitched, and under a spell; you are not able to reason things out, or to detect what is true and what is false." It was not exactly that they had been "given up to strong delusion." When God offers men the truth and they deliberately turn away from it, they stand in danger of being delivered over judicially to that which is absolutely false, but here he has something else in mind. In all likelihood these people were real Christians, but real Christians acting like men under a spell.

"O foolish Galatians, who hath bewitched you, that ye should not obey the truth, before whose eyes Jesus Christ hath been evidently set forth, crucified among you?" When once one has laid hold of the blessed truth that the Lord Jesus has been crucified on our behalf, that in itself ought to be the means of delivering us forever from such error as that into which these people had fallen. If Christ has actually given Himself for me it is because it was impossible for me to do one thing to save myself. Because I could not fit myself for the presence of God, because I could not cleanse my heart from sin, because no work of righteousness of mine could fit me for a place with the Lord, He had to come from heaven and give Himself for me on the cross. How then can I think of turning back to the ground of human merit as a means of securing salvation, or of maintaining me in a condition of salvation before God? I deserved to die, but Jesus Christ took my place, and He has settled for me. He has met all the claims of divine righteousness, and through Him I am eternally saved. Shall I go back to the law to complete the work He has done? Surely not.

The apostle now refers to the beginning of their Christian lives and says, "This only would I learn of you, Received ye the Spirit by the works of the law, or by the hearing of faith?" In the previous chapter he has shown how a man is justified before God by faith alone, and has declared that the law really is honored more in the recognition of the fact that its penalty has been met in the cross of our Lord Jesus, than by any poor effort of man to keep it as a means of salvation. Now he adds to justification by faith the truth of the reception of the Holy Spirit. He says, as it were, "Go back in your own Christian experience. You received the Holy Spirit when you believed in the Lord Jesus, when you accepted the gospel message as I brought it to you (he is referring to his own ministry among them). God gave you the Holy Spirit, not on the ground of any merit of your own, not because of any good thing that you were able to do, certainly not because of law-keeping or ritualistic observances, for you were uncircumcised Gentiles. Yet when you believed in the Lord Jesus, God gave you the Holy Spirit." Now he says, "Think it out; did you receive the Spirit by works of the law? Surely not. How then? 'By the hearing of faith.'"

"Are ye so foolish? having begun in the Spirit, are ye now made perfect by the flesh?" In other words, if the Holy Spirit came to dwell in you in the condition you were when you came to Christ, do you think you need to complete the work by your own self-effort and by putting yourself under legal rules and regulations? You who know the love of the Lord Jesus Christ have received the Holy Spirit. Some of you may say, "I wish I were sure of that." But Scripture says definitely, "After that ye believed, ye were sealed with that holy Spirit of promise" (Eph. 1:13)—you were born of the Spirit. You ask, "Do you mean that when I was born again that was the reception of the Holy Spirit?" Scripture distinguishes between new birth by the Spirit and the reception of the Holy Spirit, but there need not necessarily be any interval between our new birth and the reception of the Holy Spirit. New birth is the work of the Spirit. The Spirit Himself is the One who does the work; He comes to dwell in the man who is born again. New birth is new creation, and the Holy Spirit is the Creator. New birth is the work of God, but the Holy Spirit is God. There is a difference between being born of God and being indwelt by the Spirit of God. In past dispensations men were born of God and yet not indwelt by His Spirit, but with the coming in of the dispensation of the grace of God, when people are born again, the Holy Spirit Himself comes to dwell in them. In the case of these Galatians, if He did not approve of the work that Paul had done, if He did not approve of the stand they had taken in receiving the Lord Jesus Christ, He never would have come to dwell in them as they were. If it were necessary to be subject to the Mosaic ritual He would have made that clear and said, "I cannot come and dwell in you until these things are settled, until you submit yourselves to these regulations and rules," but He did nothing of the kind. They believed, they took their places before God as lost sinners, they turned to Him in repentance, they accepted Christ by faith as their Savior, and the Holy Spirit says, as it were, "Now I can dwell in them, they are washed from their sins in the precious blood of Christ, and I will make their bodies My temples." Do you not see what a clear argument that was in meeting the teaching of these people?

"Having begun in the Spirit, are ye now made perfect by the flesh?" He reminded them of what they went through in those early days. It meant much for people in their circumstances to step out from heathenism and take a stand against their friends and relatives, to accept the Lord Jesus Christ as their Savior, and to declare that the idols they had once worshiped were dumb images and powerless to save. To step out from all that in which they had participated for so many years meant a great deal, and exposed them to suffering, bitter persecution, and grave misunderstanding on the part of their fellow men. Yet for Jesus' sake they gladly took the step, for Jesus' sake they bore reproach, they suffered, many of them, even unto death, and those who were still living counted it all joy to have part with Christ in His rejection. But they were being brought under the power of an evil system, teaching that they were not really saved until they submitted themselves to what these Jewish legalists had put before them.

"Have ye suffered so many things in vain?" All that they had gone through for Christ's sake—was it in vain? Was it simply a profession? If not, how is it that they seem to have lost their assurance? And then he adds, "if it be yet in vain." He cannot believe that it is in vain, for he looks back and remembers the exercises they went through, the joy that came to them when they professed to receive Christ, and the love that seemed to be welling up in their hearts one for another, and for him as a servant of God and for the Savior Himself. He says, "I remember the afflictions you were ready to endure on behalf of the gospel; I cannot believe you were not converted, that it was not real. You have been misled, you have gotten into a fog, and if I can, I want by the grace of God to deliver you." He had no ill will against them, and none against the men who came down from Jerusalem, but he detested the doctrine they brought. Some people find it difficult to distinguish between a hatred of false doctrine and a love for the people themselves who have come under the influence of it. When we stand up for the truth of God and warn people against false teaching, that does not imply for one moment that we have any unkind feeling toward those taken up with that false teaching. We love such a person as one for whom Christ died, and pray that he may be delivered from his error and brought into the light of the truth.

Then the apostle reminds them that when he came among them to preach the gospel of the grace of God, there were marvelous signs and manifestations that followed. They themselves had seen him and Barnabas work wondrous miracles and some among the number had similar gifts granted to them. These miraculous evidences accompanied the testimony. "He therefore that ministereth to you the Spirit, and worketh miracles among you, doeth he it by the works of the law, or by the hearing of faith?" I think he intended them now to contrast the ministry of these false teachers who had come among them with that of his own and Barnabas when they came in the simplicity and fullness of the gospel of Christ. Are there any miraculous attestations of these false teachers? Is their testimony accredited by miraculous power? Not at all. But when Paul went preaching Christ and Him crucified, God Himself put His seal of approval upon that testimony by giving them the power to work miracles. People say, "Why not the same today?" Even today miraculous signs accompany the preaching of the truth which are not found when error is presented. When the gospel of the grace of God is preached, men and women believing it are delivered from their sins, the Holy Spirit works, creating a new life, a new nature, and sets them free. The drunkard listens to the gospel and believes it, and finds the chains of appetite are broken. The licentious man who reveled in his uncleanness like a swine in the mud, gets a sight of the Lord Jesus; his heart is stirred as he contemplates the holiness and purity of the Savior, and he bows in repentance before God, abhorring himself and his sin, and becomes pure and clean and good. The liar who has not been able to speak honest words for years hears the gospel of the grace of God and falls in love with Him who is the truth, and learns henceforth to speak right words, true words. That bad-tempered man who was a terror to his family, so that his wife shrank from him, and his children were afraid when he entered the house, is subdued by divine grace and the lion becomes a lamb. These are miracles which have been wrought down through the centuries where the gospel of the grace of God was preached. Error does not produce these things. It gives men certain intellectual conceptions in which they glory, but it does not make unclean lives clean, nor deliver from impurity and iniquity. But it is the glory of the gospel that when men truly believe they actually become new creatures in Christ Jesus. There were no such signs and wonders accompanying this law-preaching.

And so he comes back to Abraham. These false teachers had said, "God called Abraham out from among the Gentiles and gave him the covenant of circumcision, and therefore unless these Gentiles do follow him in this they cannot be saved." Even as "Abraham believed God, and it was accounted to him for righteousness." Abraham was a Gentile just as these Galatians were, and God revealed His truth to him. In verse 8 we read, "God . . . preached before the gospel unto Abraham, saying, In thee shall all nations be blessed." And Abraham believed it, and God justified him by faith. When did God preach the gospel to him? He took him outside his tent one night and said, "Look now toward heaven, and tell the stars" (Gen. 15:5). And Abraham said, "I cannot count them, they are in number utterly beyond me." And then He told him to count the sand and the dust under his feet, and Abraham said, "I cannot do that." And God said, "So shall thy seed be. In thy Seed shall all the nations of the earth be blessed."

God gave Abraham the promise of a collective seed, as numberless as the stars of the heaven, as the sand of the sea, as the dust of the ground, and also the individual Seed, the Lord Jesus Christ Himself, the son of Abraham, for in Him all the nations of the earth shall be blessed. Abraham was a childless old man, but "he staggered not at the promise of God through unbelief; but was strong in faith, giving glory to God; and being fully persuaded that, what he had promised, he was able also to perform" (Rom. 4:20–21). And when God saw this faith in Abraham He justified him. The covenant of circumcision had not yet been given to him, but he was justified by faith. What is the inference? If God can justify one Gentile by faith, can He not justify ten million by faith? If Abraham is the father of all the faithful in a spiritual sense, then we Gentiles need not fear to follow in his steps. And so the next verse goes on, "Know ye therefore that they which are of faith, the same are the children of Abraham." You see, Abraham has a spiritual seed as well as a natural seed. Those born of Abraham's lineage after the flesh are not really Abraham's sons unless born again; they must have the faith of Abraham to be his sons. But all over the world, wherever the message comes, wherever people, whether Jews or Gentiles, put their trust in that Seed of Abraham, our Lord Jesus Christ, and receive Him as Savior and Lord, God says, "Write him down a son of Abraham." And so Abraham has a vast spiritual seed. Throughout all the centuries the millions and millions of people who have believed God as he did, and trusted in the Savior in whom he trusted, will share his blessings, and will be with Abraham for all eternity.

"And the scripture, foreseeing that God would justify the heathen through faith [not through faith and works, not through faith and ordinances, not through faith and sacramental observances], preached before the gospel unto Abraham, saying, In thee shall all nations be blessed." The gospel is God's good news concerning His Son. Abraham received that good news and believed it, and if you and I have received and believed it we are linked with him, we are children of Abraham.

"So then they which be of faith are blessed with [believing] Abraham." On what are you resting for your salvation? I have received letters from people who are indignant because I have said that salvation is through faith alone. It makes one start sometimes to find that after all our gospel preaching so many people who make a Christian profession have never yet learned that salvation is absolutely of grace through faith. We almost forget that there are hundreds of people who do not believe these things. And yet how can anyone profess to believe this Book and yet insist upon salvation by human effort? In Romans we read, "If by grace, then is it no more of works: otherwise grace is no more grace. But if it be of works, then is it no more grace: otherwise work is no more work" (Rom. 11:6). Can you not see how the Holy Spirit of God shuts us up to this, that salvation is either altogether by grace or it is altogether by works? It cannot be by a combination of the two. Someone says, "But do you not remember the old story about the two preachers who were in the rowboat, who were debating as to whether salvation were by grace or by works, by faith or by works? The boatman listened to them, and when they were unable to come to a solution of the problem, one said to the boatman, 'You have heard our conversation; what do you think of this?'

"'Well,' he said, 'I have been thinking it is like this—I have two oars. I will call this one *Faith* and this one *Works*. If I pull only on this oar the boat goes round and round and does not get anywhere. If I pull on that one it goes round and round and gets nowhere. But if I pull on both I get across the river.'"

And people say that is a beautiful illustration of the fact that salvation is by faith and works. It would be if we were going to heaven in a rowboat, but we are not. We are going through in the infinite grace of our Lord Jesus Christ, and like that lost sheep that went astray and was found by the shepherd, we are being carried by the Savior home to glory, and it is not a question of working our way there. And so we come back to what Scripture says, "For by grace are ye saved through faith; and that not of yourselves: it is the gift of God: not of works, lest any man should boast" (Eph. 2:8–9). If I had to do as much as lift my little finger to save my soul I could strut up the golden streets saying, "Glory be to the Lord and to me, for by our combined efforts I am saved." No, it is no works of mine, no effort of mine, and so Jesus shall get all the glory.

> Jesus paid it all,
>> All to Him I owe;
> Sin had left a crimson stain,
>> He washed it white as snow!

Are you in perplexity and wanting the assurance of salvation? Possibly you have prayed and read your Bible, have gone to church, have been baptized and partaken of the sacrament, you have tried to do your religious duty, but you do not have peace and rest and you do not know whether your soul is saved. Turn from self and self-occupation, and fix your eyes upon the blessed Christ of God; put all your heart's trust in Him and be assured that, "Whosoever believeth in him should not perish, but have everlasting life" (John 3:16).

REDEEMED FROM THE CURSE OF THE LAW

Galatians 3:10–18

For as many as are of the works of the law are under the curse: for it is written, Cursed is every one that continueth not in all things which are written in the book of the law to do them. But that no man is justified by the law in the sight of God, it is evident: for, The just shall live by faith. And the law is not of faith: but, The man that doeth them shall live in them. Christ hath redeemed us from the curse of the law, being made a curse for us: for it is written, Cursed is every one that hangeth on a tree: that the blessing of Abraham might come on the Gentiles through Jesus Christ; that we might receive the promise of the Spirit through faith. Brethren, I speak after the manner of men; though it be but a man's covenant, yet if it be confirmed, no man disannulleth, or addeth thereto. Now to Abraham and his seed were the promises made. He saith not, And to seeds, as of many; but as of one, And to thy seed, which is Christ. And this I say, that the covenant, that was confirmed before of God in Christ, the law, which was four hundred and thirty years after, cannot disannul, that it should make the promise of none effect. For if the inheritance be of the law, it is no more of promise: but God gave it to Abraham by promise. (vv. 10–18)

Naturally one might ask, "What do we mean when we speak of the curse of the law?" Is it a curse to have good laws? Was it a curse for God to give to the people of Israel the Ten Commandments, the highest moral and ethical standard that any people had ever received and that ever had been given to mankind, until our Lord Jesus Christ proclaimed the Sermon on the Mount? Is this a curse? Surely not. It was a great blessing to Israel to have such instruction, showing them how to live and how to behave themselves, and it kept them from a great many of the sins to which the Gentile nations round about them were given. Yet we have this expression in Scripture, "The curse of the law," and read, "For as many as are of the works of the law are under the curse: for it is written, Cursed is every one that continueth not in all things which are written in the book of the law to do them."

When God gave that law, He pronounced a blessing on all who kept it, and declared that they would receive life thereby. "The man which doeth those things shall live by them" (Rom. 10:5), but on the other hand, He said, as quoted here, "Cursed is every one that continueth not in all things which are written in the book of the law to do them." Every one who recognizes in that law the divine will as to the life of man here on earth and yet fails to measure up to it comes under its curse. And who is there today who has ever kept this law? I know people say, "If we do the best we can, will that not be enough?" Scripture negates any such thought. In James we read, "Whosoever shall keep the whole law, and yet offend in one point, he is guilty of all" (2:10). We know how true that is in regard to human law. Suppose that I as a citizen of the United States violated none of the laws of my country except one. By violating that one law I have become a lawbreaker and am, therefore, subjected to the penalty of the broken law. When we speak of people being under "the curse of the law" we mean that they are subject to the penalty of the broken law, and the penalty is death, spiritual and eternal. "The soul that sinneth, it shall die" (Ezek. 18:20). Therefore the law is well called "the ministration of death" and "the ministration of condemnation" (2 Cor. 3:7, 9), for all who are under the law but have failed to keep it are under condemnation; they are condemned to death, and therefore under the curse. But our Lord Jesus Christ has died to deliver us from the curse of the law.

Can we not deliver ourselves? Though we have broken it in the past can we not make up our minds that from this moment on we will "turn over a new leaf," and be very careful to observe every precept of the moral law of God? In the first place, we could not do that. It is impossible for men with fallen natures to fully keep the holy law of God. Take that particular commandment, "Thou shalt not covet"; you cannot keep yourself from coveting though you know it is wrong to do so. You look at something your neighbor has and involuntarily your heart says, "I wish that were mine." On second thought, you say, "That is very unworthy; I should really rejoice for my neighbor"; but still, have you not coveted? The apostle Paul says that as far as the other commandments were concerned his life was outwardly blameless. He was alive without the law until the commandment came, "Thou shalt not covet." "But sin, taking occasion by the commandment, wrought in me all manner of concupiscence" (Rom. 7:8). And so he was slain by the law that he could not keep. But suppose you were able to keep it from this very day until the last day of your life, would not that undo and make up for all the wrong doing of the past? Not at all. The past failure still stands on God's record. "God requireth that which is past" (Eccl. 3:15).

"But that no man is justified by the law in the sight of God, it is evident: for, The just shall live by faith." Notice, no man is justified by the law of God, no man ever has been justified by the law of God, no man ever will be justified by the law of God. In Romans 3 we read, "Now we know that what things soever the law saith, it saith to them who are under the law: that every mouth may be stopped, and all the world may become guilty before God. Therefore by the deeds of the law there shall no flesh be justified in his sight: for by the law is the knowledge of sin" (Rom. 3:19–20). In other words, God did not give the law to save man, He gave the law to test him, to make manifest man's true condition. And that explains a passage that puzzles some, "The law . . . was added because of transgressions" (Gal. 3:19). It was really given in order to give to sin the specific character of transgression.

I was strolling across the park the other day when I suddenly looked down and saw almost at my feet a sign, "Keep off the grass." I was on the grass, but the moment I saw the sign I hurried to get onto a path. If I had continued to walk on the grass after seeing the sign, I would be a transgressor. I was not a transgressor before this, for I did not know I was doing wrong. I saw other people walking on the grass, and did not realize that there were certain sections where this was not allowed. I did not know that it was forbidden in that particular place. Until the law sin was in the world, and men were doing wrong in taking their own way, but "where no law is, there is no transgression" (Rom. 4:15). God set up His law to say, as it were, "Keep off the grass." Now if they walk on the grass they are transgressors. If men disobey God, they transgress. The sinfulness of man's heart is shown up by the fact that men do deliberately and willfully disobey. It is impossible to be justified by the law, for to be justified is to be cleared from every charge of guilt. The law brings the charge home, the law convicts me of my guilt, and the law condemns me because of that guilt.

It was written in the prophets, "The just shall live by his faith" (Hab. 2:4), so it was made known even in Old Testament times that men were to be justified, not by human effort, but by faith. Three times those words are quoted for us in the New Testament. In the epistle to the Romans the apostle says, "I am not ashamed of the gospel of Christ: for it is the power of God unto salvation to every one that believeth; to the Jew first, and also to the Greek. For therein is the righteousness of God revealed from faith to faith: as it is written, The just shall live by faith" (Rom. 1:16–17). In the epistle to the Hebrews we have exactly the same words quoted, "The just shall live by faith" (Heb. 10:38). And here we have them in the epistle to the Galatians. It has been very well said that these three epistles expound that text of six words, "The just shall live by faith."

How do men become just before God? As we have already remarked, Romans answers that question and expounds the first two words, "The just." It tells us who the just are, those who believe in the Lord Jesus Christ. But if justified by faith, how is one maintained before God in that position? Is it not now by works of their own? Galatians answers that and puts the emphasis on the next two words, "The just *shall live* by faith." And what is that power that sustains and strengthens and enables just men to walk with God through this world, living an unworldly life, even as "Enoch walked with God: and he was not; for God took him" (Gen. 5:24)? Again the answer comes to us, as in Hebrews the last two words are expounded, "The just shall live *by faith.*" It takes three epistles in the New Testament to expound one Old Testament text of only six words, "The just shall live by faith." It gives us an idea of how rich and full the Word of God is.

But if "The just shall live by faith" then men never can be justified by efforts of their own, for verse 12 tells us, "And the law is not of faith: but, The man that doeth them shall live in them." The law did not say, "The man who *believes* shall live," but, "The man who *does* shall live." The latter might seem to us to be the right thing; if a man does right he ought to live. The trouble is, man does not do right. We read, "All have sinned, and come short of the glory of God" (Rom. 3:23). If one commandment out of ten has been violated that man has forfeited all claim to life. Suppose a man falling over a precipice reached out his hand as he went over, and caught hold of a chain fastened to some stump in the cliff, and there hung on to the chain. The chain had ten links. How many would have to break to drop the man into the abyss below? Only one. The law is like that chain; when you sinned the first time you broke the link and down you went, and you are in the place of condemnation if not saved. You never can fit yourself for the presence of God by any works of righteousness that you can do. The law says, "The man that doeth these things shall live in them," but men have failed to do, and therefore are condemned to die.

Now see the glorious message of reconciliation! "Christ hath redeemed us from the curse of the law!" How did He do it? "Being made a curse for us: for it is written, Cursed is every one that hangeth on a tree." Here was One who had never violated God's law, here was the holy, eternal Son of God, the delight of the Father's heart from all eternity, who came into the world, who became Man, for the express purpose of redeeming those who were under the curse of the law. He Himself said, "The Son of man came not to be ministered unto, but to minister, and to give his life a ransom for many" (Matt. 20:28). But if He Himself has violated that law, He is subject to its penalty and never can redeem us; but how careful the Word of God has been to show that He never came under that penalty. He was holy in nature from the moment He came into the world. The angel said to Mary, His mother, "That holy thing which shall be born of thee shall be called the Son of God" (Luke 1:35). His life was absolutely pure as He went through this scene. He magnified the law and made it honorable by a life of devotion to the will of God. "[He] was in all points tempted like as we are, yet without sin" (Heb. 4:15). Sinless, though tempted; and at last God "made him to be sin for us, who knew no sin; that we might be made the righteousness of God in him" (2 Cor. 5:21). He against whom God had nothing, voluntarily took our place, went to the cross, and there paid the penalty that we should have paid. If I had to pay, eternity would be too short for it, but He, the Eternal One, hung on the cross, settled to the utmost farthing every claim that the offended law had against me, and now I receive Him, trust Him as my Savior, and what is the result? I am delivered from the curse of the law.

> Free from the law, O happy condition!
> Jesus hath bled, and there is remission,
> Cursed by the law and bruised by the fall,
> Christ hath redeemed us once for all.
>
> Now we are free—there's no condemnation,
> Jesus provides a perfect salvation;
> "Come unto Me," oh, hear His sweet call!
> Come, and He saves us once for all.

Has your soul entered into this?

I shall never forget, after struggling for so long to work out a righteousness of my own, the joy that came to me when I was led to look by faith at yonder cross, an empty cross now.

> I saw One hanging on the tree,
>   In visions of my soul,
> Who turned His loving eyes on me
>   As near His cross I stole.

I knew He was there on my behalf. He, the sinless One, was suffering there for me, the sinner, and I looked up to Him. In faith I could say, "Lord Jesus, I am Thy sin; I am Thine unrighteousness. Thou hast none of Thine own, but art bearing mine." And I looked again, and that cross was empty and my Lord's body had been laid in the tomb. "He was delivered for our offenses," and buried out of sight as I deserved to be buried out of sight. But I looked again and that tomb too was empty, and He came forth in triumph, "[He] was raised again for our justification" (Rom. 4:25). I looked not to the cross now but to the throne of God, and by faith I saw Him seated there, a Man exalted at God's right hand, the same Man who stood mute in Pilate's judgment-hall, and did not say a word to clear Himself because I could not be cleared unless He died for me.

Who would want to work out a righteousness of his own when he can have one so much better through faith in the Lord Jesus Christ? "Christ hath redeemed us from the curse of the law, being made a curse for us: for it is written, Cursed is every one that hangeth on a tree."

And now because of that, the blessing of Abraham may come to the Gentiles in Christ Jesus; we may receive the promise of the Spirit through faith. "That the blessing of Abraham might come on the Gentiles through Jesus Christ; that we might receive the promise of the Spirit through faith." What is "the blessing of Abraham?" Long ago God had said, "In thee and in thy seed shall all nations of the earth be blessed." But centuries rolled by and the nations of the Gentiles were left outside; they were outside the pale, strangers to the covenant of promise, they knew nothing of the blessing of Abraham, nor what God had promised through his seed. But now Christ has died, not for Jews only but for the Gentiles also, and because of His work the message goes out to the whole world that God can save every one who believes on the Lord Jesus, and all believers become in faith the children of Abraham and are sealed by the Holy Spirit of God. The blessing of Abraham is justification by faith for every believer, even as "Abraham believed God, and it was counted unto him for righteousness" (Rom. 4:3). The apostle draws attention to the fact that when God said to Abraham, "In thy seed shall all nations of the earth be blessed," He was not referring merely to the nation that should spring from him but to one individual Person, for it had been settled in the purpose of God from eternity that the Christ was to be born of Abraham's lineage.

"Brethren, I speak after the manner of men; though it be but a man's covenant, yet if it be confirmed, no man disannulleth, or addeth thereto." When men make covenants we expect them to live up to them. God made a covenant of unconditional grace to Abraham long years before. Later the law came in, but did that invalidate the covenant of pure grace made to Abraham? "To Abraham and his seed were the promises made. He saith not, And to seeds, as of many; but as of one, And to thy seed, which is Christ." Through the Lord Jesus, then, the blessing of the covenant goes out to every poor sinner who will believe in Him. "And this I say, that the covenant, that was confirmed before of God in Christ, the law, which was four hundred and thirty years after, cannot disannul, that it should make the promise of none effect." God was not playing fast and loose with Abraham when He gave him this unconditional covenant of grace. He did not say, "If you do thus and so, and if you do not do certain things, all the world will be blessed through your seed." But He said, unconditionally, "In thee and in thy seed shall all nations of the earth be blessed." It is not a question at all of human effort; it is not a question of something we earn.

When the apostle discusses this same subject in Romans 4, he says, in the opening verses,

> What shall we say then that Abraham our father, as pertaining to the flesh, hath found? For if Abraham were justified by works, he hath whereof to glory; but not before God. For what saith the scripture? Abraham believed God, and it was counted unto him for righteousness. Now to him that worketh is the reward not reckoned of grace, but of debt. (Rom. 4:1–4)

What does that mean? It means that if you had to do something to earn your salvation you would not be saved by grace. Suppose you work six days for an employer, and at the end of that time he comes in a supercilious kind of attitude, hands you an envelope, and says, "You have been working well the last six days, here is a little gift, I want to give you this as a token of my grace." You look at it and find it contains your wages, and you say, "Sir, I do not understand; this is not a gift. I earned this." But the man says, "I want you to feel that it is an expression of my appreciation." "No," you would say, "you owe me this; you are in my debt, for I earned this money." If I could do anything to save my soul I would put God in debt to save me, but all God does for me He does in pure grace. And so we read, "To him that worketh not, but believeth on him that justifieth the ungodly, his faith is counted for righteousness" (Rom. 4:5). And though the law came four hundred and thirty years after this promise of grace for all nations through Abraham's seed, it did not alter God's purpose; it was given only in order to increase man's sense of his need, to make him realize his sinfulness and helplessness, and lead him to cast himself on the infinite grace of God.

"For if the inheritance be of the law, it is no more of promise: but God gave it to Abraham by promise." If it comes through self-effort it is not a question of promise at all. But God gave it to Abraham by promise, and, "The promise," Peter says, "is unto you, and to your children, and to all that are afar off, even as many as the Lord our God shall call" (Acts 2:39). Perhaps, reader, you have been struggling for years to fit yourself for God's presence, you have been trying hard to work out a righteousness of your own, "trying to be a Christian." Let me beg of you, stop trying, give it up! You cannot become a Christian by trying any more than you could become the Prince of Wales by trying. You are what you are by birth. You are what you are as a sinner by natural birth, and you become a child of God through second birth, through believing on the Lord Jesus Christ. The blessing of Abraham is yours when you receive it by faith.

The Law as Child-Leader Until Christ

Galatians 3:19–29

Wherefore then serveth the law? It was added because of transgressions, till the seed should come to whom the promise was made; and it was ordained by angels in the hand of a mediator. Now a mediator is not a mediator of one, but God is one. Is the law then against the promises of God? God forbid: for if there had been a law given which could have given life, verily righteousness should have been by the law. But the scripture hath concluded all under sin, that the promise by faith of Jesus Christ might be given to them that believe. But before faith came, we were kept under the law, shut up unto the faith which should afterwards be revealed. Wherefore the law was our schoolmaster to bring us unto Christ, that we might be justified by faith. But after that faith is come, we are no longer under a schoolmaster. For ye are all the children of God by faith in Christ Jesus. For as many of you as have been baptized into Christ have put on Christ. There is neither Jew nor Greek, there is neither bond nor free, there is neither male nor female: for ye are all one in Christ Jesus. And if ye be Christ's, then are ye Abraham's seed, and heirs according to the promise. (vv. 19–29)

We have been considering in our studies of the earlier part of this chapter the relationship that the law had, the law as given at Sinai, to the unconditional promise of grace which God gave to Abraham 430 years before, and we have seen that the law coming in afterward could not add to nor take away from the covenant already made. That naturally leads to the question of verse 19, "Wherefore then serveth the law?" If the law did not add anything to what God had given by promise to Abraham, and surely it could not take anything from it, what was its purpose? Why did God give it at all? The apostle answers, "It was added because of transgressions, till the seed should come to whom the promise was made; and it was ordained by angels in the hand of a mediator." I think perhaps we may understand it better if we read it, "It was added with a view to transgressions," in order that it might make men see the specific character of transgression, and thus deepen in each soul a sense of his sinfulness and his need.

We are all so ready to excuse ourselves, to say if we had known better we would not have done the wrong thing. How often you hear people say, "I do the best I know, and endeavor to do the best I can." But where has a man or woman ever been found who could honestly utter those sentences? Have you always done the best you knew? Have you always done the best you could? If you are absolutely honest before God, you know that you have not. Again and again we have all sinned against light and knowledge, we have known far better than we have done. Thus we have failed to glorify God, and by going contrary to His revealed will we have proven ourselves not only sinners but transgressors.

Both in the original language of the New Testament and that of the Old Testament, there is a word for "sin" which literally means to "miss the mark." I remember having this brought before me when working among the Laguna Indians of New Mexico. One day my interpreter, a bright Indian, said, "I am going to spend the day hunting; would you like to go with me?"

I am no hunter, but I went with him for the exercise. He had a fine new rifle which he was very eager to try out. He gave evidence of his prowess with that weapon. Standing on one side of a canyon he would say, "Do you see that creature moving yonder?"

At first I could not possibly see it, but as he pointed it out I would see something that was just a moving speck away over on the opposite wall.

He would say, "Wait a minute," and level his rifle, and the next moment I would see the creature that looked like a small speck leap into the air and then drop down dead. He was a wonderful shot with a rifle, but when we got home he said to me, "I want to show you what I can do with our old weapon, for I have kept up with the bow and arrow. That seems so typical of our people that I have wanted to keep it up."

So we went into the field, and the Indian hunter set up a very small twig of a willow, and enacted a scene something like that described in Scott's *Ivanhoe*. He fitted the arrow to the string and said, "Now I am going to split that twig in two." Letting fly the arrow, he shot right by the twig but did not touch it. "Oh," he said, "I have sinned."

For the moment I did not ask him why he used that expression.

Then he said, "I didn't take the wind into account, as I should have done." He fitted another arrow to the string, and let it fly, and split that twig right in two. I could hardly believe that any one could do such a thing.

He said, "There! I did not sin that time."

I said to him, "Why did you use that term *sin?* You were not doing anything wrong when you did not hit that wand. Why did you say, 'I sinned,' and when you did hit it, 'I didn't sin that time'?"

"Oh," he said, "I was thinking in Gowaik (that is the language of the Laguna Indians) and speaking in English. In our language 'to sin' means 'to miss the mark.'"

"That is a very singular thing," I said, "for in the Greek and Hebrew 'to sin' is 'to miss the mark.'"

That is what is involved in the expression, "All have sinned, and come short of the glory of God" (Rom. 3:23). But in the law we have something more than that. God has set up a standard of righteousness. The law with its ten definite ordinances, "Thou shalts and thou shalt nots," makes known to man exactly what God demands of him. Now if man sins knowing the revealed will of God, if he fails to obey that law, it is evident that he is not only a sinner but a transgressor. He has definitely violated a specific command of God; he has crossed over the line, as it were, and, "Sin by the commandment might become exceeding sinful" (Rom. 7:13). That was one reason for which God gave the law—that men might have a deeper sense of the seriousness of self-will which is the very essence of sin, of rebellion against God. When God gave the law He gave it in the hands of a mediator, and Moses sprinkled the book of the covenant and also the people with the blood of the covenant, testifying to the fact that if man fails to keep his side of the covenant he must die, but also signifying that God would provide a Savior, a Redeemer.

"Now a mediator is not a mediator of one, but God is one." Two contracting parties suggest the thought of the need of a mediator, but when God gave His promise to Abraham there was only one. God gave the Word, and there was nothing to do on Abraham's part but to receive it. He did not covenant with God that he would do thus and so in order that God's promise might be fulfilled, but God spoke directly to him and committed Himself when He said, "In thee shall all nations be blessed" (Gal. 3:8). The question arises, Is the law against the promises of God by bringing in certain terms which were not in the original promise? Does the law set the promises to one side? God forbid. But a certain principle was laid down in the law which declared that "the man that doeth them shall live in them" (v. 12), and if any man had been found to do these things perfectly he could have obtained life on the ground of the law. But the law said to man, "The soul that sinneth, it shall die" (Ezek. 18:4), and no man was ever found who could keep it. "If there had been a law given which could have given life, verily righteousness should have been by the law."

A gentleman said to me in California one night, "I do not like this idea of being saved by Another. All my life I have never wanted to feel indebted to other people for anything. I do not want anybody's charity, and when it comes to spiritual things I do not want to be saved through the merits of anybody else. According to what you said tonight, if I keep the law perfectly I will live and will owe nothing to any one. Is that right?"

I said, "Well, yes, it is."

He said, "I am going to start in on that."

I said, "How old are you?"

"Around forty."

"Suppose you came to years of accountability somewhere around twelve; you are nearly thirty years too late to begin, and Scripture says, 'Cursed is every one that continueth not in all things which are written in the book of the law to do them' (v. 10). Therefore, because the law cannot give life, you will never be able to earn anything on that ground." He went away very disgruntled.

"But the scripture hath concluded all under sin." If God has concluded all under sin, must all men be lost? No, all have been concluded under sin "that the promise by faith of Jesus Christ might be given to them that believe." God would have all men recognize their sinfulness in order that all might realize their need and come to Him proving His grace. He puts all men on one common level. Romans says, "There is no difference: for all have sinned" (3:22–23). Men imagine that there are a great many differences. One man says, "Do you mean to tell me that there is no difference between a moral man and a poor reprobate in the gutter?" Of course there is a great deal of difference, not only as far as the standard of society is concerned, but also as to their own happiness and the estimate of their neighbors; but when it comes to a question of righteousness, "There is no difference: for all have sinned." All may not have sinned in the same way, they may not have committed exactly the same transgressions, but "all have sinned," all have violated God's law.

A gentleman once said to a cousin of his, "I do not like that idea about there being no difference; it is repugnant to me. Do you mean to tell me that having tried all my life to live a decent and respectable life, God does not see any difference between me and people living lives of sin and iniquity?"

She said to him, "Suppose that you and I were walking down the street together, and we passed some place of interest, perhaps a museum, that we were eager to see. We went to the window and inquired about the admission fee, and were told it was $1.00. I looked into my purse and said, 'Oh, I have left my money at home; I have only 25 cents.' You looked at your money and found you had only 70 cents. Which one of us would go in first?"

"Well," he said, "under such circumstances neither of us would get in."

"There would be no difference, and yet you have a great deal more money than I; but as far as having what was necessary to pay our way in, there is no difference."

God demands absolute righteousness of sinners before they enter heaven. "There shall in no wise enter into it any thing that defileth" (Rev. 21:27). You may have your 95 cents worth of righteousness while I do not have a nickel's worth of it, but neither of us can get in unless we have our hundred cents, and there is no difference. "There is none righteous, no, not one" (Rom. 3:10). Remember that God has said that, not some zealous, earnest preacher or evangelist, but God Himself by the Holy Spirit. And the law was given to demonstrate that fact. But if men take the place of unrighteousness before God, if they take the place of being lost sinners, and own their sin and guilt, what then? "The Scripture hath concluded all under sin, that the promise by faith of Jesus Christ might be given to them that believe." In other words, when men come to the place where they realize the fact that they cannot earn eternal life by any effort of their own, and are ready to receive it as a free gift, that moment it is theirs. "He that believeth on the Son hath everlasting life" (John 3:36). "Verily, verily, I say unto you, he that heareth my word, and believeth him that sent me, hath everlasting life, and shall not come into condemnation; but is passed from death unto life" (John 5:24).

But now the apostle shows another use for the law. Paul says in verse 23, "But before faith came," that is, "before *the* faith," because it was made known clearly and definitely that God was justifying men by faith alone in His blessed Son, "we were kept under the law"—he speaks now as a Jew—"we were kept under the law, shut up unto the faith which should afterwards be revealed." The Gentiles at that time did not have the law, but the Jews did. God gave the Jew that law, and he was looked upon as a minor child under rules and regulations. "Wherefore the law was our schoolmaster to bring us unto Christ, that we might be justified by faith." That word rendered "schoolmaster" is exactly the word that we have Anglicized by the term "pedagogue," a school teacher. But the original word was not exactly a school teacher, it really means a child leader, a child director, and was the name applied in ancient Greek households to a slave who had the care of the minor children. He was to watch over the morals of the child, protect him from association with others who were not fit for his companionship, and take him day by day from the house to the schoolroom. He there turned him over to the schoolmaster, but at the end of the day he would get him and bring him back home again. The apostle says here, and very beautifully, I think, "The law was our child leader, our child director, until Christ." That is, God did not leave His people without a code of morals until Jesus came to set before us the most wonderful moral code the world has ever known, and the law served in a very real way to protect and keep them from much of the immorality, iniquity, vileness, and corruption found in the heathen life round about them. As long as the people lived in obedience, in any measure, to that law, they were saved from a great deal of wickedness and evil.

"The law was our [child leader]," perhaps not exactly to *bring* us to Christ, but, "The law was our [child leader *until*] Christ." "The law was given by Moses, but grace and truth came by Jesus Christ" (John 1:17). Now Christ has come we have come to the door of the schoolroom of grace, and we have learned the blessed truth of justification by faith alone in Him whom God has set forth to be the propitiation for our sins. We are no longer under a child director.

We are here told that we are not only freed from the law as a means of attempting to secure justification, but are also freed from that law as a means of sanctification, for we have so much higher a standard in Christ risen from the dead, and are to be occupied with Him. As we are taken up with Him the grace of God teaches us that, "Denying ungodliness and worldly lusts, we should live soberly, righteously, and godly, in this present world" (Titus 2:12). For instance, suppose I as a Christian by some strange mishap had never even heard of the Ten Commandments. Suppose it were possible that I had never known of them, but on the other hand I had been taught the wonderful story of the gospel, and had been entrusted with some of the books of the New Testament showing how a Christian ought to live. If I walk in obedience to this revelation, I live on a higher, on a holier, plane than he who only had the Ten Commandments. Anyone having the wonderful teaching that came from the lips of the Lord Jesus Christ, and the marvelous unfolding of the epistles showing what a Christian ought to be, has this new standard of holiness, which is not the law given at Sinai, but the risen Christ at God's right hand, and as I am walking in obedience to Him my life will be a righteous life, and so, "After that faith is come, we are no longer under a schoolmaster."

Then he adds, "Ye are all the children [sons] of God by faith in Christ Jesus," from Him we receive life. To whom does God communicate eternal life? To all who put their trust in His blessed Son. "He that hath the Son hath life; and he that hath not the Son of God hath not life" (1 John 5:12). And so we can see why our Lord Jesus stresses, "Except a man be born again, he cannot see the kingdom of God" (John 3:3). There must be the impartation of the divine life. This makes us members of God's family—a new and wonderful relationship.

"For as many of you as have been baptized into Christ have put on Christ." He probably has two thoughts in mind here. Outwardly we put on Christ in our baptism. That ordinance indicates that we professedly have received the Lord Jesus Christ, but I think also he has in view the baptism of the Holy Spirit, and by that we are actually made members of Christ and, in the fullest, deepest sense, we put on Christ. And now as members of that new creation, "there is neither Jew nor Greek," national distinctions no longer come in. In this connection there is "neither Jew nor Greek, there is neither bond nor free, there is neither male nor female: for ye are all one in Christ Jesus." He does not ignore natural distinctions. Of course we still retain our natural place in society, we remain servants or masters, we remain male or female, but as to our place in the new creation, God takes none of these distinctions into account. All who believe in the Lord Jesus Christ are made one in Him, "members of his body, of his flesh, and of his bones" (Eph. 5:30). How we need to remember this!

"Ye are all one in Christ Jesus. And if ye be Christ's, then are ye Abraham's seed, and heirs according to the promise." To be "in Christ" and to be "Christ's," comes to exactly the same thing, "all one in Christ Jesus." "And if ye be Christ's [if you belong to Him], then are ye Abraham's seed, and heirs according to the promise." Because you too have believed God as Abraham did (Abraham "believed God, and it was counted unto him for righteousness." [Rom. 4:3]), it is counted to you for righteousness. And so every believer forms part of Abraham's spiritual seed. There is both the spiritual and the natural seed of Abraham. "They which be of faith are blessed with [believing] Abraham" (Gal. 3:9). I hope we are clear as to this distinction between law and grace.

Some years ago I took with me to Oakland, California, a Navajo Indian. One Sunday evening he went to our young people's meeting. They were talking about this epistle to the Galatians, about law and grace, but they were not very clear about it, and finally one turned to the Indian and said, "I wonder whether our Indian friend has anything to say about this."

He rose to his feet and said, "Well, my friends, I have been listening very carefully, because I am here to learn all I can in order to take it back to my people. I do not understand what you are talking about, and I do not think you do yourselves. But concerning this law and grace, let me see if I can make it clear. I think it is like this. When Mr. Ironside brought me from my home we took the longest railroad journey I ever took. We got out at Barstow, and there I saw the most beautiful railroad station with a hotel above it that I have ever seen. I walked all around and saw at one end a sign, 'Do not spit here.' I looked at that sign and then looked down at the ground and saw many had spitted there, and before I think what I am doing I have spitted myself. Isn't that strange when the sign say, 'Do not spit here'? I come to Oakland and go to the home of the lady who invited me to dinner today and I am in the nicest home I have ever been in my life. Such beautiful furniture and carpets I hate to step on them. I sank into a comfortable chair, and the lady said, 'Now, John, you sit there while I go out and see whether the maid has dinner ready.' I look around at the beautiful pictures, at the grand piano, and I walk all around those rooms. I am looking for a sign; the sign I am looking for is, 'Do not spit here,' but I look around those two beautiful drawing rooms, and cannot find a sign like this. I think, What a pity when this is such a beautiful home to have people spitting all over it—too bad they don't put up a sign! So I look all over that carpet but cannot find that anybody has spitted there. What a funny thing! Where the sign says, 'Do not spit,' a lot of people spitted; here where there is no sign, nobody spitted. Now I understand! That sign is law, but inside the home it is grace. They love their beautiful home and want to keep it clean. I think that explains this law and grace business," and he sat down.

THE ADOPTION OF SONS

Galatians 4:1–7

Now I say, that the heir, as long as he is a child, differeth nothing from a servant, though he be lord of all; but is under tutors and governors until the time appointed of the father. Even so we, when we were children, were in bondage under the elements of the world: but when the fulness of the time was come, God sent forth his Son, made of a woman, made under the law, to redeem them that were under the law, that we might receive the adoption of sons. And because ye are sons, God hath sent forth the Spirit of his Son into your hearts, crying, Abba, Father. Wherefore thou art no more a servant, but a son; and if a son, then an heir of God through Christ. (vv. 1–7)

In this section of the epistle the apostle makes a very interesting distinction, which, if thoroughly understood, will help greatly in enabling us to see the relative place of Old Testament believers and that of those in the present glorious dispensation of the grace of God. We need to remember that in all dispensations it was necessary that men be born again in order to become the children of God, and new birth has always been, on the part of adults at least, by faith in the divine revelation. We are told in James 1:18, "Of his own will begat he us with the word of truth, that we should be a kind of firstfruits of his creatures." What is true of us in this age has been true of believers in all ages. Each one was begotten by the Word of truth. Of course, in the case of infants not yet come to years of accountability, God acts in sovereignty, regenerating them by His divine power apart from personal faith in the Word when they are too young to know it. Jesus has said, "It is not the will of your Father which is in heaven, that one of these little ones should perish" (Matt. 18:14), but it is just as necessary that children be born again as in the case of adults, for, "That which is born of the flesh is flesh; and that which is born of the Spirit is spirit" (John 3:6). There must be new birth on the part of every person who would enter the kingdom of God. But there are great dispensational distinctions marked out in Holy Scripture. In Old Testament times believers were all God's children, but they were not definitely recognized as His sons. In this age it is different. All of God's children are also His sons. Do you ask what is the difference? Well, the distinction is one that we today perhaps would not think of making, but when Paul wrote the epistle to the Galatians all his readers would understand it very clearly. In that day, minor children were not recognized as their father's heirs until, when they came of age, he took them down to the forum, answering to our courthouse, and there officially adopted them as his sons. From that time on they were no longer considered as minor children, but recognized as heirs. Old Testament saints, the apostle shows us, were in the position of children. New Testament saints, since the coming of the Holy Spirit at Pentecost, are acknowledged by God as His sons by adoption. The Holy Spirit Himself is the Spirit of adoption. When He is received in faith, at the very moment of our conversion we are marked out as God's sons and heirs. This is confirmed in Romans 8:14–17:

> For as many as are led by the Spirit of God, they are the sons of God. For ye have not received the spirit of bondage again to fear; but ye have received the Spirit of adoption, whereby we cry, Abba, Father. The Spirit itself beareth witness with our spirit, that we are the children of God: and if children, then heirs; heirs of God, and joint-heirs with Christ; if so be that we suffer with him, that we may be also glorified together.

The divinely-directed reasoning of the apostle in these first seven verses in Galatians 4 is very striking and beautiful in its orderly presentation of the theme. He tells us, "Now I say, that the heir, as long as he is a child, differeth nothing from a servant [that is, a bondman], though he be lord of all." Take a young child in the home before he has attained his majority. He may be heir actually to vast wealth, but he is not permitted to have his own way, nor enter into the possession of his patrimony. He is to be kept in the place of subjection for discipline and training. His place in the home is practically no different than that of a servant. In fact, he himself has to be subject to the servant, as verse 2 tells us; he is under guardians and stewards, or tutors, until the time appointed of the father. This is all perfectly plain and does not take an erudite mind to understand it. Then note the application. The apostle shows that the people of Israel, God's earthly people, were in this state of nonage. The apostle Paul identifies himself with these as a Jew and says, "Even so we, when we were children, were in bondage under the elements [or principles] of the world." That is, they were under the law, and the law speaks to man in the flesh. It was given by God in order to impress upon him his duties and responsibilities. It had no power in itself to produce the new life, though it could guide the children of God and show them the path they should take through the world. It was really, however, an almost intolerable bondage to those who did not enter into the spiritual side of it. But now since the new age has come in, the age of grace, a wonderful change has been brought about. We read: "But when the fulness of the time was come, God sent forth his Son, [born] of a woman, [born] under the law, to redeem them that were under the law, that we might receive the adoption of sons." "The fulness of the time" was, of course, the completion of the prophetic periods as given in the Old Testament. One would think particularly of the great prophecy of the seventy weeks of Daniel. When at last the time had arrived that Messiah was destined to appear, God fulfilled His Word by sending His Son into this scene to be born of a woman, and that woman an Israelite under law.

Now observe one thing here. We meet certain professed Christians today who deny what is called the Eternal Sonship of Christ. They tell us He was not Son from eternity. They admit He was the Word, as set forth in John 1:1, but they say He became the Son when He was born on earth. Verse 4 definitely denies any such teaching. "God sent forth his Son, [to be born] of a woman." He was the Son before He ever stooped from the heights of glory to the virgin's womb. It was the Son who came in grace to become Man in order that we might be saved. This same truth is set forth in 1 John 4:9–10: "In this was manifested the love of God toward us, because that God sent his only begotten Son into the world, that we might live through him. Herein is love, not that we loved God, but that he loved us, and sent his Son to be the propitiation for our sins." Nothing could be clearer than the two definite statements in these verses. God sent His Son, sent Him into the world, sent Him from heaven, even as John 3:16 declares:

"God so loved the world, that he gave his only begotten Son." We dishonor the Lord Jesus Christ if we deny His Eternal Sonship. If He be not the Eternal Son, then God is not the Eternal Father. Someone has well asked, "Had the Father no bosom till Jesus was born in Bethlehem?" He came from the bosom of the Father, to be born into this world, in order that He might be our Kinsman-Redeemer.

He was born under the law. He took His place before God here on earth as an Israelite, subject to the law of God. He kept that law perfectly; sinless Himself, He never could come under its curse because of His own failure. Therefore, He was able to go to the cross and give Himself up to death to bear the curse of the broken law, that He might redeem them that were under the law, "that we," says the apostle, "might receive the adoption of sons." He met all that was against His people and brought them out into a place of full liberty where God could publicly own them as His sons, no longer children in the servant's place but heirs of God, joint-heirs with Jesus Christ. The testimony to this was the giving of the Holy Spirit. So in verse 6 we read, "And because ye are sons, God hath sent forth the Spirit of His Son into your hearts, crying, Abba, Father." This is true of all believers, for we need to remember that since the bringing in of the new dispensation in all its fullness, every believer is indwelt by the Holy Spirit, and thus sealed and anointed. "If any man have not the Spirit of Christ," we are told, "he is none of his" (Rom. 8:9). So there is no such person in the world today as a true Christian who is not indwelt by the Spirit of God. We have the Spirit of the Son, and because He dwells in our hearts we now look up with adoring love into the face of God and cry "Abba, Father." "Abba" is the Hebrew word for "Father." Our English word is the translation of the Greek *pateer,* and so we have Jew and Gentile united through grace, addressing God as members of one family, as His children by birth and His sons by adoption, and crying, "Abba, Father."

The apostle's conclusion follows very naturally: "Wherefore thou art no more a servant, but a son; and if a son, then an heir of God through Christ." The old condition, which prevailed throughout the centuries before Jesus came into the world and died for all our sins upon the cross, rose again for our justification, ascended to heaven, and in unity with the Father sent the Holy Spirit, that has come to an end. Believers are no longer in the servant's place, but by the reception of the Spirit are God's recognized sons, and so heirs of all His possessions through Christ Jesus our Lord.

In this connection it is interesting to notice that after the resurrection of the Lord Jesus from the dead, He said to Mary, "Go to my brethren, and say unto them, I ascend unto my Father, and your Father; and to my God, and your God" (John 20:17). In this He fulfilled the prophecy written so long before, "I will declare thy name unto my brethren" (Ps. 22:22). Though the Holy Spirit had not yet come, the Lord anticipates the full glory of the new dispensation by recognizing all the redeemed as His brethren, and thus He speaks of "My Father and your Father, My God and your God." Notice, He does not say, *our* Father and *our* God. There was good reason for this. God was His Father in a unique sense; He was His Father from eternity. This is not true of us. He is our Father when we receive Christ in faith as our Savior. And so in regard to the other expression, "My God." It is written, "In the beginning was the Word, and the Word was with God, and the Word was God." Therefore God was His God in a different sense to that in which He is our God. He is our God because He is our Creator. We are merely creatures, while He Himself created all things. And so while there cannot be exactly the same relationship, yet the same Person who is His Father and His God is now our Father and our God, because we are sons of God through faith in Christ Jesus. Oh, may our hearts enter more into the preciousness of this, and as we realize something of the dignity of this wonderful place that God has given us, may we seek grace to so live in this scene as to bring glory to His name.

Remember, there is a certain sense in which He has entrusted the honor of His name to us. He said to Israel of old, "Thou shalt not take the name of the LORD thy God in vain." This did not refer to what we call swearing or profanity, but they were called by the name of the Lord and were responsible to magnify His name. Instead of that, the apostle Paul says of them, "The name of God is blasphemed among the Gentiles through you." That is, the Gentiles saw so much that was wicked and corrupt in the behavior of God's earthly people that they said, "If these people are like their God, then He must be a very unholy Being indeed." Oh, my brethren, are we so behaving ourselves that men, "seeing our good works, glorify our Father which is in heaven?" Do they say, as they behold the grace of God in our lives, "How marvelous must be the love and the holiness of the God to whom these people belong, and whose sons they profess to be!" It is as we walk in obedience to His Word that we magnify the grace which has saved us and put us into this blessed place of sons and heirs.

THE ELEMENTS OF THE WORLD

Galatians 4:8–20

Howbeit then, when ye knew not God, ye did service unto them which by nature are no gods. But now, after that ye have known God, or rather are known of God, how turn ye again to the weak and beggarly elements, whereunto ye desire again to be in bondage? Ye observe days, and months, and times, and years. I am afraid of you, lest I have bestowed upon you labour in vain. Brethren, I beseech you, be as I am; for I am as ye are: ye have not injured me at all. Ye know how through infirmity of the flesh I preached the gospel unto you at the first. And my temptation which was in my flesh ye despised not, nor rejected; but received me as an angel of God, even as Christ Jesus. Where is then the blessedness ye spake of? for I bear you record, that, if it had been possible, ye would have plucked out your own eyes, and have given them to me. Am I therefore become your enemy, because I tell you the truth? They zealously affect you, but not well; yea, they would exclude you, that ye might affect them. But it is good to be zealously affected always in a good thing, and not only when I am present with you. My little children, of whom I travail in birth again until Christ be formed in you,

I desire to be present with you now, and to change my voice; for I stand in doubt of you. (vv. 8–20)

Howbeit then, when ye knew not God, ye did service unto them which by nature are no gods." We have seen in this epistle that the Galatians, who had been brought out of heathen darkness into the light and liberty of the gospel through the ministry of the apostle Paul, had fallen under the charm—shall I say?—of certain Judaizing teachers who were carrying them into subjection to the law of Moses, telling them that unless they were circumcised and kept the law of Moses they could not be saved, that while they began in faith, they had to complete their salvation through works of their own, acquiring merit by obedience to the commands of the law. The apostle has been showing them that the law could only condemn, could only kill, could not justify, could not give life, neither could it sanctify, and that our sanctification is as truly by faith as is our justification.

Now he reasons with them, trying to show the folly of their course in giving up Christianity with all its liberty and light for the twilight and bondage of Judaism. "Why," he says, "you were heathen when I came to you. You were enslaved to heathen customs, you served those that you esteemed to be gods who really are not gods, you were worshipers of idols, and you know that in those days you were misled by pagan priest craft. There were certain things you could not eat, places you could not go, things you could not touch. There were different kinds of offerings that you had to bring, there were charms against evil spirits, and amulets, and talismans. You were slaves to worldly customs in those days of your heathenism. The thing that amazes me is that you should be willing to go into another bondage after having known something of the liberty of grace."

"But now, after that ye have known God, or rather are known of God, how turn ye again to the weak and beggarly elements, whereunto ye desire again to be in bondage?" Notice that expression, "After that ye have known God, or rather are known of God." There are the two sides to it. We often say to people, "Do you know Jesus?" But it means more to realize that Jesus knows you, to be able to say, "Thank God, He knows me, and He knew about me in my sin, and He loved me and gave Himself for me." We sometimes say, "Have you found Jesus?" Of course the Word of God says, "Seek, and ye shall find," and the Lord bids us to "call upon Him while He is near," but it is a more wonderful truth that He seeks us. We have heard of the little boy who was approached by a Christian worker who said to him, "My boy, have you found Jesus?" And the little fellow looked up with a perturbed expression and said, "Why, please, sir, I didn't know He was lost, but I was, and He found me." That is it.

> I was lost, but Jesus found me,
>> Found the sheep that went astray;
>> Threw His loving arms around me,
>> Drew me back into His way.

God knew me long before I knew Him. He knows me now, since I have trusted Christ, as His child, and Paul says, "Isn't it a shame that after you have known God, or rather have been known of God, after you have come into this blessed relationship with Him as your Father, if you really know what it is to be born again, isn't it strange that you would turn now to as legal a system as that from which you were delivered when first brought to a saving knowledge of the Lord Jesus Christ?" "How turn ye again to the weak and beggarly elements, whereunto ye desire again to be in bondage?" Someone might say, "But what do you mean? They were turning to law, to observing Jewish feasts and Jewish Sabbath, Jewish ceremonies. But they never knew those things in their heathen days. Why does he say, 'How turn ye *again*?" The principle was exactly the same. Why do the heathen go through their forms and ceremonies? Because they hope to gain merit and save their souls. Why did the Jews go through all their rites and ceremonies? That they might please God in that way, and so gain merit and eventually save their souls. The principle is just the same, whether you try to save yourself by offering your own child or the dearest thing you have on a heathen altar, whether you keep the seventh-day Sabbath, as some people do today, and thereby hope to save themselves, or whether you observe the heathen feast days and hope to please the heathen gods thereby. The Jewish festivals have been fulfilled in Christ, and we are not going back to them, hoping to please God by their observance. They had their place once, and men of faith could observe them in obedience to the Word of God, but that place is not theirs now, because "Christ is the end of the law for righteousness to every one that believeth" (Rom. 10:4). All these ceremonies were merely shadows of things to come. Now that the reality is come, why go back to the shadow? We are not going to be occupied with the type since we have the Antitype; we are not going to be occupied with pictures when we have the Reality. The worldly principle, of course, is to try to merit salvation by works of your own.

There are only two religions in the world, the true and the false. All forms of false religion are alike, they all say, "Something in my hand I bring," the only difference being in what that something is. But the true religion, the revelation from heaven, leads a man to sing, "Nothing in my hand I bring." Christianity says, "Not by works of righteousness which we have done, but according to his mercy he saved us, by the washing of regeneration, and renewing of the Holy Ghost" (Titus 3:5). We see Christians today who turn to symbols and pictures as a means of helping them spiritually, but they are just going back to the elements of the world. If you were to ask a heathen, "Is this idol your god?" some would say, "Yes," but an intelligent heathen would reply, "No, it is not exactly that I consider that idol as my god, but it represents my god; it helps me to enter into communion with my god." You see just the same thing in Christendom where some churches are filled with images. They are not images of Mars, Jupiter, Venus, Isis, or Osiris, but images just the same—images of Saint Joseph, Saint Barnabas, Saint Paul, the twelve apostles, the blessed Virgin Mary, and even of Christ. Candles are burning in front of them and people bow before them. We ask, "Why do you not worship God? Why worship these images?" And they answer, "We do not worship them; we reverence them, and they are simply aids to worship. These images help to stir up our spirits and help us to worship."

I heard a Protestant minister speaking to a group of ministers and he said, "I find that it is very helpful to have before me a very beautiful picture of the thorn-crowned Christ." He mentioned a painting by a certain artist, and said, "I have that framed; and when I want to come to the Lord I like to drop everything else and sit and contemplate that picture for a while, and I begin to realize more and more what He has done for me. That draws out my heart in worship and adoration." "How turn ye again to the weak and beggarly elements, whereunto ye desire again to be in bondage?" There is no painter on earth who can paint my Christ. You need to go to the Bible to get that picture. If you want to be stirred up and put in a worshipful spirit, sit down over your Bible and read the fifty-third chapter of Isaiah, or the account in the Gospels of what Christ accomplished, and as you are occupied with the truth of God your heart will be drawn out in worship. You do not need pictures to help you to worship. These are just the "weak and beggarly elements" of the world. In the dispensation of the grace of our Lord Jesus Christ we are to worship in "spirit and in truth."

So the apostle says, "I am sorry to see you go back to these things"—"Ye observe days, and months, and times, and years." That is, they were going back to the Jewish Sabbath and other holy days and festivals, the Jewish Sabbatical year and the year of Jubilee. But, you see, these things are not binding on us today. Why? Because the Sabbath day of the Jews has found its fulfillment in Him who said, "Come unto me, all ye that labour and are heavy laden, and I will give you rest" (Matt. 11:28). "There remaineth therefore a rest (a true Sabbath-keeping) to the people of God" (Heb. 4:9). We have found our Sabbath in Christ, and so we observe the first day of the week, the day of His resurrection, not in order to gain merit but because we are glad to have the privilege of coming together as a company of worshiping believers and to take advantage of the opportunity to preach the gospel of the grace of God. That seventh-day Sabbath was the memorial of Israel's deliverance from Egypt. That does not apply to us, but we have found its fulfillment in Christ. Some may ask, "Are you quite certain that the Sabbath of the law is included among the shadows?" Yes, turn to Colossians 2:16–17: "Let no man therefore judge you in meat, or in drink, or in respect of an holy day, or of the new moon, or of the sabbath days: which are a shadow of things to come; but the body is of Christ." Do you not see?—it was the Sabbath of old, one day's rest in seven. Now I have Jesus, and I have seven days' rest in seven. I have rest in Him continually and am delivered from the Sabbath of the law.

Then there were sacred months. There was the month in which they had the Passover and the Feast of Firstfruits. Then the seventh month, in which was the great day of Atonement and the Feast of Tabernacles. But all of which those months and feasts speak has been fulfilled in Christ. He is the true Passover: "Christ our passover is sacrificed for us: therefore let us keep the feast, not with old leaven, neither with the leaven of malice and wickedness; but with the unleavened bread of sincerity and truth" (1 Cor. 5:7–8). The Feast of Firstfruits had its fulfillment in the resurrection of Christ, and it was He who said, "Except a corn of wheat fall into the ground and die, it abideth alone: but if it die, it bringeth forth much fruit" (John 12:24). Christ fell into the ground in death, and now has become the firstfruits of them that slept, and we worship with adoring gratitude for all that this means to us. The great day of Atonement has had its fulfillment in the cross. The Lord Jesus Christ was the sacrificed Victim whose precious blood makes atonement for the soul. We read, "The life of the flesh is in the blood: and I have given it to you upon the altar to make an atonement for your souls: for it is the blood that maketh an atonement for the soul" (Lev. 17:11). That is all fulfilled in Jesus. And He is the true fulfillment of the Feast of Tabernacles, the feast which carries us on to His coming back again when He will bring in everlasting righteousness. They were all given to point forward to the coming of the blessed Son of God, and His wondrous work.

"Ye observe days, and months, and times, and years." Many in Israel had fallen into the evil habit of consulting astrologers and others, and so were known as observers of times, but that was distinctly contrary to God's mind, and He links it up with demons. Christians have nothing to do with anything like that. Then they observed sacred years. There was the Sabbatical year; every seventh year had to be set apart as a Sabbath to the Lord. You cannot pick out certain parts of the law and keep them only; if you are bound to keep the seventh-day Sabbath, you are bound to keep the seventh-year Sabbath also. But Paul says that as Christians we are delivered from all this. It was only bondage and we are free from it.

"I am afraid of you, lest I have bestowed upon you labour in vain." He really stood in doubt as to whether they were truly converted. He remembered how they had confessed their sins, and the joy they had, and now he says, "Was that not genuine?" One may often feel like that about people. Some make a good start and apparently seem to be real Christians, but the next thing you know they are taken up with some most unscriptural thing, and you wonder whether it was all a mistake. If people are saved, they are sealed by the Holy Spirit. He is the Spirit of Truth and He comes to guide them into all truth. Thank God, sometimes they are recovered, and then you know they were real, but if never recovered, we read, "They went out from us, but they were not of us; for if they had been of us, they would no doubt have continued with us: but they went out, that they might be made manifest that they were not all of us" (1 John 2:19).

Now he turns directly to these converts of his, and in the most tender way he says, "Brethren, I beseech you, be as I am; for I am as ye are: ye have not injured me at all." What does he mean? He is practically saying, "There was a time in my life when I observed all these things that you are going into now; when all my hope of heaven was based upon working out a righteousness of my own; and I was very punctilious about all these things that you now are taking up. I observed the Passover, I kept the Feast of Firstfruits, the ordinances of the great day of the Atonement, and kept the Feast of Tabernacles. I did all these things that you are undertaking to do. I was careful about meats and drink, I looked upon certain foods as unclean and would have nothing to do with them, but I came to you as one of you. You did not know anything about the law, and I came to you as a man utterly delivered from the law of Moses, completely freed from it. I wish you would come over to where I am. Take your place now with me; I am not under law but under grace, and I want you to be under grace rather than under law." Before God, they were actually so, of course, if truly saved, but he would have them so in spirit.

He tells us elsewhere how he stood:

> Unto the Jews I became as a Jew, that I might gain the Jews; to them that are under the law, as under the law, that I might gain them that are under the law; to them that are without law, as without law, (being not without law to God, but under the law to Christ,) that I might gain them that are without law. . . . I am made all things to all men, that I might by all means save some. (1 Cor. 9:20–22)

Let me illustrate Paul's position. He stands in the center between the two extremes. Over to the right are those under the law, the Jews; to the left are those without the law, the Gentiles, who do not know anything about the law of Moses. Now he says, "I do not belong in either company since I am saved by grace, but stand here between the two, and being regenerated I am subject to Christ. In order that I may reach the Jew I go over there where he is, and am willing to sit down with him and partake of the kind of food he eats, and to go with him to his synagogue, in order that I may have an opportunity to preach to him. And I will use the law of Moses to show him his sin, and the prophets to show him the Savior. Then I go to the Gentiles, but I do not preach the law of Moses to them." He could say, "When I came among you I took my place as a man not under law but in the liberty of grace, and preached Christ to you as the Savior of all who believe. I wish you would appreciate that enough to stand with me. You leave me and go to the place God took me out of before He saved me. Do you not see the mistake you are making? You are giving up grace for law."

"Ye know how through infirmity of the flesh I preached the gospel unto you at the first. And my temptation which was in my flesh ye despised not, nor rejected; but received me as an angel of God, even as Christ Jesus." He sought to touch their hearts by reminding them of those early days when he came to Antioch in Pisidia, and to Iconium, Lystra, and Derbe, and preached the Word among them. All of these were Galatian cities. Did he come with pomp and ceremony, marvelous costumes, and candles and images? No, nothing like that. He came not as a great and mighty ecclesiastic, as one professing to have authority over them, but as a lowly man preaching Christ and Him crucified. "Ye know how through infirmity of the flesh I preached the gospel unto you at the first."

Paul was used of God to heal many sick people, but he never healed himself, and did not ask anybody to heal him except God. He prayed for deliverance three times, but God said, "I am not going to deliver you but—'My grace is sufficient for thee,'" and Paul answered, "Most gladly therefore will I rather glory in my infirmities, that the power of Christ may rest upon me" (2 Cor. 12:9). He was a sick man for years as he preached the gospel. He would come in among people, weak and tired and worn, and if there was not money enough to support him he would go to work and make tents to earn money for bread, and then at night would go and look for people to whom to preach Christ. He commended the gospel to these Galatians by his self-denying service and his readiness to suffer. As they (in those days, poor heathen) looked upon him they wondered that he should so love them, and they marveled at his message, and believed it, and were saved. Now he says, "You have lost all that; you do not care anything about me any more; you have gone off after these false teachers, and you have lost your joy." "Where is then the blessedness ye spake of? for I bear you record, that, if it had been possible, ye would have plucked out your own eyes, and have given them to me." I take it that the suffering he endured had to do with his eyes. He probably had some affliction of the eyes that made it difficult for him to read and to see an audience, and it made his appearance mean when he stood upon the platform. Possibly they said, "Poor Paul! If we could give him our eyes we would gladly do so!" That is the way they once felt. "Am I therefore become your enemy, because I tell you the truth?" It was these evil teachers that had upset them.

"They zealously affect you, but not well; yea, they would exclude you, that ye might affect them." In other words, they have come to make a prey of you with their false teaching, trying to affect you adversely in order that you might rally around them, for they want to get up a little party of their own. They are not seeking your good, but trying to extend their own influence. "It is good to be zealously affected always in a good thing, and not only when I am present with you." That is, it is good for a man to be zealous in what is right, it is good to go after people with the truth and bring them into the light, and they who had started in the truth should have continued in it.

And now in his deep affliction he exclaims, "My little children, of whom I travail in birth again until Christ be formed in you." In other words, I remember when you were saved, I went through the very pangs of birth in my soul, and now I am going through it all again because I am in such anxiety about you. "I desire to be present with you now, and to change my voice; for I stand in doubt of you." In other words, "I am writing some strong things to you, but I would like to talk tenderly, lovingly, to you if I were only there. I am not sure about you." False religion never can give certainty, but the blessed, glorious gospel of the grace of God does. It fully assures us of complete and final salvation if we believe God. Who then would turn away deliberately from the liberty that we have in Christ to the bondage of some false system?

LECTURE 11

A DIVINE ALLEGORY

Galatians 4:21–31

Tell me, ye that desire to be under the law, do ye not hear the law? For it
is written, that Abraham had two sons, the one by a bondmaid, the
other by a freewoman. But he who was of the bondwoman was born
after the flesh; but he of the freewoman was by promise. Which things
are an allegory: for these are the two covenants; the one from the mount
Sinai, which gendereth to bondage, which is Agar. For this Agar is mount
Sinai in Arabia, and answereth to Jerusalem which now is, and is in
bondage with her children. But Jerusalem which is above is free, which
is the mother of us all. For it is written, Rejoice, thou barren that bearest
not; break forth and cry, thou that travailest not: for the desolate hath
many more children than she which hath an husband. Now we, brethren, as Isaac was, are the children of promise. But as then he that was
born after the flesh persecuted him that was born after the Spirit, even
so it is now. Nevertheless what saith the scripture? Cast out the bondwoman and her son: for the son of the bondwoman shall not be heir
with the son of the freewoman. So then, brethren, we are not children
of the bondwoman, but of the free. (vv. 21–31)

"Tell me, ye that desire to be under the law, do ye not hear the law?" We have already noticed that while the Galatians were a Gentile people who had been saved by grace, they had fallen under the influence of certain Judaizing teachers who were trying to put them under the law. They said, "Except ye be circumcised after the manner of Moses, ye cannot be saved" (Acts 15:1), and so in this letter the apostle Paul has taken up the great question of Law and Grace and has been expounding it, clarifying it, making clear that salvation is not by works of the law but entirely by the hearing of faith.

Undoubtedly these Jewish teachers who had gotten into the Christian company were referring the believers back to the Old Testament, and they could give them Scripture after Scripture in which it seemed evident that the law was the supreme test, and that God had said, "The man which doeth those things shall live by them" (Rom. 10:5), and, "Cursed is every one that continueth not in all things which are written in the book of the law to do them" (Gal. 3:10). And so they sought to impress upon these believers the importance of endeavoring to propitiate God, of gaining divine favor by human effort.

Now he says, "You desire to be under the law, do you? Do you want to put yourself under the law of Moses? Why do you not hear the law? Why do you not carefully read the books of the law and see just what God has said?" He uses the term *law* here in two different ways. In the first instance as referring to Moses' law, the law given at Sinai with the accompanying rules and regulations, statutes and judgments, that were linked with it, but in the second, as referring to the books of the Law. "Tell me, ye that desire to be under the law [the legal covenant], do ye not hear the law [the books of the law in which God tells us of the covenants]?"

Then he turns them back to Genesis and says, "For it is written, that Abraham had two sons, the one by a bondmaid, the other by a freewoman." We know that story. Abraham's wife was Sarah, and God had promised that Abraham and Sarah should be the parents of a son who was to be the precursor of the coming Seed in whom all nations of the earth should be blessed, but the years passed by and it seemed as though there was to be no fulfillment of that promise. Finally, losing hope, Sarah herself suggested that they should descend to the lower custom of the people of the nations around them, and that Abraham should take another woman, not exactly to occupy the full status of a wife, but one to be brought into the home as a concubine. Abraham foolishly acceded to that and took Hagar. As a result of that union a son was born who was called Ishmael, and Abraham fondly hoped that he would prove to be the promised one through whom the Messiah should come into the world. But God said, "No, this is not the one. I told you you should have a child of Sarah, and this one is not the promised seed." Abraham pleaded, "O that Ishmael might live before thee!" (Gen. 17:18). But God said, as it were, "He can have a certain inheritance, but he cannot be the child of promise. In due time Sarah herself shall have a child, and in that child My covenant will stand fast."

The apostle now shows us that these events had a symbolic meaning. He does not mean to imply that they did not actually take place as written. They did. Scripture says in 1 Corinthians 10:11, speaking of Old Testament records, "Now all these things happened unto them for [types]: and they are written for our admonition, upon whom the ends of the world are come." Notice, "All these things happened." Some people say they did not happen, that they were just myths, or folklore, or something like that, but the Holy Spirit says, "All these things happened." And so what you read in the Word concerning different Old Testament characters, the nations, cities, and so on, all these are to be received as historic facts. During the last hundred years when the voice of archeology has been crying out so clearly and loudly, not one thing has been discovered to refute anything written in Scripture, while thousands of discoveries have helped to bear witness to and authenticate the Bible record. It does not need to be authenticated, of course, as far as faith is concerned, for we believe what God has said. However, these important discoveries have helped in a large measure to shut the mouths of skeptics who would not believe the statements of Scripture to be true. Abraham lived, Sarah lived, Hagar was a real personage, the two sons were real personages. From Ishmael came the Arabs, from Isaac, the Hebrews. From the beginning the two boys did not get on together, and these nations were not friendly. That explains the trouble in Palestine today. They could not get on in the beginning, and cannot today. But the apostle undertakes to show that these mothers and their sons had symbolic significance.

"But he who was of the bondwoman was born after the flesh [and so he speaks of all who are only born after the flesh]; but he of the freewoman was by promise [Isaac was the child of grace]." It would have been absolutely impossible from a natural standpoint for Abraham and Sarah to become parents at the time Isaac was born. It was a divine manifestation, a miracle. Isaac was a child of promise, and hence the child of grace. The apostle tells us that these things are an allegory. All through the Word God has used allegories in order that we might receive great moral, spiritual, and typical lessons from these incidents, and here the Spirit of God Himself unfolds one of them for us.

"Which things are an allegory: for these are the two covenants; the one from the mount Sinai, which gendereth to bondage, which is Agar. For this Agar is mount Sinai in Arabia, and answereth to Jerusalem which now is, and is in bondage with her children. But Jerusalem which is above is free, which is the mother of us all." These two women represent the two covenants: Sarah, the Abrahamic covenant, and Hagar, the Mosaic covenant. What was the difference between these two? The Abrahamic covenant was the covenant of sovereign grace. When God said to Abraham, "In thee and in thy seed shall all nations of the earth be blessed," He did not put in any conditions whatsoever. It was a divine promise. God said, "I am going to do it; I do not ask anything of you, Abraham, I simply tell you what I will do." That is grace. Grace does not make terms with people; grace does not ask that we do anything in order to procure merit. Many people talk about salvation by grace who do not seem to have the least conception of what grace is. They think that God gives them the grace to do the things that make them deserving of salvation. That is not it at all. We read, "Being justified freely by his grace" (Rom. 3:24), and that word *freely* literally means "gratuitously." The same word is translated "without a cause" in another portion of Scripture. It is said of the Lord Jesus Christ that the Scripture was fulfilled which was written concerning Him, "They hated me without a cause" (John 15:25). Jesus never did anything to deserve the bad treatment that men gave Him, and you and I cannot do one thing to deserve the good treatment that God gives us. Jesus was treated badly by men freely; we who are saved are treated well by God freely. I hope that you understand this wonderful fact, and that your soul is thrilling with the joy of it! What a marvelous thing to be saved by grace! One reason that God saves people by grace is that, "It is more blessed to give than to receive," and He must have the more blessed part.

Years ago a wealthy lady in New York built a beautiful church. On the day of dedication her agent came up from the audience to the platform and handed the deed of the property to the Episcopal Bishop of New York. The bishop gave the agent one dollar for the deed, and by virtue of the one dollar, which was acknowledged, the property was turned over to the Episcopal Church. You say, "What a wonderful gift!" Yes, in a certain sense it was, for the passing over of one dollar was simply a legal observance. But after all, in the full Bible sense it was not a gift, for it cost one dollar; and so the deed was made out not as a deed of gift but as a deed of sale. It was sold to the Episcopal Church for one dollar. If you had to do one thing in order to be saved, if you had even to raise your hand, to stand to your feet, had but to say one word, it would not be a gift. You could say, "I did thus and so, and in that way earned my salvation," but this priceless blessing is absolutely free. "If by grace, then is it no more of works: otherwise grace is no more grace. But if it be of works, then is it no more grace: otherwise work is no more work" (Rom. 11:6). That is what the Spirit of God tells us in the Word.

And so we see the covenant of grace illustrated in Sarah. God had said to Sarah, "You shall have a child, and that child will be the means of blessing to the whole world." It seemed impossible that that could ever be, but in God's good time His Word was fulfilled, at last through Isaac came our Lord Jesus Christ who brought blessing to all mankind. Hagar, on the other hand, was a bondwoman, and she speaks of the covenant of law, of the Mosaic covenant, made at Mount Sinai, for there God said, "The man that doeth [those things] shall live in them," but no man was ever found who could keep that perfectly, and therefore on the ground of law no one ever obtained life. Sarah, who typifies grace, became the mother of the child of promise; Hagar typifies law, and became the mother of the child of the flesh. The law speaks only to the flesh, while the believer is the child of promise and has been born of divine power. "Except a man be born again, he cannot see the kingdom of God" (John 3:3). Why is it that people generally are so ready to take up with legality and so afraid of grace? It is because legality appeals to the natural mind.

I remember going through Max Muller's set of translations of Oriental sacred literature in thirty-eight large volumes. I read them through in order to get an understanding of the different religious systems in oriental lands, and found that though they differed in ten thousand things, they all agreed on one thing, and that is that salvation was to be won by self-effort, the only difference being as to what the effort was. All taught salvation by works, and every religion except that which is revealed from heaven sets people doing something or paying something in order to win divine favor. This appeals to the natural man. He feels intuitively that God helps those that help themselves, and that if he does his best, surely then God will be interested enough to do something for him. But our best amounts to absolutely nothing. "All our righteousnesses are as filthy rags" (Isa. 64:6), and the sooner we learn that we have no goodness of our own, that we have nothing to present to God with which to earn our salvation, the better for us. When we learn that, we are ready to be saved by grace alone. We come to God as poor, needy, helpless sinners, and through the work that the Lord Jesus Christ has done for our salvation we who believe in Him become the children of promise.

Hagar typified Jerusalem, which is here on earth because Jerusalem at that time was the center of the legal religion. But Sarah typifies Jerusalem above "which is the mother of us all," or literally, "our mother." The law is the earthly system, it speaks to an earthly people, to men after the flesh, whereas grace is a heavenly system which avails to children of promise. Jerusalem above is "our mother." Why? Because Christ is above. Christ has gone up yonder, and having by Himself made purification for sins He has taken His seat on the right hand of the Majesty in the heavens and there He sits exalted, a Prince and Savior, and from that throne grace is flowing down to sinful men.

> Grace is flowing like a river,
>> Millions there have been supplied;
> Still it flows as fresh as ever,
>> From the Saviour's wounded side;
>> None need perish,
> All may live since Christ has died.

Have you trusted this Savior? Have you received that grace? Can you say, "Yes, I am a citizen of heaven; Jerusalem above is my mother"? Even Abraham looked for that heavenly city. God promised him an inheritance on earth, and some day his children will have that. They are trying to get it now after the flesh, and are having a very hard time. Some day in accordance with the promise, they shall have it, and then it will be all blessing for them. That will be after their eyes are opened to see the Lord Jesus Christ as their Messiah. A great many people are troubled about Palestine. I am deeply interested in what is going on over there, and recognize in it a partial fulfillment of the Word, but the reason why the Jews were driven out of Palestine nineteen hundred years ago was because they "knew not the time of their visitation," and when their own Savior came they rejected Him. They said, "We have no king but Caesar." And when Pilate asked, "What shall I do with Jesus which is called Christ?" they cried, "Away with him, away with him, crucify him" (John 19:15), "His blood be on us, and on our children" (Matt. 27:25). How terribly that malediction has been answered through the centuries. That does not excuse the wickedness of the persecution of the Jews, but it is an evidence of divine judgment. They would not have the Savior, and they have been under Caesar's iron heel ever since. But now they are going back to Palestine. Have they changed in their attitude, in their thoughts? Have they turned to God and confessed the sin of crucifying the Lord of glory? No. Then how can they expect blessing as they go back to the land? No wonder there is trouble, trouble which will continue and increase until the dark and dreadful days of the Great Tribulation. They are but the children of Hagar, but some day when the church has been caught up to be with the Lord, and God turns back to Israel, a remnant from them will be saved. "They shall look upon me whom they have pierced, and they shall mourn for him, as one mourneth for his only son" (Zech. 12:10), and when they own as Savior and Lord, Him whom once they rejected, He will cleanse them from their sins; He will take them back to the land; He will bring them into blessing; He will destroy all their foes; and they themselves will become a means of blessing to the whole earth. That is the divine program as laid down in the Word of God.

I should like to urge any Jewish friends to search their own Scriptures. Will you not turn to your own Bible and read Isaiah 53, Psalm 22, Psalm 69, the last three chapters of the book of Zechariah, and then if you have a New Testament, read the epistle to the Hebrews and the gospel of Matthew, and see if the Spirit of God will not show you what is the whole trouble with Israel today? All their troubles have come upon them because they sought the blessing not after the Spirit but after the flesh, and so refused the promised Seed when He came. And you Gentiles, if you are seeking salvation by church membership, by observing ordinances, by charity, by your own good works, prayers, and penances, can you not see that you too are seeking the blessing after the flesh when God would give it to you on the ground of pure grace? Oh, that you might become children of Sarah, of the covenant of grace, who can say, "Thank God, Jerusalem above is our mother." "Our [citizenship]," says the apostle, "is in heaven; from whence also we look for the Saviour, the Lord Jesus Christ" (Phil. 3:20). And Abraham, we are told, "looked for a city which hath foundations, whose builder and maker is God" (Heb. 11:10). Abraham is in heaven, and all his spiritual children who have died in the past are with him there. The Lord Jesus tells of the poor beggar, the child of Abraham, who died and was carried by the angels to Abraham's bosom. All the redeemed who have passed off the scene are in this same glorious paradise where Abraham is, and by-and-by, when Jesus comes, we all shall join that glad throng.

And then, not only now but through the millennial age, how many will be the children of God! So the apostle quotes from Isaiah 54:1: "Rejoice, thou barren that bearest not; break forth and cry, thou that travailest not: for the desolate hath many more children than she which hath an husband." What a strange Scripture! First notice its character. The chapter that precedes it is Isaiah 53. There we have the fullest, the most complete prophecy of the coming into the world of the Lord Jesus, His suffering and death and resurrection, that is to be found anywhere in the Bible. Isaiah seems to see Him suffering, bleeding, and dying on the cross, and he says: "He was wounded for our transgressions, he was bruised for our iniquities: the chastisement of our peace was upon him; and with his stripes we are healed. All we like sheep have gone astray; we have turned every one to his own way; and the LORD hath laid on him the iniquity of us all" (Isa. 53:5–6), and the prophet closes that chapter with the wonderful words,

"He bare the sin of many, and made intercession for the transgressors" (v. 12). And then the very next word, when you come to chapter 54, is *"Sing!"* There is enough there to make you sing: "He bare the sin of many, and made intercession for the transgressors. Sing!" Of what shall we sing? Of the matchless grace that God has manifested in Christ. Paul translated that word, *sing,* "rejoice." Why? Because Jesus has died, the sin question is settled, and now God can let free grace flow to poor sinners. Grace in the past had been like a woman who was forsaken and alone, and longed to be the mother of children, but wept and mourned alone. And on the other hand here is legality typified by another woman, and she has thousands of children, people who profess to be saved by human effort, saved by their own merits. Yes, legality is a wonderful mother, she has a past family, and poor grace does not seem to have any children at all. But now the gospel goes forth, and what happens? Grace, the one forsaken, neglected, becomes the mother of more children than legality. "For it is written, Rejoice, thou barren that bearest not; break forth and cry, thou that travailest not: for the desolate hath many more children than she which hath an husband." And so grace now has untold millions of children, and there will be millions more in the glorious age to come.

> Millions have reached that blissful shore,
> Their trials and their labors o'er,
> And still there's room for millions more.
> Will you go?

"Now we, brethren, as Isaac was, are the children of promise." Are you sure that is true of you? Have you believed God's promise? He has promised a full, free, and eternal salvation to every one who trusts His Son. We who have believed are children of promise. But the children of legality cannot understand this. No one hates grace as much as the man who is trying to save himself by his own efforts.

"But as then he that was born after the flesh persecuted him that was born after the Spirit, even so it is now." During the dark ages, for more than one thousand years, the doctrines of grace were practically lost to the church, and many were trying to save themselves by penances, by long weary journeys, by thousands and thousands of prayers repeated over and over, by giving of their wealth to endow churches and build monasteries. The children of legality were a great host, and God opened the eyes of Martin Luther, John Knox, John Calvin, William Farel, and a host of others, and they found out that while men had been trying to save themselves by human effort it was the will of God to save poor sinners by grace. Luther took hold of the text, "The just shall live by faith," and the truth began to ring out all over Germany and Europe and then spread to Britain, and soon bitter persecution broke out and people cried, "Put them to death, these people who believe in salvation by grace, who do not believe that they can be saved by penances and human merit; burn them, starve them, shoot them, behead them, do everything possible to rid the world of them!" They do not get rid of them in those ways today, but the world still hates and detests the people who are saved by grace. If you come into a community where people are going on in a smug self-righteousness, imagining they are going to heaven by church attendance, because they were baptized as babies, were confirmed at twelve years of age, have given of their money, and have attended to their religious duties, and you ask, "Are you saved?" their answer will be, "Nobody can ever know until they get to the judgment seat, but I am trying to be." "Well," you say, "you can be sure"; and you tell them of salvation by grace, and they exclaim, "What is this? What detestable fanaticism!" and at once they will begin to persecute you. The children of the flesh cannot stand the children of the Spirit.

"Nevertheless what saith the scripture? Cast out the bondwoman and her son: for the son of the bondwoman shall not be heir with the son of the freewoman." God says, "My children are the children of promise; My children are those who are saved by grace." Do you know the blessedness of the reality of it in your own soul?

"So then, brethren," the apostle concludes, "we are not children of the bondwoman, but of the free." In other words, we have nothing to do with the legal covenant but we are the children of the covenant of grace.

> Grace is the sweetest sound
>> That ever reached our ears,
> When conscience charged and justice frowned,
>> 'Twas grace removed our fears.

PART 3

PERSONAL

Galatians 5–6

LECTURE 12

FALLING FROM GRACE

Galatians 5:1–6

Stand fast therefore in the liberty wherewith Christ hath made us free, and be not entangled again with the yoke of bondage. Behold, I Paul say unto you, that if ye be circumcised, Christ shall profit you nothing. For I testify again to every man that is circumcised, that he is a debtor to do the whole law. Christ is become of no effect unto you, whosoever of you are justified by the law; ye are fallen from grace. For we through the Spirit wait for the hope of righteousness by faith. For in Jesus Christ neither circumcision availeth any thing, nor uncircumcision; but faith which worketh by love. (vv. 1–6)

In chapters 5 and 6 we have the third division, the practical part, of this letter. He shows us what the result should be in our daily lives if we have laid hold of the blessed truth that salvation is altogether by grace through faith in Christ Jesus, and so begins like this, "Stand fast therefore." Wherefore? Because of the finished work of Christ through which all who believe have been not only delivered from the judgment due to their sins, not only delivered from the penalty of the broken law, but delivered from the law itself and en-lawed to Christ. The believer now walks in a place that was never known before. He is down here in this world, it is true, but he is neither without law, nor yet under law, but is subject to the Lord Jesus Christ, and so is brought into a glorious liberty—liberty, of course, not to do the will of the natural man, not to obey the dictates of the flesh, but liberty to glorify God, to adorn the doctrines of Christ by a holy, triumphant life as he passes through this scene. This is the liberty into which Christ has brought us, and now to go back to some legalistic system such as that of Judaism or those prevailing in Christendom today, is to become "entangled again with the yoke of bondage."

Through the centuries that the Jews were under the law, not one of them found salvation through practicing the ceremonial law or obeying the law given at Mount Sinai, because every man failed, and it put them all under condemnation. But Christ has brought us into liberty. How foolish then to go back under law which only engenders bondage. Paul could say, "I was in that bondage once, but I was delivered from it. You heathen people never knew that bondage, but you do know something of the liberty of Christ. Are you going now into the bondage out of which God delivers every Jew He saves? It is folly to take a step like that. But if you mean to do it, you had better go the whole length, for you cannot take certain commands and say, 'I will obey those things,' for God says, 'Cursed is every one that continueth not in all things which are written in the book of the law to do them'" (Gal. 3:10).

"Behold, I Paul say unto you, that if ye be circumcised, Christ shall profit you nothing." That is, if they depended upon the rite of circumcision for the salvation of their souls they were ignoring Christ. He is not saying that if somebody had been misled for the moment and had accepted the teaching of these Judaizers, he lost Christ, but if their dependence was upon these things, they have set Christ at naught. "For I testify again to every man that is circumcised, that he is a debtor to do the whole law." If you take the first step, go the whole length, for the law is one. You cannot take from it what you please and reject the rest. "Christ is become of no effect unto you, whosoever of you are justified by the law; ye are fallen from grace." Of course the real meaning is, that if one is seeking justification by law, he is seeking to be right with God on the basis of his own human efforts. You say, "Well, God commanded His people to do them." Yes, in the Old Testament, but we read that "the law was our schoolmaster [our child leader] unto Christ," but now that Christ has come we are no longer under the child leader. If you go back to law, you set Christ to one side; you cannot link the two principles of law and grace.

In Romans we are told that if salvation is "by grace, then is it no more of works: otherwise grace is no more grace. But if it be of works, then is it no more grace: otherwise work is no more work" (Rom. 11:6). It must be one or the other. Either you earn your salvation by efforts of your own, or you accept it as the free gift of God. If you have trusted Christ as your Savior you have received it as a gift. If you did anything to deserve it, if you worked for it, if you purchased it, it would not be a gift. So we read, "To him that worketh is the reward not reckoned of grace, but of debt. But to him that worketh not, but believeth on him that justifieth the ungodly, his faith is counted for righteousness" (Rom. 4:4–5). Therefore, if you turn back to law after you have known Christ, you are deliberately setting your Savior to one side. "Ye are fallen from grace."

That is an expression that a great many people are interested in. A man came to a friend of mine, a Methodist minister, and said, "I understand that you Methodists believe in falling from grace; is that so?"

He said, "I understand that you Presbyterians believe in horse-stealing."

"No, we do not."

"Well, don't you believe that it is possible for a man to steal horses?"

"Yes, but we wouldn't do it."

"Well, we believe it is possible for men to fall from grace, but we do not believe in doing it."

But what do we mean by falling from grace? Here we have the expression in Scripture, "Ye are fallen from grace." Really, a better translation is, "Ye are fallen away from grace"—you have turned away from grace. Does this mean that if a man is once a Christian but falls into some kind of sin, he loses his salvation and is no longer a Christian? If it meant that, every believer ceases to be a Christian every day, because there is not a person anywhere that does not fall into some kind of sin every day—sins of thought, of word, or of deed. But falling from grace is not sinking into sin, into immorality or other evildoing, but it is turning from the full, clear, high Christian standard of salvation by grace alone to the low level of attempting to keep one's salvation by human effort. Therefore, a man who says, "I am saved by grace, but now my continuance depends on my own effort," has fallen from grace. That is what it is to "fall from grace."

I do not care what it is you imagine you have to do in order to keep saved; whatever it is, you put yourself on legal ground if after believing on the Lord Jesus Christ you think that your salvation is made more secure by baptism, by taking the Lord's Supper, by giving money, by joining the church. If you do these things in order to help save your soul, you have fallen from grace—you fail to realize that salvation is by grace alone, God's free unmerited favor. Someone asks, "Don't you believe in doing those things?" Indeed, I do; not in order to save my soul, but out of love for Christ.

> I would not work my soul to save,
> That work my Lord has done;
> But I would work like any slave
> From love to God's dear Son.

Christian obedience is not on the principle of law but of love to Christ.

It is the grace of God working in the soul that makes the believer delight in holiness, in righteousness, in obedience to the will of God, for real joy is found in the service of the Lord Jesus Christ. I remember a man who had lived a life of gross sin. After his conversion one of his old friends said to him, "Bill, I pity you—a man that has been such a highflier as you. And now you have settled down, you go to church, or stay at home and read the Bible and pray; you never have good times any more."

"But, Bob," said the man, "you don't understand. I get drunk every time I want to. I go to the theater every time I want to. I go to the dance when I want to. I play cards and gamble whenever I want to."

"I say, Bill," said his friend, "I didn't understand it that way. I thought you had to give up these things to be a Christian."

"No, Bob," said Bill, "the Lord took the 'want to' out when He saved my soul, and He made me a new creature in Christ Jesus."

We do not make terms with the Lord and say, "If You will save me, I won't do this, and I will do that," but we come throwing up our hands and saying, "Lord, I cannot do a thing to save myself; Thou must do it in Thine own free grace or I am eternally lost." Now if as Christians we stoop down from that high level and still try to make ourselves acceptable to God by some human effort, we have fallen from grace. Yes, we do believe it is possible to fall from grace, and we also believe that about three-fourths of Christendom have fallen from grace. I do not mean that they won't get to heaven, but I do mean that many real Christians have come down to a very low level. They are so occupied with their own efforts instead of with the glorious finished work of our Lord Jesus Christ.

"For we through the Spirit." Everything for the believer is through the Spirit. The Holy Spirit has come to dwell in us, and God works His works in us by the Spirit. And so instead of human efforts, instead of trying to do something in order to earn divine favor, we yield ourselves to the Holy Spirit of God that He may work in and through us to the glory of our Lord Jesus Christ. "For we through the Spirit wait for the hope of righteousness by faith." What is the hope of righteousness? It is the coming again of our Lord Jesus Christ and our gathering together unto Him. We are now made the righteousness of God in Christ, and yet every day we mourn over our failures; we do not rise to the heights we desire. Every night we have to kneel before God and confess our sins. But we are looking on in glad hope to the time when Jesus will come back again and transform these bodies of our humiliation, and then we shall be fully like Him.

> Soon I'll pass this desert dreary,
> Soon will bid farewell to pain,
> Nevermore be sad or weary,
> Never, never sin again.

When he shall appear, we shall be like him; for we shall see him as he is. (1 John 3:2)

"For in Jesus Christ neither circumcision availeth any thing, nor uncircumcision; but faith which worketh by love." Whether a man is a Jew or a Gentile, it does not make any difference, whether he has been a rigid law-keeper or an idolater, there is no difference, "For all have sinned, and come short of the glory of God" (Rom. 3:23). When people put their trust in the Lord Jesus Christ the Holy Spirit comes to dwell in them, and they are said to be "in Christ," and, "There is therefore now no condemnation to them which are in Christ Jesus" (Rom. 8:1), for we are forever linked up with His Son, the Lord Jesus Christ. Our human works and religious ceremonies count for nothing as far as justifying the soul. What does count? "Faith which worketh by love." And as we walk in fellowship with the Lord Jesus Christ, as our hearts are taken up with Him, as faith makes Christ real ("Faith is the substance of things hoped for, the evidence of things not seen." [Heb. 11:1]), we shall find that it is the substantiating of the things for which we hope, the assured conviction of the reality of things that our eyes have never seen. Faith tells us Jesus lives, faith tells us that the sin question is settled, that we are in Christ. As we go on in faith looking to Him, drawing from Him new supplies of grace day by day, faith works by love, and love is the fulfilling of the law, and therefore we do not need to be under the law in order to live aright. It is the only natural thing now for Christians to seek to live for the glory of our Lord Jesus Christ.

A physician came into a room where I was visiting a family where a dear child was very ill. She was the apple of the mother's eye. The doctor said, "Now, Mrs.

So-and-So, there is one thing I would suggest. Because of the condition the little one is in, I would not let anyone else take care of her but yourself. It is going to mean a great deal to the child to have you care for her. She is in a very nervous condition." Do you think that mother found that a hard law to obey? Her mother-heart led her to respond at once, "Yes, Doctor, I will see that no one else looks after the baby. I will do all I can for her." Was that legality? No, it was "faith working by love." So with the Christian. All our obedience springs from heart-devotion to the Lord Jesus Christ. We delight to do good, we delight to help others, we delight to preach His Word, to minister to those in need and distress, we delight in what Jesus Himself calls "good works," because we love Christ and we want to do those things of which He approves. Anything else than this is to "fall from grace."

Faith Working by Love

Galatians 5:7–15

Ye did run well; who did hinder you that ye should not obey the truth? This persuasion cometh not of him that calleth you. A little leaven leaveneth the whole lump. I have confidence in you through the Lord, that ye will be none otherwise minded: but he that troubleth you shall bear his judgment, whosoever he be. And I, brethren, if I yet preach circumcision, why do I yet suffer persecution? then is the offense of the cross ceased. I would they were even cut off which trouble you. For, brethren, ye have been called unto liberty; only use not liberty for an occasion to the flesh, but by love serve one another. For all the law is fulfilled in one word, even in this; Thou shalt love thy neighbour as thyself. But if ye bite and devour one another, take heed that ye be not consumed one of another. (vv. 7–15)

Paul now goes on to show that Christian liberty is not license to live after the flesh, but it is liberty to glorify God. Notice how he pours out his heart to them as he thinks of their defection. He says, "Ye did run well." That is, he looks back over their earlier years and reminds himself of their first devotion and joy, how consistent they were, how they sought to glorify the Lord. But their testimony has been marred, their earlier love has been lost, they no longer are such devoted, active servants of the Lord Jesus Christ as once they were. They have been turned aside by false teaching.

"Ye did run well; who did hinder you that ye should not obey the truth?" What was it that turned them aside? It was their acceptance of the idea that although they were justified by faith they could be sanctified only by the law, and that is a very common error today. A great many people think that while the law cannot justify, yet after all, when one is justified, it is obedience to the law that sanctifies. But the law is as powerless to sanctify as it was to justify. It is of no use to try to put the old nature under law. You have two natures, the old, the carnal, and the new, the spiritual. That old nature is just as black as it can be, and the new is as white as it can be. The old is just as evil as it can be, and the new is as good as it can be. It is of no use to say to the old nature, "You must obey the law," because the carnal mind is not subject to the law of God. On the other hand, you do not need to say that to the new nature, because it delights in the law of God. So our sanctification is not of the law. These Galatians had lost sight of this.

And so in verse 8 the apostle says, "This persuasion cometh not of him that calleth you." The word translated "persuasion" might be better rendered "persuasibleness." This persuasibleness, this readiness on your part to be persuaded by these false teachers, "cometh not of him that calleth you." People are as easily changed in their religious views as they are in their political views. They are one thing one day, and another thing the next. They start out all right, and then the first false teacher that comes along gets their attention, and if he quotes a few Scripture verses they say, "It sounds all right; he has the Bible for it," and so they go from one thing to another and never get settled anywhere. The apostle says that this readiness to be persuaded by human teachers is not of God. If you were walking with God you would be listening to His voice and hearing His Word, and would be kept from "overpersuasibleness."

"A little leaven leaveneth the whole lump," we are told in verse 9. This same sentence is found in 1 Corinthians 5:6, where Paul warns the saints against the toleration of immorality in their midst. An evil man was among them. He was living in sin and they seemed powerless to deal with it, like some churches today who have never had a case of discipline for years, tolerating all kinds of wickedness. They do not dare to come out and deal with it. These Corinthians were glorying in the fact that they were broad-minded enough to overlook this man's adultery and incest, and Paul says to them, "If you are going to do this, you must face the fact that 'a little leaven leaveneth the whole lump.' Others looking on will say, 'If the church of God does not take a stand against these things, why should we be so careful?'"

Here in Galatians, the apostle is not speaking of wickedness in the life but of false doctrine, and says that if they do not deal with it in the light of God's Word they will find that it too is like leaven, and "a little leaven leaveneth the whole lump," and the time will come when they will have lost altogether the sense of the grace of God. It is interesting to notice that in the Word of God leaven is always a picture of evil. A great many people do not see that. They talk about "the leaven of the gospel." In Matthew where the Lord Jesus says, "The kingdom of heaven is like unto leaven, which a woman took, and hid in three measures of meal, till the whole was leavened" (Matt. 13:33), their idea is that the three measures of meal represent the world, and the woman is the church putting the leaven, the gospel, into the world, and by-and-by the whole world will be converted. We have been at it now for nearly two thousand years, and instead of the world getting converted, the professing church is getting unconverted.

Think of issuing a decree to blot out the name of Jehovah from all texts written on the walls of any church in Germany—Germany, the land of the Reformation; Germany, where Luther led the people away from the darkness of corruption—and think of that country attempting to blot out the name of Jehovah today! We are not converting the world very fast. Think of Russia where the gospel was introduced over fifteen hundred years ago, and today every effort is being made to destroy the testimony that remains in that land. It will take millennium after millennium if ever the world is to be saved by our testimony. But that is not our program. We read, "When the Son of man cometh, shall he find faith on the earth?" (Luke 18:8). "As it was in the days of Noe, so shall it be also in the days of the Son of man" (Luke 17:26). Corruption and vileness filled the world in the days of Noah, and so today corruption and vileness fill the world. "They did eat, they drank, they married wives, they were given in marriage, until the day that Noe entered into the ark, and the flood came, and destroyed them all" (Luke 17:27). We see the same things happening now, and some day the Lord's people are going, not into the ark, but they are going to be caught up to meet the Lord in the air, and then the awful flood of judgment will be poured out on this poor world. The parable does not mean that the gospel will go on until the whole world is converted; it means the very opposite. The three measures of meal represented the meal offering, and the meal offering was the food of the people of God and typified Christ, our blessed, holy Savior. There was to be no leaven in the meal offering, for that was a type of evil. The leaven is the evil teaching corrupting the truth. Jesus indicated three kinds of leaven. He said, "Beware of the leaven of Herod, beware of the leaven of the Pharisees, beware of the leaven of the Sadducees." The leaven of Herod was political corruption and wickedness, that of the Pharisees was self-righteousness and hypocrisy, and that of the Sadducees was materialism. Of any of these it may be said, "A little leaven leaveneth the whole lump." The thing that stops its working is to expose it to the action of fire, and when we judge these things in the light of the gospel of Christ they can work no longer.

But though Paul warns these Galatians he does not give them up. He feels sure that they will come out all right, for he knows how real they were in the beginning. "I have confidence in you through the Lord, that ye will be none otherwise minded: but he that troubleth you shall bear his judgment, whosoever he be." What a solemn word that is! God has said, "Be not deceived; God is not mocked: for whatsoever a man soweth, that shall he also reap" (Gal. 6:7). And we are told, "There is no respect of persons with God" (Rom. 2:11). How that ought to keep our hearts as we see men in high places today guilty of heinous crimes against civilization. We shudder as we see how hopeless it is for the nations to contend with these men and their evil principles. How the tyrants of earth still defy God! But, depend upon it, He is going to take things in His own hands one of these days, and judgment is coming as surely as there is a God in heaven. For God has said, regarding Abraham's seed, "Cursed be every one that curseth thee, and blessed be he that blesseth thee" (Gen. 27:29), and the man who is dealing cruelly with Abraham's seed is already under the curse of God. That judgment some day will fall. We can be sure of that. There is no way out, because God has decreed it. Men may trifle with God for the moment, they may question because He seems to wait a long time, but the Greeks used to say, "The mills of the gods grind slowly, but they grind exceeding small." In every aspect of life the truth remains that God is a God of judgment, and, "By him actions are weighed" (1 Sam. 2:3).

Paul then says, "And I, brethren, if I yet preach circumcision"—suppose I preached all these legalistic things, would I be persecuted as I am now? Surely not. But if I did that, I would not be true to my great commission. "Why do I yet suffer persecution? then is the offense [the scandal] of the cross ceased." What does he mean by "the scandal of the cross"? It was a scandalous end to a human life to have to die on a cross. The cross was like the gallows today. Cicero said, "The cross, it is so shameful it never ought to be mentioned in polite society." Just as a person having a relative who had committed murder and was hung for it would not want to speak about it, so people felt about the cross in those days. Yet the Son of God died on a cross. Oh, the shame of it! The Holy One, the Eternal Creator, the One who brought all things into existence, went to that cross and died for our sins. Paul practically says, "You are setting that cross at naught if you introduce any other apparent means of salvation in place of the death Jesus died to put away sins." And then he cries, "I would they were even cut off which trouble you." Or literally, "I would they would cut themselves off that trouble you," these men who would pervert the gospel of Christ.

In verse 13 he comes back to the theme of liberty, "For, brethren, ye have been called unto liberty"—you have been set free, you are no longer slaves, you are free men—"only use not liberty for an occasion to the flesh." Do not say, "Well, now, I am saved by grace and, therefore, am free to do as I like." No, but, I am saved by grace and so I am free to glorify the God of all grace! I have liberty to live for God, I have liberty to magnify the Christ who died for me, and I have liberty to walk in love toward all my brethren. It is a glorious liberty this, the liberty of holiness, of righteousness. "But by love serve one another." Having been called into this liberty be willing to be a servant. Our blessed Lord set us the example; He took that place on earth: "If I then, your Lord and Master, have washed your feet; ye also ought to wash one another's feet" (John 13:14). Through love we delight to serve. Look at that mother caring for her little babe. She has to do many things her heart does not naturally delight in. Is her service a slavery as she waits upon her babe? Oh, no; she delights to do that which love dictates, and so in our relation to one another, how glad we ought to be to have the opportunity of serving fellow saints. "By love serve one another."

"For all the law is fulfilled in one word." It is as though he says, "You talk about the law, you insist that believers should come under the law; why don't you stop to consider what the law really teaches?" "All the law is fulfilled in one word, even in this: Thou shalt love." The man who loves will not break any of the commandments. If I love God as I should, I will not sin against Him. Look at Joseph, exposed to severe temptation, greater perhaps than many another has gone through, and yet his answer to the temptress was, "How shall I do this great wickedness and sin against God?" He loved God and that kept him in the hour of temptation. And when it comes to dealing with our fellows, if we love our neighbors as ourselves we won't violate the commandments. We won't lie to one another, we won't bear false witness, no one will commit adultery, there will be no violation of God's law, we will not murder. No wrong will be done to another if we are walking in love. "All the law is fulfilled in one word, even in this: Thou shalt love thy neighbour as thyself." The Holy Spirit who dwells in every believer is the Spirit of love, and the new nature is a nature which God Himself has implanted; God is love and therefore it is natural for the new nature to love. When you find a believer acting in an unloving way, doing an unkind thing, you may be sure that it is the old nature, not the new, that is dominating him at that moment. Oh, to walk in love that Christ may be glorified in all our ways! It was said of early Christians, even by the heathen about them, "Behold how they love one another!" Can that always be said of us? Or must it be said, "Behold how they quarrel; behold how they criticize; behold how they backbite one another; behold how they scandalize one another." What a shame if such things could be said of us! "All the law is fulfilled in one word, even in this: Thou shalt love."

Now on the other hand, if one fails in this, "If ye bite and devour one another, take heed that ye be not consumed one of another." If you would tear one another's reputations to pieces, find fault with one another, quarrel with one another, be careful, for the natural result will be that you will be "consumed one of another." Do you know why many a testimony that was once bright for God today is in ruins? It is because of a spirit of quarrelsomeness, fault-finding, and murmuring comes in among the people of God, and God cannot bless that. If you and I are guilty of that, we ought to get into God's presence and examine our ways before Him; yea, plead with Him to search our hearts, and confess and judge every such thing as sin in His sight in order that we may be helpers and not hinderers in His service.

"If ye bite and devour one another, take heed that ye be not consumed one of another." "Well," someone says, "I always hate myself if I say anything unkind, and I make up my mind never to do it again." The trouble is that you have not yielded that tongue of yours to the Lord Jesus Christ. You remember the word, "Present your bodies a living sacrifice, holy, acceptable unto God, which is your reasonable service" (Rom. 12:1). A number of people have presented almost every part of their bodies except their tongues. They have kept the tongues for themselves, and they allow them to wag on and on until gradually they bring in a lot of sorrow and grief among the people of God. Won't you say, "Lord, this tongue of mine was given me to glorify Thee; I have used it so often to find fault with others, to injure the reputation of a brother or a sister, to speak unkindly or discourteously about other people. Lord Jesus, I give it to Thee, this tongue that Thou hast bought with Thy blood. Help me to use it from this time on solely to glorify Thee. And in using it to glorify Thee, I shall be using it to bless and help others, instead of to distress and hinder them."

You may never yet have come to Jesus, and possibly you are saying, "Is there a power such as you speak of that can lift a person above a life of sin, enabling him to so live?" Yes, there is; come to the Lord Jesus Christ, put your trust in

Him, receive Him as your Savior, enthrone Him as Lord of your life, and you will find that everything will be different, everything will be new. You will have a joy, a gladness, that you have never been able to find in all the devious ways of this poor world. He says, "Behold, I stand at the door, and knock: if any man hear my voice, and open the door, I will come in to him, and will sup with him, and he with me" (Rev. 3:20). Fling wide the door of your heart today, and say:

> Come in, my Lord, come in,
>   And make my heart thy home.
> Come in, and cleanse my soul from sin,
>   And dwell with me alone.

He will be so glad to come in and take control, and everything will be made new in the light of His presence.

LECTURE 14

LIBERTY, NOT LICENSE

Galatians 5:16–26

This I say then, Walk in the Spirit, and ye shall not fulfil the lust of the flesh. For the flesh lusteth against the Spirit, and the Spirit against the flesh: and these are contrary the one to the other: so that ye cannot do the things that ye would. But if ye be led of the Spirit, ye are not under the law. Now the works of the flesh are manifest, which are these; adultery, fornication, uncleanness, lasciviousness, idolatry, witchcraft, hatred, variance, emulations, wrath, strife, seditions, heresies, envyings, murders, drunkenness, revellings, and such like: of the which I tell you before, as I have also told you in time past, that they which do such things shall not inherit the kingdom of God. But the fruit of the Spirit is love, joy, peace, longsuffering, gentleness, goodness, faith, meekness, temperance: against such there is no law. And they that are Christ's have crucified the flesh with the affections and lusts. If we live in the Spirit, let us also walk in the Spirit. Let us not be desirous of vain glory, provoking one another, envying one another. (vv. 16–26)

The present section of this epistle brings before us the truth, in a very marked way, of the two natures in the believer. It is important to remember that when God saves us He does not destroy the carnal nature which we received at our natural birth. The new birth does not imply the elimination of that old carnal nature, neither does it imply a change in it, but rather the impartation of an absolutely new nature born of the Holy Spirit of God, and these two natures abide side by side in the believer in the Lord Jesus Christ. This explains the conflict that many of us have known since we have been converted. In fact, I need not have said, "many of us," for all converted people know at one time or another something of that conflict between the flesh and the Spirit. Jesus said, "That which is born of the flesh is flesh"—that is, the old nature—"that which is born of the Spirit is spirit"—that is the new nature, and these two natures abide side by side until we receive the redemption of the body which will be at the coming again of our Lord Jesus Christ, when He will transform this body of our humiliation and make it like unto the body of His glory. Then we will be delivered forever from all inward tendency to sin. Until then we have to learn, and sometimes by very painful experiences, that the carnal nature, that old nature, "is not subject to the law of God, neither indeed can be" (Rom. 8:7).

That old nature is so corrupt, so vile, that it can never be sanctified, and the new nature is so pure, so holy, that it does not need to be sanctified. So there is no mention in Scripture of the sanctification of the old nature. What is it then that needs to be sanctified? It is the man himself, and he is sanctified as he learns to walk in accordance with the dictates of the new nature. He is directed by the Holy Spirit of God, for the believer is not only born of the Spirit but indwelt by the Spirit.

We are not to confound new birth by the Spirit with the reception of the Spirit. New birth is the operation of the Spirit of God. He it is who produces the new birth through the Word. We receive the Word in faith, we believe the Word, and the Spirit of God through the Word brings about new birth. The apostle James says, "Of his own will begat he us with the word of truth" (James 1:18). The apostle Peter says, "Being born again, not of corruptible seed, but of incorruptible, by the Word of God, which liveth and abideth for ever. . . . And this is the word which by the gospel is preached unto you" (1 Peter 1:23, 25). And when I believe that Word I am born again; that is an inward change. It is the impartation of a new life; it is eternal life. But there is something more than that. It was always true in all dispensations, from Adam down to the day of Pentecost, that wherever people believed God's Word they were born again, but the Holy Spirit Himself as a divine Person had not then come to dwell within them. Now since Pentecost, upon believing, we are sealed with the Holy Spirit of God. He creates the new nature, and then comes to indwell the one who is thus born again, and as the believer learns to recognize the fact that the Spirit of God dwells within him, and as he turns everything over to His control, he finds deliverance from the power of inbred sin.

Notice how the apostle puts it here: "This I say then, Walk in the Spirit, and ye shall not fulfil the lust [or, the desire] of the flesh." It is so easy to fulfill the desire of the flesh. We must not link with that word *lust* the idea that it always means things base and unclean. The word itself simply means "desire," and whatever the desire of the flesh is, it is always hateful to God. Here may be one who desires all kinds of carnal indulgences, and we have no difficulty in realizing the vileness of that, but here is another who desires worldly fame, the praise and adulation of his fellows, and that is also the lust of the flesh, or mind, and is as obnoxious to God as the other. Any kind of a carnal or fleshly desire is a lust, and if we would be delivered from walking according to these selfish lusts we must walk in the Spirit.

It is one thing to have the Spirit indwelling us and quite another to walk in the Spirit. To walk in the Spirit implies that the Holy Spirit is controlling us, and we can walk in the Spirit only as our lives are truly surrendered to Christ. Somebody says, "Well, then, I understand you mean to tell us that all believers possess the Holy Spirit, but that many of us have never received the second blessing, and are not filled with the Spirit." I do not find the term, "second blessing," in Scripture, though I admit that in the lives of many Christians there is an experience that answers to what people call "the second blessing." Many Christians have lived for years on a rather low, somewhat carnal, worldly plane. They love the Lord, they love His Word, they love to attend the ordinances of His house, they enjoy Christian fellowship, and seek to walk as upright men and women through this world, but they have never truly yielded themselves and all their ransomed powers wholly to the Lord. There is something they are keeping back, some controversy with God, and as long as this continues there will always be conflict and defeat, but when one comes to the place where he heeds the Word, "I beseech you therefore, brethren, by the mercies of God, that ye present [that you surrender, hand over] your bodies a living sacrifice, holy, acceptable unto God, which is your reasonable service" (Rom. 12:1)—when one makes that surrender there is indeed in the life what answers to a kind of second blessing; that is, the Spirit of God is now free to take possession of that believer, and operate through him and use him for the glory of God in a way He could not do as long as that man or woman was not wholly surrendered to the Lord. We speak a great deal about "full surrender," and yet, I am afraid, some of us use the term in a very careless way. It is of no use to speak of being fully surrendered to God if I am still seeking my own interest. If I am self-centered, if I am hurt because people do not praise me, or if I am lifted up because they do, then the Spirit of God does not have His way with me. If Christ Himself is not the one object before my soul, if I cannot say, "For me to live is Christ," if my great concern is not that Christ should be magnified in me whether by life or by death, then I am not yet wholly surrendered to Him. If I cannot say from the heart, "Not my will, but Thine," there is no use in talking about being surrendered to Christ. The surrendered believer is no longer seeking his own but the things which belong to Christ Jesus. That is the man who "walks in the Spirit." "Walk in the Spirit, and ye shall not fulfil the lust of the flesh."

The conflict is shown in verse 17: "For the flesh lusteth [or desireth] against the Spirit, and the Spirit against [or contrary to] the flesh: and these are contrary the one to the other." It is not exactly, "So that ye *cannot* do the things that ye would," for God has made provision that we might do the things that we would, but it should be rendered, "So that ye *may not* do the things that ye would." Here is conflict in the believer's breast. The flesh desires one thing, the Spirit another, and as long as there is not a full surrender to the will of God these two are in constant warfare, and therefore the believer may not do the things that he would. I rise in the morning and say, "Today I will not allow that tongue of mine to say one unkind thing, one un-Christlike word." But some unexpected circumstances arise, and almost before I know it I have said something for which I could bite my tongue. The thing I never meant to do I did. And, on the other hand, things I meant to do I did not do. What does that tell me? There is conflict. The Spirit of God has not His complete right of way in my heart and life, and because of this conflict I may not do the things that I would. I am hindered, and my life is not a life of full surrender as God intended it to be. How many of us know this experimentally. Oh, the defeated lives, the disappointed lives, even of people who are real Christians, who know the blessedness of being saved by the precious blood of the Lord Jesus Christ and who long to glorify God, and yet are constantly defeated. Why? Because the Spirit of God does not have His supreme place in their lives.

"But if ye be led of the Spirit, ye are not under the law." We are not to think that the way of deliverance is by law-keeping. I may say, "From now on I mean to be very careful, I will obey God's law in everything. That surely will result in my practical sanctification." But no, I am disappointed again. I will find that the will to do good is present with me, but how to perform it is another thing, and so I have to learn that my sanctification is no more through the law than my justification. What then? He tells us, "If ye be led of the Spirit, ye are not under the law." If you yield to the Spirit of God, if He has the control of your life, if you are led by Him, then the righteousness of the law is fulfilled in us who walk not after the flesh but after the Spirit. And in order that we may not misunderstand, he brings before us the lusts of the flesh, that we may be able to drag these things out into the light, that we may see them in all their ugliness, so that if any of them have any place in our hearts and lives we may judge them in the presence of God. We often run across people today who say that they do not believe in the depravity of human life, but these are the things that come from the natural man; and even the believer, if he is not careful, if he is not walking with God as led by the Spirit, may fall into some of them.

"Now the works of the flesh are manifest [they are evident], which are these; adultery, fornication, uncleanness, lasciviousness." Maybe some of you think or say, "I wish he would not use those words; I do not like them; they are nasty words." My dear friends, let me remind you, there is nothing the matter with the words; it is the sins that are expressed in these words that are so nasty. Many people who do not like the words are living in the sins, and God drags things out into the light and calls sin by name. There are people living in the sin of adultery who do not like to hear their wickedness called by name. Take the words of the Lord Jesus, "Whosoever shall put away his wife, saving for the cause of fornication, causeth her to commit adultery: and whosoever shall marry her that is divorced committeth adultery" (Matt. 5:32). There are those who are committing adultery according to that passage, and others who are contemplating it. If you have allowed yourself any unholy love, permitting yourself any unholy familiarity with one with whom you have no right to seek to enter the married relationship, you yourself are guilty in God's sight of the sin that is mentioned here. "Fornication, uncleanness, lasciviousness"—that is, vile, filthy thoughts indulged in. You cannot hinder evil thoughts coming into your mind, but you can help indulging in them. Lasciviousness is indulging in thoughts that are unclean and vile and unholy. People sometimes come to me in great distress and say, "Evil thoughts come to me, even when I am praying, and I wonder sometimes whether I am really converted or not." That is the flesh manifesting itself. These things may come to you, but do you indulge in them? A Welshman said, "I cannot help it if a bird alights on top of my head, but I can help it if he builds his nest in my hair," and so you may not be able to help it if evil thoughts come surging into your mind, but you can help indulging in those thoughts.

Idolatry, putting anything in the place of the true and living God. *Witchcraft.* "Oh," you say, "that is outmoded. They used to burn witches." But what is witchcraft? It is a word that implies "having to do with the dead," and I think that Chicago has a good many witches in it. Often while passing along the street I see such signs as "Spiritualist medium," or something like that, people pretending to have traffic with the dead. That is witchcraft, and it is an abomination in the sight of God. *Hatred.* This is a sin which we all have to guard against. Scripture says, "Whosoever hateth his brother is a murderer" (1 John 3:15). Hatred comes from the old nature. *Variance*—quarrelsomeness. There are many of us who would shrink from those first sins, but we are not very easy to get along with, we are dreadfully touchy, and this is as truly an evidence of the old nature, as those other "works of the flesh." *Emulations,* a constant desire to excel other people, to get the admiration of others. Here is a preacher who has some little gift, and he is upset because some other preacher has greater recognition. Here is one who sings a little, and someone else who also sings excites more admiration, and there is trouble about it. Here is a Sunday school teacher, and some other teacher seems to be preferred before her, and she is in a frenzy and almost ready to quit her work. Trace these things back to their source and you will find they all come from the flesh, and therefore they should be judged in the sight of God. And then, *wrath.* That is anger. There is an anger that is holy, but that wrath to which you and I usually give way is very unholy. The only holy anger is anger with sin. "Be ye angry, and sin not" (Eph. 4:26). The old Puritan said, "I am determined so to be angry as not to sin, therefore to be angry at nothing but sin." And then *strife,* resulting in "seditions." The two words are intimately linked together. All these things are sinful. *Heresies,* a school of opinion set up opposed to the truth of God. *Envyings.* Scripture says, "Be content with such things as ye have" (Heb. 13:5). Someone has a better house than I have, someone else has a better car than mine, and I envy him. The Arab said, "Once I felt bad and I complained because I had no shoes, until I met a man who had no feet." There is not one of us but has far more than he deserves. Why should we envy anyone else? Suppose some people have magnificent mansions and I have only a hut.

> A tent or a cottage, why should I care?
> They're building a palace for me over there!

"Be content," says the Spirit of God, "with such things as ye have." When you reach that place life will be very much happier for you.

Murders. Think of putting murder with such sins as emulations and envyings! Many a murder has resulted from these very sins, and, you know, murder does not consist in sticking a knife into a man or blowing his brains out with a revolver. You can murder a man by your unkindness. I have known many a person who died of a broken heart because of the unkindness of those from whom they had a right to expect something different. God give us to manifest so much of the love of Christ that we will be a blessing to people instead of a curse to them. Then *drunkenness.* Surely I do not need to speak of this to Christians. This too is a work of the flesh. Then *revelings.* The world calls it "having a good time" in a carnal way. "And such like: of the which I tell you before, as I have also told you in time past, that they which do such things shall not inherit the kingdom of God." Here he uses the present continuous tense: "That they that are in the habit of doing such things, they whose lives are characterized by such things." If people are characterized by these things, they prove that they are not Christians at all. Real Christians may fall into them, but they are miserable and wretched until they confess them, but unsaved men revel in them and go on without judging them. These things come from the flesh. Now we have the opposite—the fruit of the Spirit. "But the fruit of the Spirit is love, joy, peace, longsuffering, gentleness, goodness, faith, meekness, temperance: against such there is no law." You notice the word here is *fruit,* for we do not read in the Bible of the "fruits" of the Spirit, but of the "fruit." This ninefold fruit springs from the new nature as one is actuated by the Holy Spirit of God. *Love,* the very essence of the divine nature. *Joy*—Scripture says, "The joy of the Lord is your strength" (Neh. 8:10). *Peace,* that is more than happiness, that is a deep-toned gladness that is unruffled and untroubled by all the trials of earth. *Longsuffering,* this leads you to endure uncomplainingly. *Gentleness,* some of us are so gruff and so rough, but the Christian should cultivate the meekness, the gentleness of Christ. *Faith,* in the sense of confidence in God. *Meekness.* We are not meek by nature; the natural man is always pushing himself forward. The spiritual man says, "Never mind me, recognize others; I am willing to remain in the background." Wherever you find this pushing spirit you may know that one is still walking in the flesh. When you find the desire to give godly recognition to others you will find one walking in the Spirit. And then, *temperance* is just "self-control," the whole body held under in subjection to the Spirit of God. "Against such there is no law." You do not need law to control a man thus walking in the Spirit.

"And they that are Christ's have crucified the flesh with the affections and lusts." It does not say, "They that are Christ's *[should]* crucify the flesh." They have done so when they put their trust in the Lord Jesus. They trusted in the

One crucified on their behalf, and therefore can say, "I am crucified with Christ: nevertheless I live" (Gal. 2:20). It is a settled thing. If you have crucified the flesh, if you have recognized the fact that Christ's crucifixion is yours, then do not live in that to which you have died. "If we live in the Spirit, let us also walk in the Spirit." If we have this new life, if linked up now with our risen Christ, then let Him control our ways, let us be yielded to Him, let us walk in the Spirit, let us not be desirous of fame or glory, let us not seek anything that would lead to empty boasting, provoking one another, saying and doing things that may pain others needlessly, or envying one another.

Some of you may say, "That is a tremendously high standard, and I am afraid I can never attain to it." No, and I can never attain to it in my own strength, but if you and I are yielded to the Holy Spirit of God and allow Him to make these things real in our lives, then we will indeed attain to the ideal set before us here, but it will not be ourselves, it will be Christ living in us manifesting His life, His holy life, in and through the members of our body. God give us to know the reality of it!

GRACE IN ACTION

Galatians 6:1–10

Brethren, if a man be overtaken in a fault, ye which are spiritual, restore such an one in the spirit of meekness; considering thyself, lest thou also be tempted. Bear ye one another's burdens, and so fulfil the law of Christ. For if a man think himself to be something, when he is nothing, he deceiveth himself. But let every man prove his own work, and then shall he have rejoicing in himself alone, and not in another. For every man shall bear his own burden. Let him that is taught in the word communicate unto him that teacheth in all good things. Be not deceived; God is not mocked: for whatsoever a man soweth, that shall he also reap. For he that soweth to his flesh shall of the flesh reap corruption; but he that soweth to the Spirit shall of the Spirit reap life everlasting. And let us not be weary in well doing: for in due season we shall reap, if we faint not. As we have therefore opportunity, let us do good unto all men, especially unto them who are of the household of faith. (vv. 1–10)

We are now to consider a number of special admonitions having to do with the manifestation of grace, in our attitude toward our brethren generally and toward the world outside, for where grace is active in the soul there will always be kindly consideration of others. Where a spirit of censoriousness prevails, or where malice and bitterness fill the heart, one may be certain that, for the time being at least, the one who manifests such a disposition has lost the sense of his debtorship to the grace of God.

In the first instance, we have the case of a brother who has failed, though not willfully. The Spirit of God says, "Brethren, if a man be overtaken in a fault." He did not set out with intention to sin. He was not endeavoring to stifle his conscience, but sudden temptation proved too much for him, as for instance, in the case of the apostle Peter, who really loved the Lord, but when challenged as to being one of His disciples was so filled with fear that he denied the One he had declared he would never forsake. It is important to distinguish between willful, deliberate sin, when one has put away a good conscience and definitely embarked upon a course of evil, and sudden and unexpected failure because of overwhelming temptation taking one off his guard. How many fall under such circumstances! Perhaps it is the power of appetite or of fleshly passion. It may be a question of a quick temper or unjudged pride and vanity. One goes on unconscious of danger, finds himself in circumstances for which he was not prepared, and before he realizes what is transpiring, he has sinned against the One who loves him most. It is easy for others who do not understand the hidden springs of action to blame such a one very severely, particularly if his fault is of such a character as to reflect discredit upon the testimony of the Lord. The easiest way in such a case is to insist on immediate excision, excommunicating the wrongdoer from all church privileges. But here a better way is unfolded to us. Paul writes, "Ye which are spiritual, restore such an one in the spirit of meekness; considering thyself, lest thou also be tempted." It is no evidence of spirituality to give way to harsh judgment, but rather to manifest compassion for the one who has failed and to seek to bring him back to fellowship with God. It is only in the spirit of meekness that this can be done. A hard, critical spirit will drive the failing one deeper into sin and make it more difficult to recover him at last. But a loving, tender word, accompanied by gracious effort to recover, will often result in saving him from further declension.

If we remember what we ourselves are and how easily we too may fall, we will not be over-stern in dealing with others. It is not that we are called upon to excuse sin. That must be dealt with faithfully, for we are told in the law, "Thou shalt in any wise rebuke thy neighbour, and not suffer sin upon him." But we are to point out the way of deliverance; considering our own need of divine help continually in order that we may be kept from sin, we will know better how to deal with those who in the hour of temptation have missed their path.

Then we have a precious word as to that mutual concern for others which should ever characterize believers: "Bear ye one another's burdens, and so fulfil the law of Christ." The law of Christ is the law of love, and love seeks to help others in their distress and share the load with them. If anyone thinks himself superior to such service and stands upon his dignity, he is but manifesting his own littleness, for "if a man think himself to be something, when he is nothing, he deceiveth himself."

Each one should recognize his own individual responsibility to God, and therefore he is to be careful that his own work is in accordance with God's revealed mind, as indicated in His Word. As he thus walks obediently he will know that joy which comes from fellowship with God and will not depend on others for his happiness. It is a recognized principle of Scripture that each man must bear his own responsibility, and this is the meaning of verse 5, where the word *burden* suggests something quite different to its use in verse 2.

Verse 6 lays down a principle of wide application: "Let him that is taught in the word communicate unto him that teacheth in all good things." If God has used another to instruct and help me in the way of life, I, on my part, should be glad to do what I can to be of help and assistance to him. It is not simply that preachers entirely given to the work of the Lord should be sustained by the gracious gifts of those to whom they minister, though that is involved in it, but it is a constant giving and receiving in all walks of life. He who seeks only to be benefited by others and is not concerned about sharing with them, will have a Dead Sea kind of a life. It is said that nothing can live in that body of water because it has no outlet, and though millions of tons of fresh water pour into it every week, evaporation and mineral deposits make it so bitter and acrid that it cannot sustain life. He who is more concerned about giving to others than about receiving for himself will be constantly fresh and happy in his own experience and will enjoy all the more the good things ministered to him.

It is a remarkable fact that it is in this connection, what we might call the principle of "giving and receiving," that the Holy Spirit directs our attention most solemnly to the kindred law of "sowing and reaping." It never pays to be forgetful of the future. He who acts for the present moment only is like one who is indifferent to the coming harvest, and so either thinks to save by sparse sowing, or else recklessly strews obnoxious seeds in his field, sowing wild oats, as people say, and yet hopes to reap a far different kind of harvest. We reap as we sow. This is insisted on again and again in Scripture. Here we are told, "Be not deceived; God is not mocked: for whatsoever a man soweth, that shall he also reap." Elsewhere our Lord has laid down the same principle. He asks, "Do men gather grapes of thorns, or figs of thistles?" (Matt. 7:16). And He declares that "every good tree bringeth forth good fruit; but a corrupt tree bring forth evil fruit" (Matt. 7:17). Israel sowed the wind, the prophet exclaimed, and he predicted they would reap the whirlwind (Hos. 8:7). Men who sow wickedness reap the same, asserted Eliphaz (Job 4:8). This is so self-evident that it needs no emphasis. Yet how easily we forget it, and how readily we hope that in some strange, unnatural transformation our sinful folly will be so overruled as to produce the peaceable fruits of righteousness. But whether it be in the case of the unsaved worldling, or the failing Christian, the inexorable law will be fulfilled— we reap what we sow. How important then that we walk carefully before God, not permitting ourselves any license which is unbecoming in one who professes to acknowledge the Lordship of Christ. "For he that soweth to his flesh shall of the flesh reap corruption; but he that soweth to the Spirit shall of the Spirit reap life everlasting" (v. 8). It is not that we *earn* everlasting life by our behavior; we receive it as a gift when we believe on the Lord Jesus Christ (John 3:36). But we now have eternal life in dying bodies, and in a scene of contrariety, where everything about us is opposed to that new and divinely-implanted nature which we were given in regeneration. Soon, at our Lord's return, we shall enter into life in all its fullness, and then, at the judgment seat of Christ, we shall reap according to our sowing. They who live for God now will receive rich reward in that day. And they who yield now to the impulses of the flesh and are occupied with things that do not glorify God will suffer loss.

How timely then the admonition: "Let us not be weary in well doing," coupled with the sure promise, "for in due season we shall reap if we faint not." We are so apt, having begun in the Spirit, to seek to finish in the flesh, as in the case of these Galatians. But only that which is of the Spirit will be rewarded in the day of manifestation. That which is of the flesh—even though seemingly religious— will only produce corruption and bring disappointment at last.

In closing this section the apostle reverts to the general principle of verse 6, now extending it to include all men everywhere. The spiritual man is one who sees things from God's standpoint, therefore he cannot be insular, self-centered, of indifferent to the needy souls all about him. "As we have therefore opportunity, let us do good unto all men, especially unto them who are of the household of faith." Thus we will imitate Him whose life was laid out in doing good, both to the unthankful and the godless, and to the little flock who waited for the consolation of Israel. As we seek, by the power of the indwelling Spirit, to maintain the same attitude toward our fellow men, whether sinners or saints, we fulfill the righteousness of that law which says, "Thou shalt love thy neighbour as thyself." We do not need to put ourselves under the law to do this. We only need to recognize our relationship to the glorified Christ, who is the Head of that new creation to which, by grace, we belong.

Are we ever on the watch for such opportunities to manifest the goodness of God to those with whom we come in contact, and thus magnify the Lord, whose we are and whom we serve? Having been so wondrously dealt with ourselves, how can we do other than seek to exemplify in our dealings with others the mercy and loving-kindness which has been shown toward us?

This is indeed to live on a higher plane than law. It is the liberty of grace, which the Holy Spirit gives to all who recognize the Lordship of Christ.

LECTURE 16

GLORYING IN THE CROSS

Galatians 6:11–18

Ye see how large a letter I have written unto you with mine own hand. As many as desire to make a fair show in the flesh, they constrain you to be circumcised; only lest they should suffer persecution for the cross of Christ. For neither they themselves who are circumcised keep the law; but desire to have you circumcised, that they may glory in your flesh. But God forbid that I should glory, save in the cross of our Lord Jesus Christ, by whom the world is crucified unto me, and I unto the world. For in Christ Jesus neither circumcision availeth any thing, nor uncircumcision, but a new creature. And as many as walk according to this rule, peace be on them, and mercy, and upon the Israel of God. From henceforth let no man trouble me: for I bear in my body the marks of the Lord Jesus. Brethren, the grace of our Lord Jesus Christ be with your spirit. Amen. (vv. 11–18)

There is something about verse 11 that I think lets us right into the heart of the apostle Paul. He was some distance away from Galatia when word came to him that Judaizing teachers had come in among the different assemblies, and were teaching the believers that unless they were circumcised and kept the law they could not be saved. He saw that this meant to step down from the truth of grace altogether. The believer does not obey in order to be saved, but because he is saved. He delights to glorify the One who has redeemed him, and his obedience springs from a heart filled with gratitude to that One who gave His life for him. He does not try to make himself fit or to keep himself fit for heaven. The apostle was so much disturbed by what he heard that he sat right down and penned this letter. It glows with the white heat of his burning zeal for the gospel of God. As we have already remarked, it was not a usual thing for men to write their own letters in those days. Letter-writing was a distinct occupation, as it is still in the different cities of the East, and if a man had a good deal to do he would engage one of these professional letter-writers just as here and now a man who has much correspondence engages a stenographer. He would not attempt to handle it all himself. And so ordinarily the apostle dictated his letters to various persons. They wrote them out, and he signed them and sent them on. But in this case apparently he had no amanuensis close at hand, and he was so stirred in his spirit that he felt he could not lose a moment in getting a letter off, and so sat right down and wrote it himself. He refers to this in verse 11, "Ye see how large a letter I have written unto you with mine own hand." It is not really a large letter. Compared with the epistle to the Romans this is a very short one. It is not more than one-third the length of 1 Corinthians, and only about one-half the length of 2 Corinthians. Compared with other writings in the New Testament it is brief indeed, but we get help here if we consult a more critical translation. It should read, "You see with what large characters I have written unto you with mine own hand." And that indicates not only that he was not used to letter-writing, but we gather besides that he had some kind of affliction with his eyes, and was not able to see well. You remember the time he was on trial in Jerusalem, and the high priest commanded him to be smitten on the mouth, and indignantly he shouted out, "God shall smite thee, thou whited wall" (Acts 23:3), and somebody said, "Do you speak evil of God's high priest?" At once he apologized and said, "I did not know that he was the high priest." He ought to have known, for there Ananias stood, doubtless in his priestly robes, but if Paul were at the other end of the room with poor eyesight he might not have recognized the man. And then there are other Scripture passages that give similar suggestions. He had already said in this letter, "I bear you record, that, if it had been possible, ye would have plucked out your own eyes, and have given them to me" (Gal. 4:15). They would not have wanted to do that unless his sight were poor. So I take it that possibly this was the affliction which he had to endure for many years, and therefore when he sat down to write he was like a half-blind person writing in big sprawling letters. And realizing that he was not sending a neat manuscript such as an amanuensis would have prepared, he apologized for it by saying, "You see with what large characters I have written unto you with mine own hand." I think that manuscript with its large letters ought to have touched the hearts of those Galatians, and should have made them realize how truly he loved them, how concerned he was about them, that he could not wait to write them in the ordinary way, but must send off this epistle as quickly as it could be produced.

Then he concludes with these words, "As many as desire to make a fair show in the flesh, they constrain you to be circumcised." If it could have been possible to keep the Christians within the fold of Judaism and make of them one more Jewish sect, they would have been saved from a great deal of persecution they had to suffer. And so the apostle says, "These emissaries from Jerusalem going about among you have not your good at heart, but they want to make a fair show in the flesh; they want to show a great many adherents to what they teach, but do not take the place of separation to the name of the Lord Jesus Christ. I could go with them and make a fair show in the flesh, too, and would not have to suffer persecution for the cross of Christ." That cross was not only the place where the Lord Jesus suffered for our sins but is the symbol of separation. It told out the world's hatred of the Son of God, and Paul had identified himself with the One whom the world spurned, and therefore he gloried in that cross.

When people take legal ground and tell you that salvation is by human effort, they themselves never live up to their own profession. You may have heard some say, "I do not think people have to be saved by the blood of the Lord Jesus Christ; I think if everybody does the best they can, that is all that can be expected." Did you ever see a man who did the best he could do? Have you always done the best you knew? You know you have failed over and over again, even in those things that you knew to be right, things you did not do that you should have done, and things you did that you knew you should not have done. Therefore, to talk about being saved by doing the best you can is absurd. No man has ever done his best, except, of course, our holy, spotless Savior, the Lord Jesus Christ.

Somebody says, "It is gospel enough for me to follow the Sermon on the Mount." That is saying a good deal. Did you ever see a man who did that, or have you done it? Test yourself by it. Read Matthew 5–7, and just test yourself honestly; check yourself, and see how far you fall short of the precious precepts of this wonderful address given by the Lord Jesus Christ. There is no question but that you and I ought to live up to it. It indicates the type of life that should characterize every believer. But if you have not lived up to the Sermon on the Mount, either as a matter of attaining or maintaining salvation, at once you put yourself out of court. You have not lived it out, and I am afraid you never will, and therefore you can be very thankful indeed that God is saving poor sinners by grace. Someone else says, "I believe if we keep the law God gave at Sinai (it is holy, just, and good, the apostle himself tells us), it is all that God or man could require of us." So far as actual living is concerned, I suppose it is; but again I put the question, Have you kept it? Do you know of any one who has ever kept it? Let us keep in mind the words, "Whosoever shall keep the whole law, and yet offend in one point, he is guilty of all" (James 2:10). So on this ground there is no hope for any of us. "If we fail," some say, "God has provided the sacraments." But those who talk in that way are never certain that they are keeping the sacraments correctly. How do you know that you are keeping them perfectly? You may fail in purity of purpose as you take the Lord's Supper or in baptism. Even they who count on being saved through self-effort do not keep the law perfectly. We all fail, and therefore we need to recognize the fact that salvation is only through the free, matchless grace of God.

They would like to have you follow on in their ways in order that they might glory in your flesh, says the apostle. Men like to get a following, they like to have people join with them in any particular stand they take. It ministers to the pride of the natural heart to be able to head up a large group.

In opposition to all this human effort Paul sets the cross of our blessed Savior: "But God forbid that I should glory, save in the cross of our Lord Jesus Christ, by whom the world is crucified unto me, and I unto the world." When he said these words he was not thinking just of the wooden instrument on which Jesus died, and he certainly was not thinking of a cross on a steeple of a church, or on an altar of a church, nor yet of a cross dangling from a chain at the waist or throat, or worn as an ornament. When he wrote of "the cross of our Lord Jesus Christ," he was thinking of all that is involved in the crucifixion of the blessed Savior on that tree. The cross of Christ is the measure of man's hatred to God. Think of it! God sent His Son into the world! Millions of people talk about it at the Christmas season, and the merchants today are encouraging people to observe His birth so that they may sell more goods. You will find that even a Jewish merchant will wish you a merry Christmas if you purchase something from him. But remember this, the world has already told us what it thinks of Christ. It may celebrate His birth by gifts one to another, they may put on glorious concerts and have great festivals in the name of the Christ born in Bethlehem, but this world has shown what it thinks of Jesus by hurrying Him to a Roman cross. When Pilate asked, "What shall I do then with Jesus which is called Christ?" they cried out with one accord, "Let him be crucified" (Matt. 27:22), and that is the Christ they profess to worship today, the Christ they have crucified. They will even celebrate Christmas in the taverns of our cities, celebrate the birth of Christ by drinking and carousing on Christmas Eve and Christmas Day, and they will call that keeping the birth of Jesus. But the Christ of Bethlehem is the Christ of the cross, and the world has given its sentence concerning Him. They said, "We will not have this man to reign over us." "Well," the apostle says, "I glory in siding with the Man whom the world rejected." When he says, "God forbid that I should glory, save in the cross of our Lord Jesus Christ," it is just another way of saying, "My boast, my joy, my delight is in the One whom the world has crucified."

Then the cross of Christ was the place where God has told out His love in utmost fullness. "Herein is love, not that we loved God, but that he loved us, and sent his Son to be the propitiation for our sins" (1 John 4:10). When man did his worst, God did His best. When man said, "Away with him, crucify him!" God accepted Him as the substitute for sinners, and the judgment that our sins deserved fell on Him. God made His soul an offering for our sin. And so when Paul says, "I glory in the cross of our Lord Jesus," he means, I glory in the love that gave Jesus to die for me, a sinner.

But he has shown that Christ's death is my death and I am to take my place with Him, recognizing His death as mine. In 2:20 we read, "I am crucified with Christ: nevertheless I live; yet not I, but Christ liveth in me: and the life which I now live in the flesh I live by the faith of the Son of God, who loved me, and gave himself for me." When Paul says, "I glory in the cross of Christ," he means this then: I accept the cross of Christ as my cross; I accept His death as my death; I take my place with Him as one who has died to the world, to sin, and to self, and henceforth I am not under law but under grace. Law crucified my Savior. He met its claims upon that cross, and now, having satisfied all its demands, I am delivered from its authority and am free to walk before God in grace, seeking to glorify Him in a life of happy obedience because I love the One who died there to put away my sin. All this, and much more, is involved in the expression, "God forbid that I should glory, save in the cross of our Lord Jesus Christ, by whom," he says, "the world is crucified unto me, and I unto the world."

Christian, have you taken that stand? Do you realize that Christ's cross means absolute separation from the world that rejected Him? That is what we confess in our baptism; that is what Christian baptism means. I have heard of many a believer who pondered a long time before taking the step of being buried in baptism because he was afraid he would not be able to live out what was set forth in this beautiful ordinance, and, of course, apart from Christ we could not. But what is involved? A recognition that I have died with Him, that I have been buried with Him, and that this is an end of me as a man after the flesh. Therefore, I have been raised with Christ to walk in newness of life.

I remember some brethren who were talking about a Christian's relationship to oath-bound secret societies. (This Book tells me concerning the Lord Jesus that He said, "In secret have I said nothing" [John 18:20], therefore I know that He never was inside of an oath-bound secret order, and He has called upon me to be a follower of Him.) One of these brethren said to the other, "You belong to such-and-such an order."

"Oh, no," he said, "I do not."

"Why, you do; I was there the night you were initiated, and once a member of that you are a member until death."

"Exactly; I quite admit what you say, but I buried the lodge member in Lake Ontario."

He meant that in his baptism the old order came to an end.

I have heard of a dear young woman once a thorough worldling, but at last she was brought to a saving knowledge of the Lord Jesus. Her friends came on her birthday one evening to give her a surprise party and wanted to take her with them to a place of ungodly worldly amusement. She said, "It is good of you to think of me, but I could not go with you; I never go to those places."

"Nonsense," they said, "you have often gone with us."

"But," she said, "I have buried the girl that used to go to those places. 'Not I, but Christ liveth in me.'"

Christian baptism should speak of separation from the world that crucified the Lord Jesus Christ. Look at Israel. They had been slaves to Pharaoh, and there is old Pharaoh on the other side of the sea, shouting, "You come back here and serve me; put your necks under the yoke of bondage again." And I think I hear them say, "Good-bye, Pharaoh; the Red Sea rolls between us; we have been crucified to Egypt and Egypt to us." That is it, "I [have been] crucified with Christ: nevertheless I live; yet not I, but Christ liveth in me." And so the world is crucified to me and I to the world. Let me say a word of warning here. Many a Christian has judged the vile, filthy, corrupt, polluted things of the world who has never judged the brilliant, cultured, esthetic world. But the brilliant, cultured world is just as vile in the sight of God as the corrupt, disgusting, filthy world that many walked with, in days before they were converted. You can get out of fellowship with God by association with the cultured world, as truly as by going down into the world's base and ungodly places of vulgar amusement.

Oh, Christian, keep close to the footsteps of the flock of Christ, and do not let them meet you in any other field. Here is real circumcision. Circumcision was an ordinance that signified the death of the flesh. "For in Christ Jesus neither circumcision availeth any thing, nor uncircumcision, but a new creature," or, literally, "a new creation." And that is the whole thing. You and I through the cross have passed out of the old creation, if saved, and are now in the new creation of which Christ is the glorified Head. See to it that in your associations, in your pleasure, in your amusement, in your religious life, you keep in that sphere where Christ is owned as Head and Lord.

And then he adds, "And as many as walk according to this rule"—what rule? He has not laid down any rule. Yes, he has said we are a new creation. That is the way to test everything that may be put before me. Is it of the new creation or is it of the old? If it is of the old, it has nothing for me. I belong to the new and am to walk according to this rule. "As many as walk according to this rule, peace be on them, and mercy," for they will always need mercy. They will never attain perfection in this life, but God never forgets His own. Sometimes we may drift so far that we forget Him, we may even feel as though our hearts are utterly dead toward Him, as though He has forsaken us, but remember what He says, "I will never leave thee, nor forsake thee" (Heb. 13:5). There is a double negative in the original, it is, "I will never, never leave thee, nor forsake thee." It is unthinkable that the blessed Lord should ever give up one who has put his trust in Jesus, and so He always deals with us in mercy, restoring our souls when we fail.

Then the apostle uses a very peculiar expression, "And upon the Israel of God." Who does he mean by "the Israel of God"? I do not think he is referring to the church as such, for he has just referred to that when speaking of the new creation. I think he recognizes as the true Israel those of God's earthly people who really accept the testimony of God and who own their sin and trust the Savior whom God has provided. "They are not all Israel, which are of Israel" (Rom. 9:6). That a man happens to be born of the seed of Abraham does not make him a son of Abraham. Because a man happens to be born of Israel this does not make him an Israelite. He must have the faith of Abraham to be blessed with faithful Abraham, and he must receive the Savior who came through Israel if he is going to be a true Israelite.

Now that these Judaizers have made so much of a distinguishing mark upon the body through an ordinance and have said that a man that did not bear that mark was unclean and unfit for Christian fellowship, Paul says, I have a better mark than anything you may talk about. "From henceforth let no man trouble me: for I bear in my body the marks of the Lord Jesus." What did he mean by that? His very body had been wounded many times for Jesus' sake, when those cruel stones fell on him at Lystra, when beaten with stripes his body was branded; but he glories in these things and says, "I bear in my body the marks of the Lord Jesus." Someone has said, "When we get home to heaven God is not going to look us over for medals but for scars." I wonder whether we have received any scars for Jesus' sake. Many of them are not physical scars, they are scars of the heart, but it is a great thing to have the brand-marks of the Lord Jesus.

And now Paul closes this epistle without any salutations. Most of his letters contain a great many salutations to various people, but here he does not send any special message to any of them because, you see, they were playing fast and loose with the things of God, and he would not, after giving them this stern message, placate them by sending cordial salutations to the brethren in Christ as though nothing had happened to hinder fellowship. So he merely says, "The grace of our Lord Jesus Christ be with your spirit. Amen." God grant that every one of us may enjoy that grace!